ULTIMATE MUSIC THEORY
GLORY ST. GERMAIN ARCT RMT MYCC UMTC

Edited by Shelagh McKibbon-U'Ren RMT UMTC

BASIC RUDIMENTS ANSWER BOOK

UltimateMusicTheory.com

Enriching Lives Through Music Education - The Way To Score Success!

ISBN: 978-0-9813101-4-5

Ultimate Music Theory Ltd. © COPYRIGHT 2021 Gloryland Publishing. All Rights Reserved.

ULTIMATE MUSIC THEORY: *The Way to Score Success!*

The Ultimate Music Theory workbooks are for all Musicians.

The more we understand the universal language of music, the more we are capable of communicating our ideas through performing and writing music, interpreting musical compositions of others, and developing a deeper appreciation of music. It is through music education that we progress from student to musician and are able to enjoy and understand music at a more comprehensive level.

Respect Copyright 2021 Glory St. Germain
All rights reserved. No part of this publication may be reproduced or transmitted in any form or by any means, electronic or mechanical, including photocopying, recording, or any information storage and retrieval system, without permission in writing from the author/publisher.

Published in 2021 by Gloryland Publishing

GlorylandPublishing.com

UltimateMusicTheory.com

Library and Archives Canada Cataloguing in Publication St. Germain, Glory 1953-
Ultimate Music Theory Series / Glory St. Germain

Gloryland Publishing - Ultimate Music Theory Series:

GP - UP1	ISBN: 978-0-9809556-6-8	Ultimate Prep 1 Rudiments
GP - UP1A	ISBN: 978-0-9809556-9-9	Ultimate Prep 1 Rudiments Answer Book
GP - UP2	ISBN: 978-0-9809556-7-5	Ultimate Prep 2 Rudiments
GP - UP2A	ISBN: 978-0-9813101-0-7	Ultimate Prep 2 Rudiments Answer Book
GP - UBR	ISBN: 978-0-9813101-3-8	Ultimate Basic Rudiments
GP - UBRA	ISBN: 978-0-9813101-4-5	Ultimate Basic Answer Book
GP - UIR	ISBN: 978-0-9813101-5-2	Ultimate Intermediate Rudiments
GP - UIRA	ISBN: 978-0-9813101-6-9	Ultimate Intermediate Answer Book
GP - UAR	ISBN: 978-0-9813101-7-6	Ultimate Advanced Rudiments
GP - UARA	ISBN: 978-0-9813101-8-3	Ultimate Advanced Answer Book
GP - UCR	ISBN: 978-0-9813101-1-4	Ultimate Complete Rudiments
GP - UCRA	ISBN: 978-0-9813101-2-1	Ultimate Complete Answer Book

♫ **Note:** The Ultimate Music Theory Program includes the UMT Workbook Series, Exam Series & Supplemental Series to help students successfully prepare for international theory exams.

Ultimate Music Theory Basic Rudiments
Table of Contents

Lesson 1	Music Notation - Notes, Rests and Values	5
	Lesson 1 Review Test - Score: _____ / 100%	19
Lesson 2	Accidentals - Sharp, Flat and Natural Signs	22
	Lesson 2 Review Test - Score: _____ / 100%	27
Lesson 3	Semitones, Enharmonic Equivalents and Whole Tones	30
	Lesson 3 Review Test - Score: _____ / 100%	35
Lesson 4	Major Scales and the Circle of Fifths - Major Keys	38
	Lesson 4 Review Test - Score: _____ / 100%	54
Lesson 5	Intervals - Perfect, Major and Minor	59
	Lesson 5 Review Test - Score: _____ / 100%	66
Lesson 6	Circle of Fifths - Minor Keys and Minor Scales	70
	Lesson 6 Review Test - Score: _____ / 100%	81
Lesson 7	Triads - Major and Minor: Tonic, Subdominant and Dominant	86
	Lesson 7 Review Test - Score: _____ / 100%	91
Lesson 8	Simple Time - Duple, Triple and Quadruple	95
	Lesson 8 Review Test - Score: _____ / 100%	111
Lesson 9	Identifying the Key of a Melody - Major or Minor	116
	Lesson 9 Review Test - Score: _____ / 100%	118
Lesson 10	Transposition - Up or Down One Octave	123
	Lesson 10 Review Test - Score: _____ / 100%	125
Lesson 11	Analysis - Musical Compositions	130
	Lesson 11 Review Test - Score: _____ / 100%	132
Lesson 12	Musical Terms, Definitions and Signs	137
	Lesson 12 Final Basic Exam - Score: _____ / 100%	140
Guide & Chart	UMT Guide & Chart - Basic Rudiments Flashcards	146

Score: 60 - 69 Pass; **70 - 79** Honors; **80 - 89** First Class Honors; **90 - 100** First Class Honors with Distinction

Ultimate Music Theory: *The Way to Score Success!*

ULTIMATE MUSIC THEORY: *The Way to Score Success!*

The focus of the **Ultimate Music Theory** Series is to simplify complex concepts and show the relativity of these concepts with practical application. These workbooks are designed to help teachers and students discover the excitement and benefits of a music theory education.

Ultimate Music Theory workbooks are based on a proven approach to the study of music theory that follows these **4 Ultimate Music Theory Learning Principles**:

- ♪ **Simplicity of Learning** - easy to understand instructions, examples and exercises.

- ♪ **Memory Joggers** - tips for all learning styles including visual, auditory, and kinesthetic.

- ♪ **Tie it All Together** - helping musicians understand the universal language of music.

- ♪ **Make it Relevant** - applying theoretical concepts to pedagogical studies.

The **Ultimate Music Theory**™ Rudiments Workbooks, Supplemental Workbooks and Exams help students prepare for successful completion of internationally recognized theory examinations.

BONUS - Convenient and easy to use Ultimate Music Theory Answer Books - Identical to the student workbooks for quick, easy & accurate marking. UMT Answer Books available for all levels.

♫ **Note:** Each Ultimate Music Theory Rudiments Workbook has a corresponding Supplemental Workbook Level to enhance knowledge of analysis, develop a deeper understanding of music history, provide a proven step-by-step system in melody writing, and much more!

The Ultimate Music Theory Series includes these EXCLUSIVE BONUS features:

Ultimate Music Theory Guide & Chart - a convenient summarization to review concepts.

12 Comprehensive Review Tests & Final Exam - retention of concepts learned in previous lessons.

♫ **Notes:** point out important information and handy memory tips.

80 Music Theory Flashcards - Musical Terms & Signs, Rhythms, Key Signatures, Time Signatures, Note Naming, Dynamics, Tempos, Articulation, Triads, Chords, etc. (each workbook is different).

Ultimate Music Theory FREE Resources - Music History Videos, Worksheets, Music Theory Blogs, Free Ultimate Music Theory Teachers Guide & Free Teach Basic Rudiments Online Mini-Course.

Go To: **UltimateMusicTheory.com** Today!

Enriching Lives Through Music Education

Lesson 1 Music Notation - Notes, Rests and Values

TREBLE CLEF and BASS CLEF

A **STAFF** consists of **FIVE** lines and **FOUR** spaces.

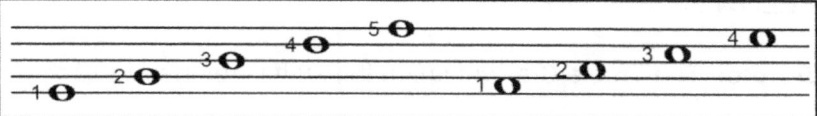

1. Drawing the **TREBLE CLEF** or **G Clef**. Copy the following:
   a) Draw a "J" through the staff. Start above the staff and end in the space below the staff.
   b) Draw a "P" to line 4. Continue circling to the left and draw a "d" to line 1.
   c) Continue to circle up to line 3. Curl around and cross line 2. This is the "G" line.
   d) This creates a **LANDMARK** for the note "G" in the **Treble Clef**.

2. a) The Treble Clef **SPACE** notes are: **F A C E**. Copy and name the space notes.
   b) The Treble Clef **LINE** notes are: **E G B D F**. Copy and name the line notes.

F A C E F A C E   E G B D F E G B D F

3. Drawing the **BASS CLEF** or **F Clef**. Copy the following:
   a) Draw a black **dot** on line 4. This is the "F" line.
   b) Draw half of a heart. Curl up to line 5. End in space 1.
   c) Draw a **dot** in SPACE 4 (above the "F" line) and a **dot** in SPACE 3 (below the "F" line).
   d) This creates a **LANDMARK** for the note "F" in the **Bass Clef**.

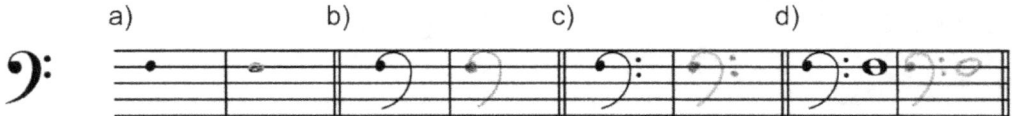

4. a) The Bass Clef **SPACE** notes are: **A C E G**. Copy and name the space notes.
   b) The Bass Clef **LINE** notes are: **G B D F A**. Copy and name the line notes.

A C E G A C E G   G B D F A G B D F A

THE TREBLE CLEF

The **TREBLE CLEF** or **G CLEF** curls around line 2 (the "**G**" line) and indicates the location of G above Middle C. Middle C is written on its own line called a Ledger Line. Middle C and D are written **BELOW** the Treble Clef.

♪ **Note:** The Treble Clef written on the staff is referred to as the **Treble Staff** or **Treble Clef**.

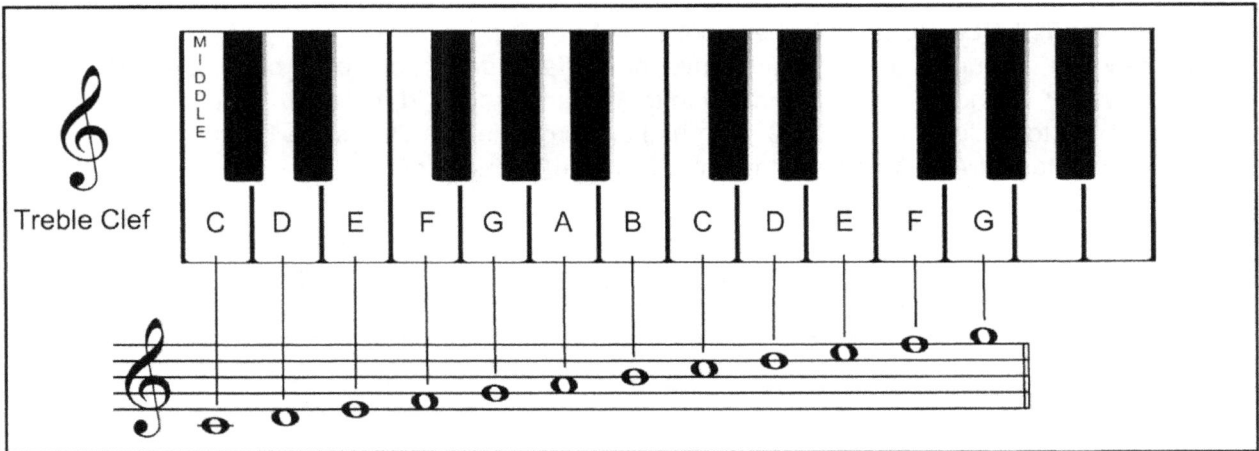

1. Draw a Treble Clef at the beginning of each measure. Write the notes Middle C and D below the Treble Staff.

2. Name the following notes in the Treble Clef.

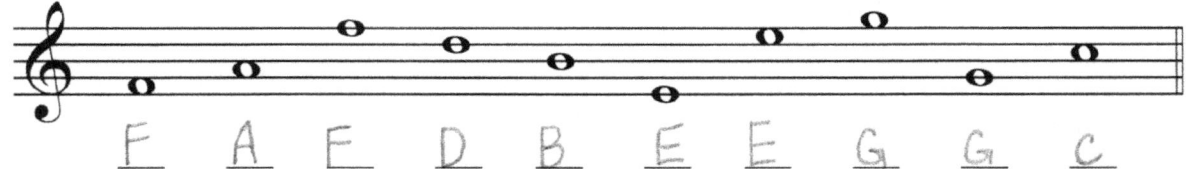

F   A   E   D   B   E   E   G   G   C

3. Write the following notes in the Treble Clef.

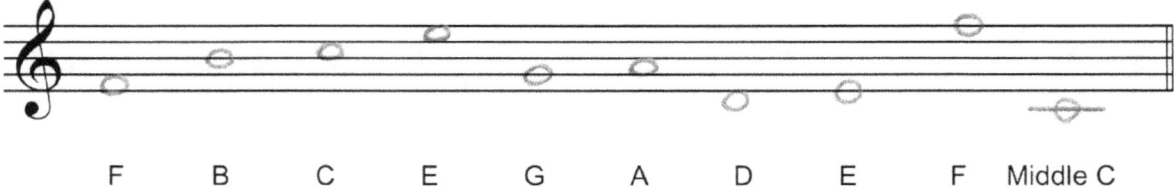

F   B   C   E   G   A   D   E   F   Middle C

THE BASS CLEF

The **BASS CLEF** or **F CLEF** has 2 dots, one in the space above and one in the space below line 4 (the "**F**" line), and indicates the location of F below Middle C. Middle C and B are written **ABOVE** the Bass Clef.

♫ **Note:** The Bass Clef written on the staff is referred to as the **Bass Staff** or **Bass Clef**.

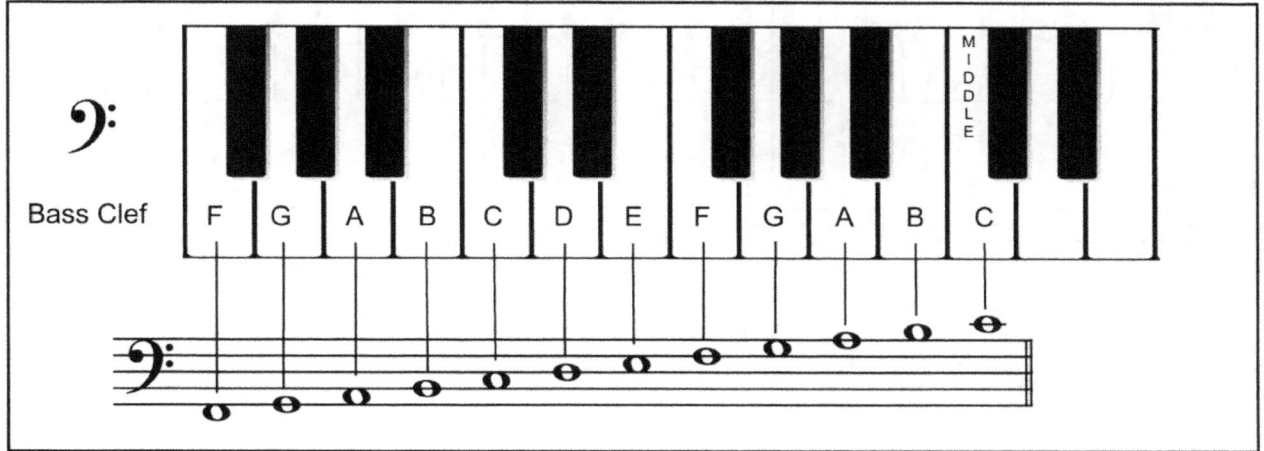

1. Draw a Bass Clef at the beginning of each measure. Write the notes Middle C and B above the Bass Staff.

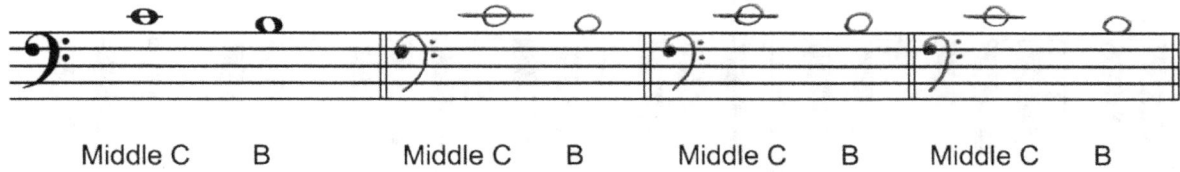

    Middle C   B   Middle C   B   Middle C   B   Middle C   B

2. Name the following notes in the Bass Clef.

  F   C   A   F   D   G   G   A   B   E

3. Write the following notes in the Bass Clef.

  F   B   C   E   G   A   D   B   F   Middle C

LANDMARK F-A-C-E and G-B-D LINE NOTES in the TREBLE CLEF

LANDMARK F-A-C-E groups and **LANDMARK G-B-D** groups identify the LINES in the Treble Clef.
Ledger Lines are short lines used above or below the staff to extend the range of the staff.

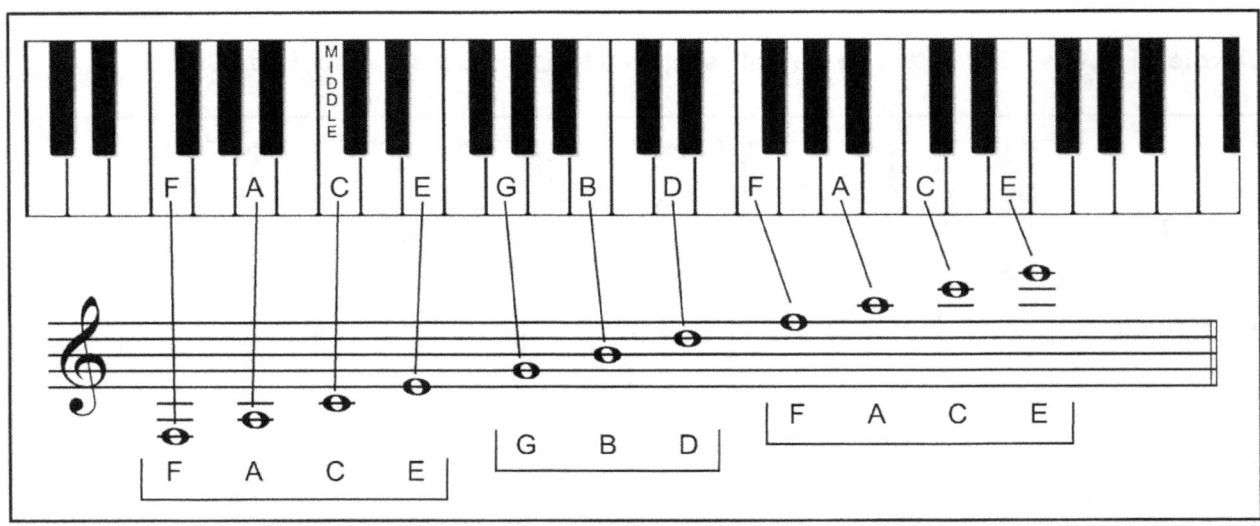

1. a) Name the following line notes in the Treble Clef.
   b) Draw a line from each note in the Treble Clef to the corresponding key on the keyboard (at the correct pitch).
   c) Name the key directly on the keyboard.

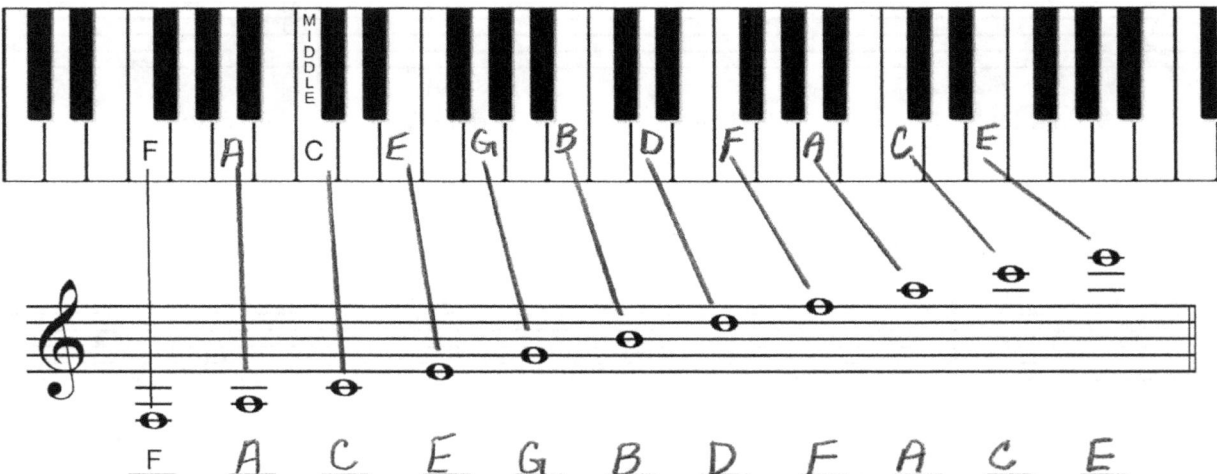

F A C E G B D F A C E

2. Name the following line notes in the Treble Clef.

C F G A B E A D E C F

LANDMARK G-B-D and F-A-C-E SPACE NOTES in the TREBLE CLEF

LANDMARK G-B-D groups and **LANDMARK F-A-C-E** groups identify the SPACES in the Treble Clef. **Ledger Lines** must be equal distance from the staff and are used as needed.

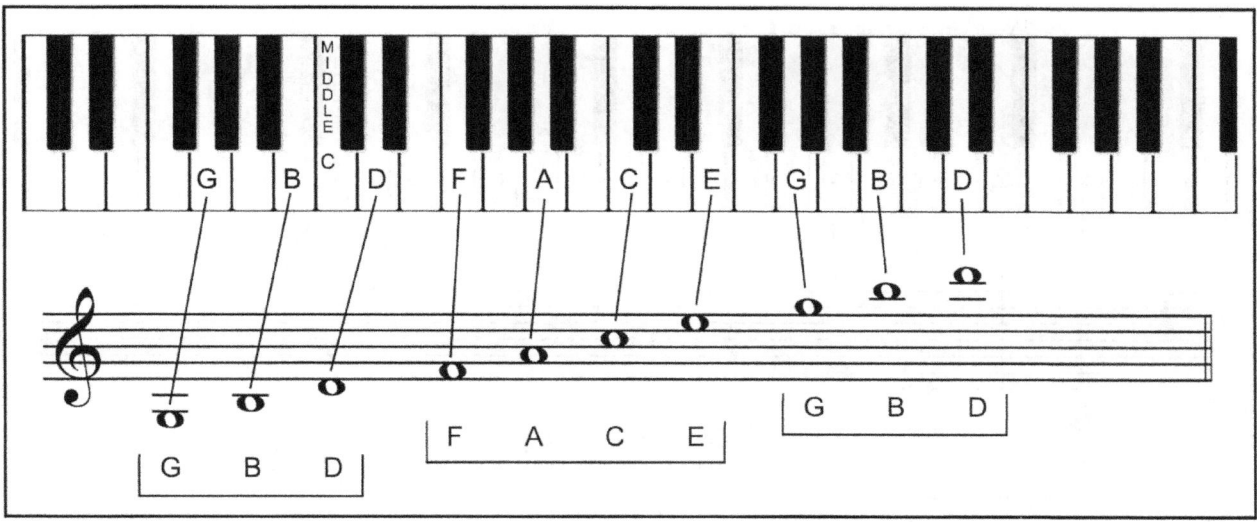

1. a) Name the following space notes in the Treble Clef.
   b) Draw a line from each note in the Treble Clef to the corresponding key on the keyboard (at the correct pitch).
   c) Name the key directly on the keyboard.

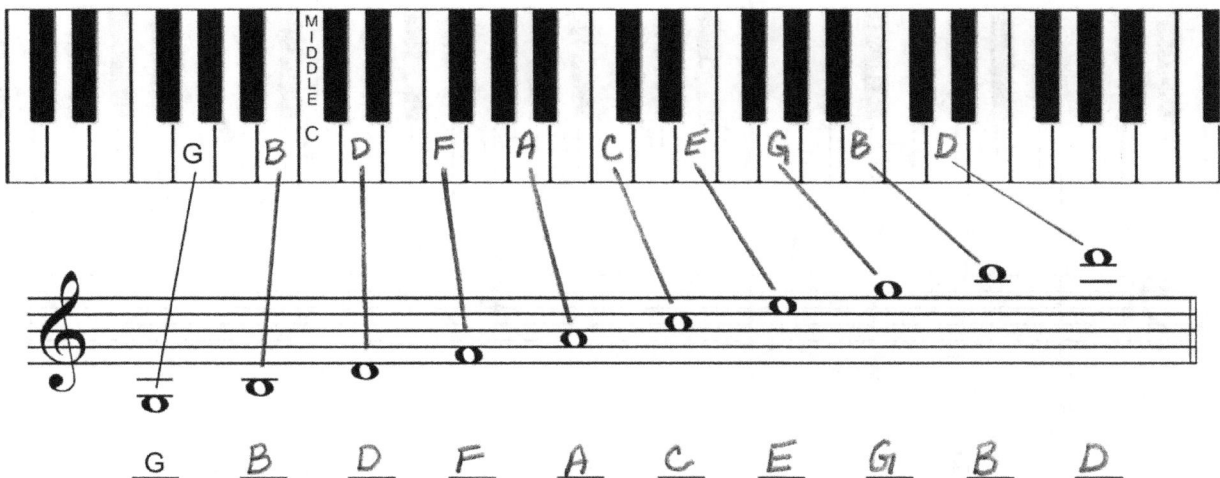

G B D F A C E G B D

2. Name the following space notes in the Treble Clef.

F B C G G B E A D D

LANDMARK F-A-C-E and G-B-D LINE NOTES in the BASS CLEF

LANDMARK F-A-C-E groups and **LANDMARK G-B-D** groups identify the LINES in the Bass Clef.
Ledger Lines are short lines used above or below the staff to extend the range of the staff.

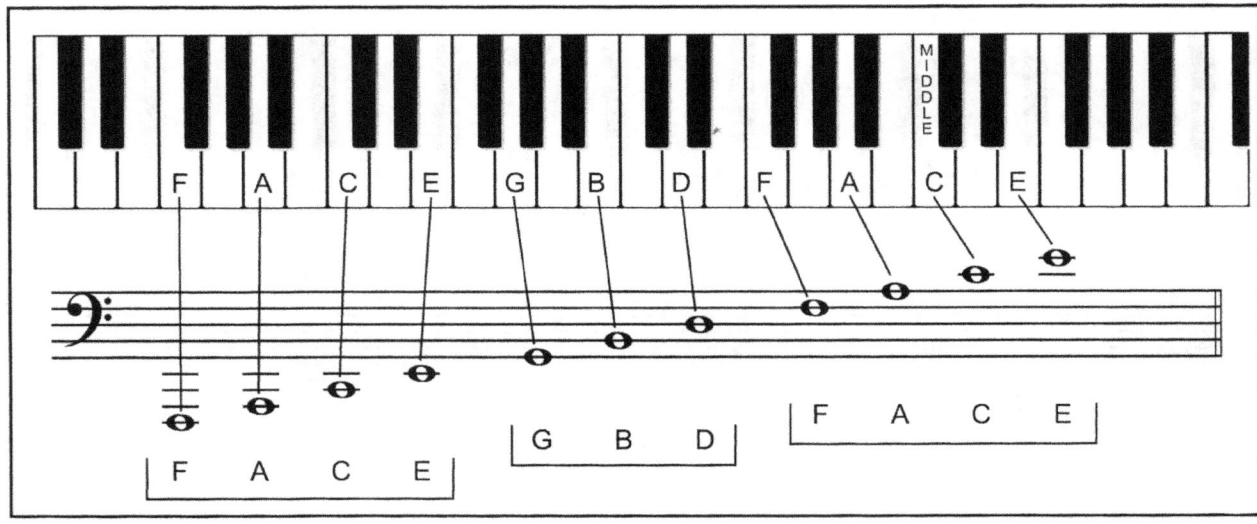

1. a) Name the following line notes in the Bass Clef.
   b) Draw a line from each note in the Bass Clef to the corresponding key on the keyboard (at the correct pitch).
   c) Name the key directly on the keyboard.

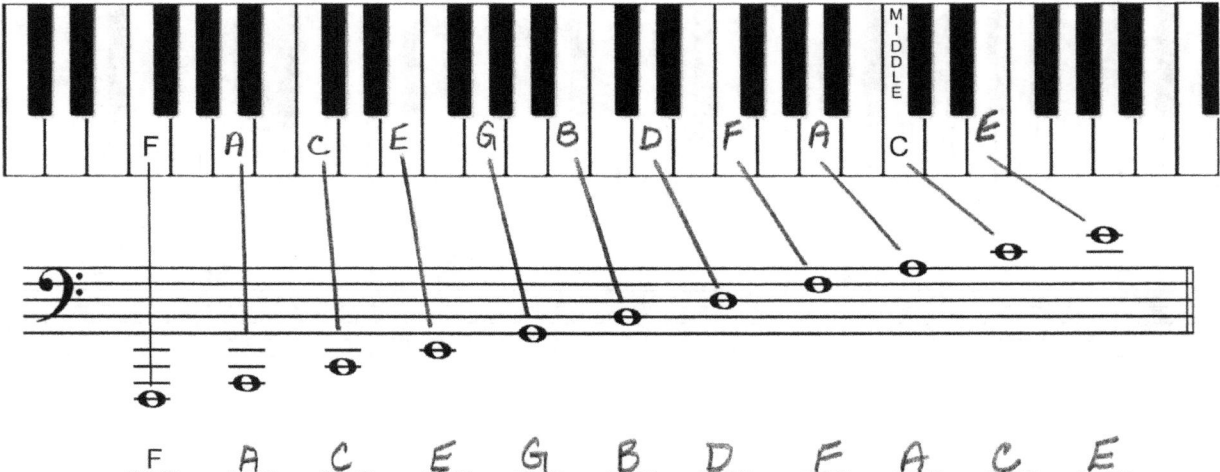

F A C E G B D F A C E

2. Name the following line notes in the Bass Clef.

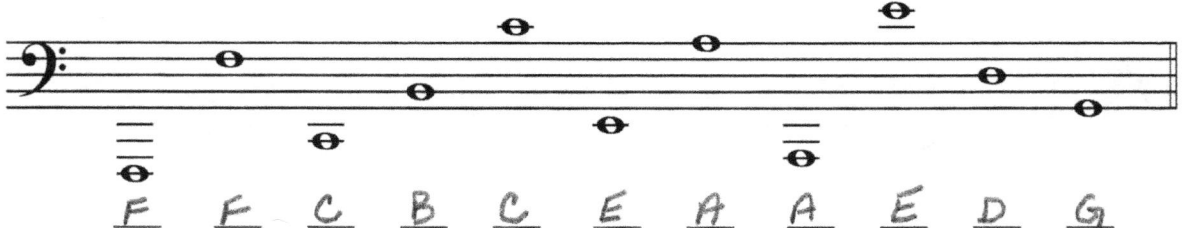

F F C B C E A A E D G

LANDMARK G-B-D and F-A-C-E SPACE NOTES in the BASS CLEF

LANDMARK G-B-D groups and **LANDMARK F-A-C-E** groups identify the SPACES in the Bass Clef.
Ledger Lines must be equal distance from the staff and are used as needed.

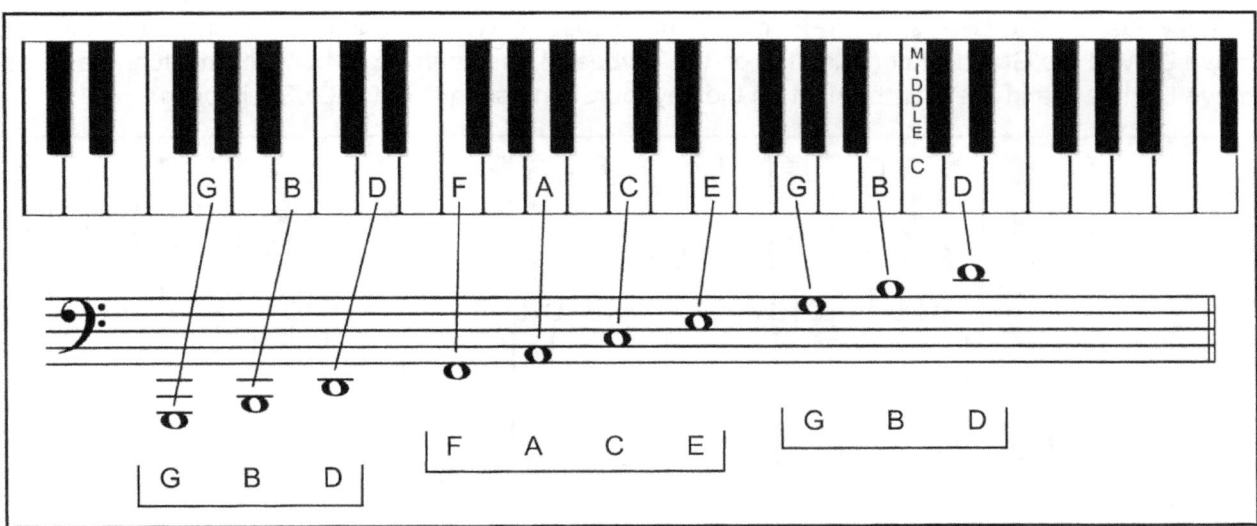

1. a) Name the following space notes in the Bass Clef.
   b) Draw a line from each note in the Bass Clef to the corresponding key on the keyboard (at the correct pitch).
   c) Name the key directly on the keyboard.

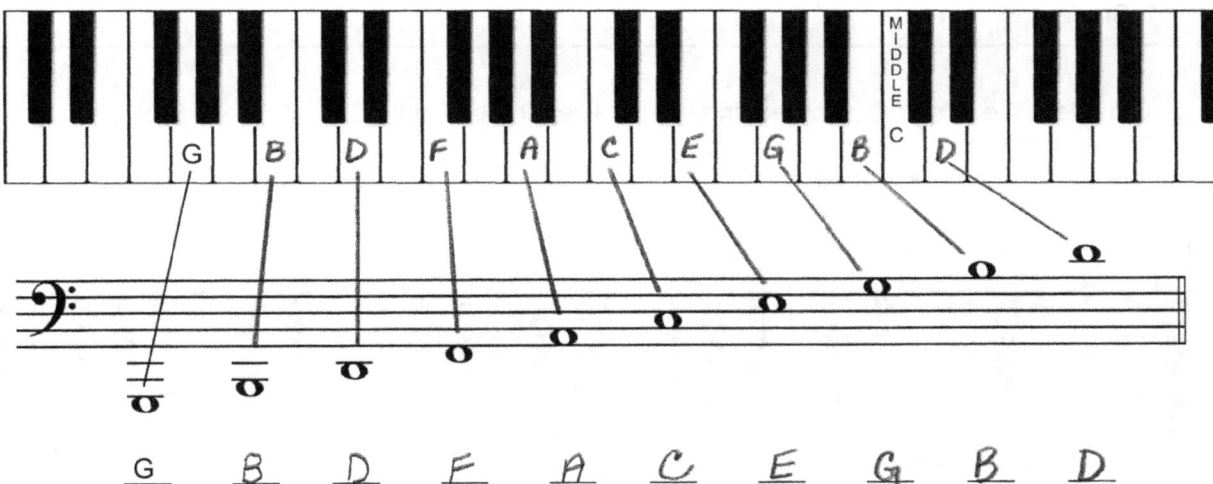

G B D F A C E G B D

2. Name the following space notes in the Bass Clef.

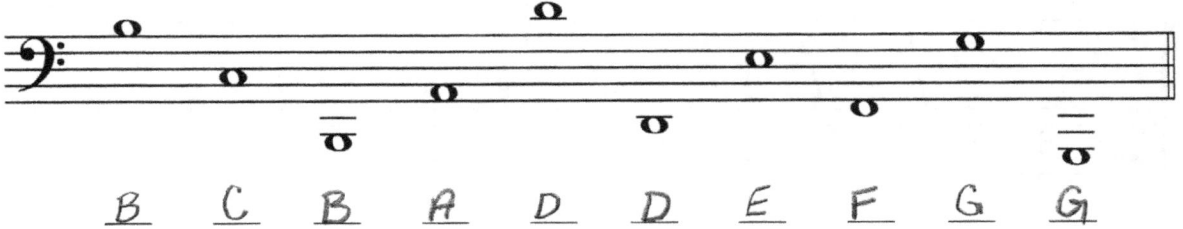

B C B A D D E F G G

THE GRAND STAFF

The **GRAND STAFF** is made up of the Treble Clef and the Bass Clef joined together by a BRACE or BRACKET and a bar line. Middle C can be written in both the Treble Clef and the Bass Clef.

Notes written on the **GRAND STAFF** correspond to specific **PITCHES** on the keyboard. As notes move DOWN the Grand Staff (to the left on the keyboard), the sounds get LOWER in pitch. As notes move UP the Grand Staff (to the right on the keyboard), the sounds get HIGHER in pitch.

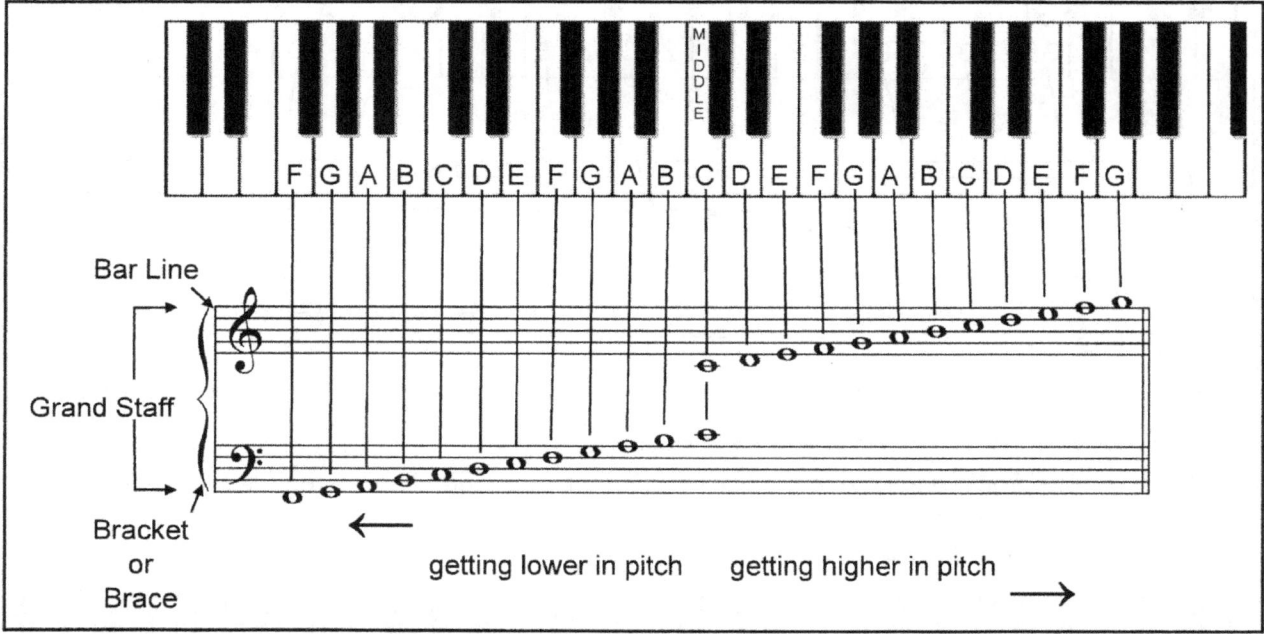

1. a) Complete the Grand Staff by adding the bar line, brace, Treble Clef and Bass Clef.
   b) Name the following notes on the Grand Staff.
   c) Draw a line from each note on the Grand Staff to the corresponding key on the keyboard (at the correct pitch).
   d) Name the key directly on the keyboard.

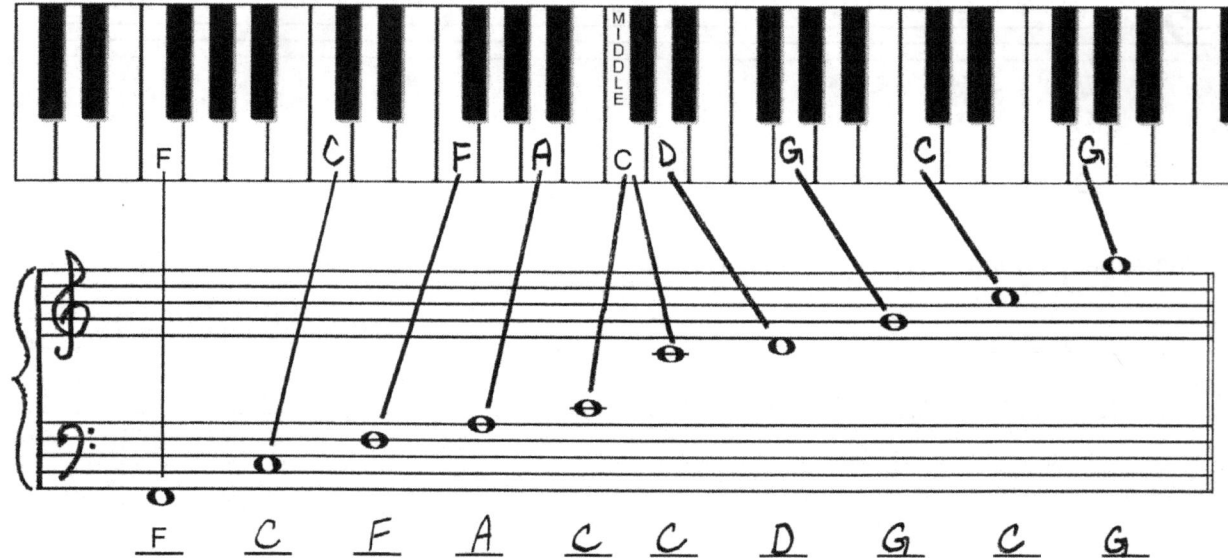

F   C   F   A   C   C   D   G   C   G

BAR LINES, MEASURES and DYNAMICS

BAR LINES are lines (single thin lines) that divide the music into equal **MEASURES** of time.
A measure is the space (area of music) between two bar lines.

A **DOUBLE BAR LINE** (two thin bar lines together) indicates the end of a section.
A **DOUBLE BAR LINE** (a thin bar line and a thick bar line together) indicates the end of the piece of music. The double bar line at the end of a piece is also called a final bar line.

Measure numbers can be written inside a small box above the top left of each measure.

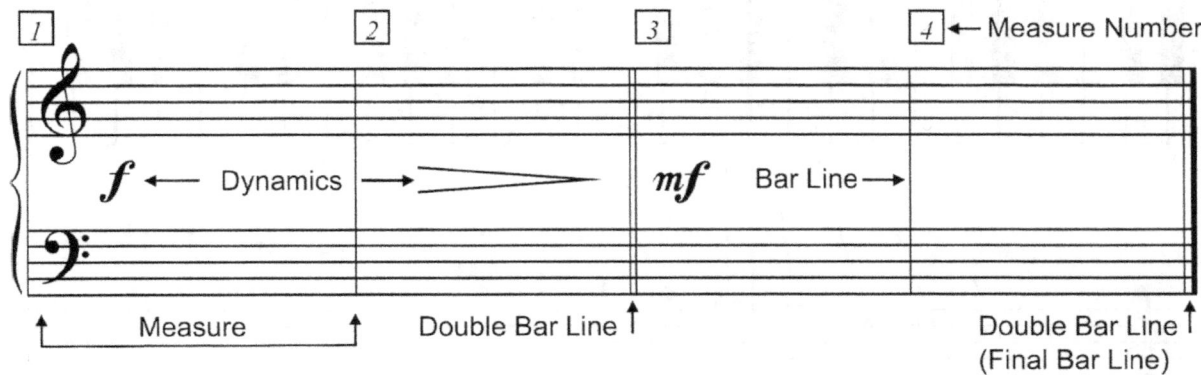

DYNAMICS refer to the varying degrees of loudness or softness. Dynamic markings are symbols or signs written in music to indicate different volumes of sound.

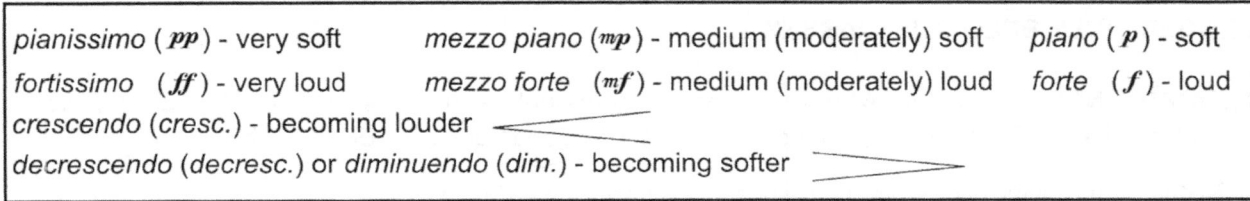

♪ **Note:** Dynamic markings are written **BELOW** the Treble Staff, **ABOVE** the Bass Staff and in the **MIDDLE** of the Grand Staff.

1. a) Complete the Grand Staff by adding the bar line, brace, Treble Clef and Bass Clef.
   b) Number each measure in the box above the staff.
   c) Draw a double bar line (final bar line) at the end of the Grand Staff.
   d) Add the dynamic signs for "*piano*" in measure 1 and for "*crescendo*" in measure 3.

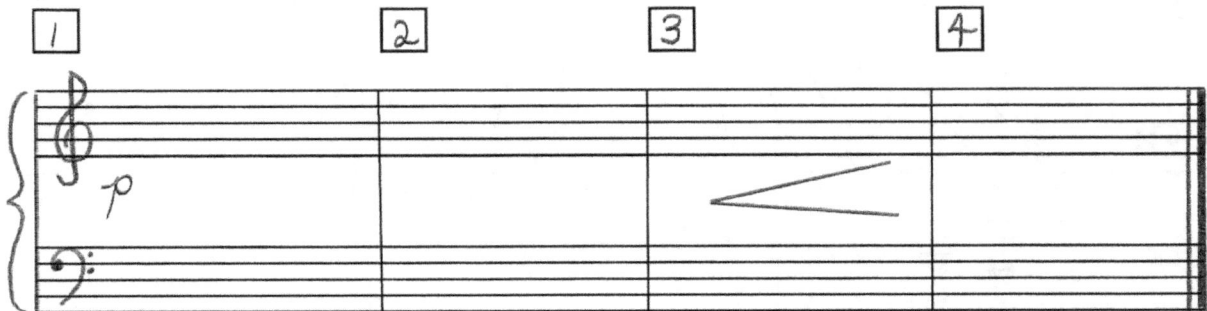

LEDGER LINES ABOVE the TREBLE CLEF

LEDGER LINES are used to extend the range of notes above the Treble Clef. As the notes move **UP** the Treble Clef (to the right on the keyboard) the sounds get **HIGHER** in pitch.

♪ **Note:** When using ledger lines, the note "**C**" appears 4 times in the Treble Clef.

1. a) Name the following notes in the Treble Clef.
   b) Name the key directly on the keyboard.

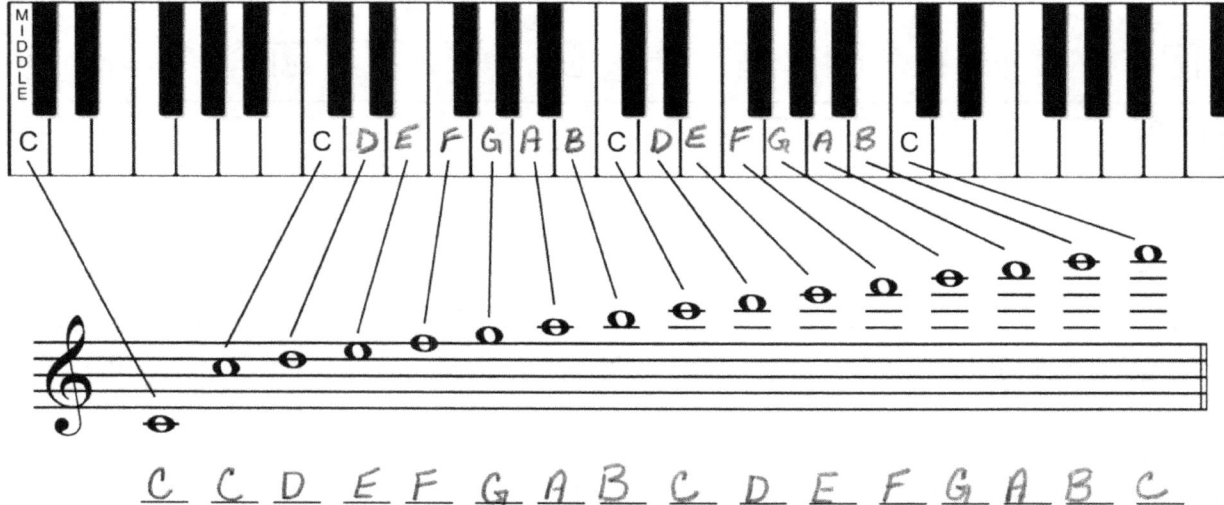

C C D E F G A B C D E F G A B C

LEDGER LINES BELOW the BASS CLEF

LEDGER LINES are used to extend the range of notes below the Bass Clef. As the notes move **DOWN** the Bass Clef (to the left on the keyboard) the sounds get **LOWER** in pitch.

♪ **Note:** When using ledger lines, the note "**C**" appears 4 times in the Bass Clef.

2. a) Name the following notes in the Bass Clef.
   b) Name the key directly on the keyboard.

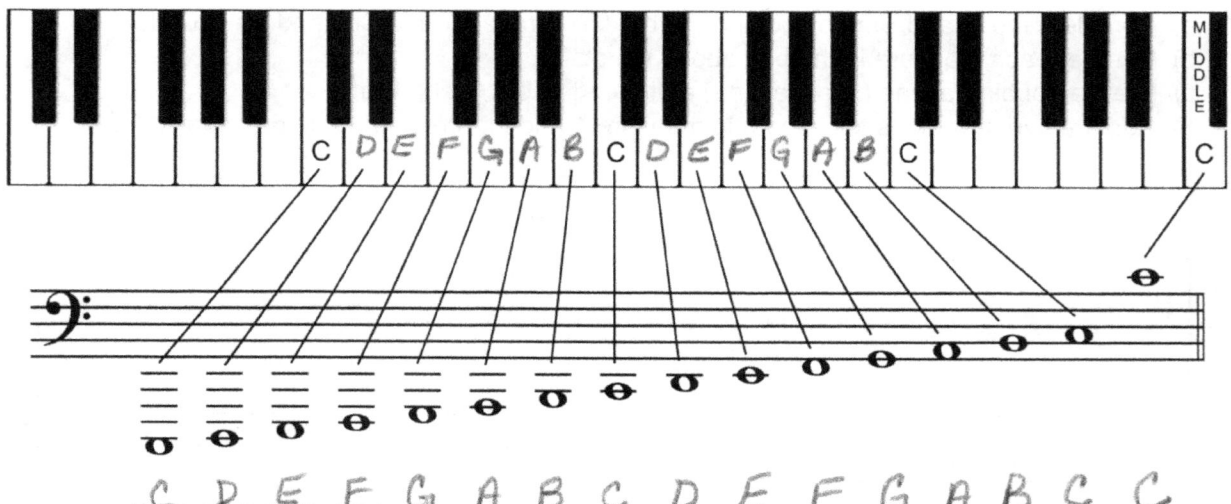

C D E F G A B C D E F G A B C C

SAME PITCH, ALTERNATE CLEF

The notes written with ledger lines **BELOW** the Treble Clef are at the **SAME PITCH** as the corresponding notes in the Bass Clef. The notes written with ledger lines **ABOVE** the Bass Clef are at the **SAME PITCH** as the corresponding notes in the Treble Clef.

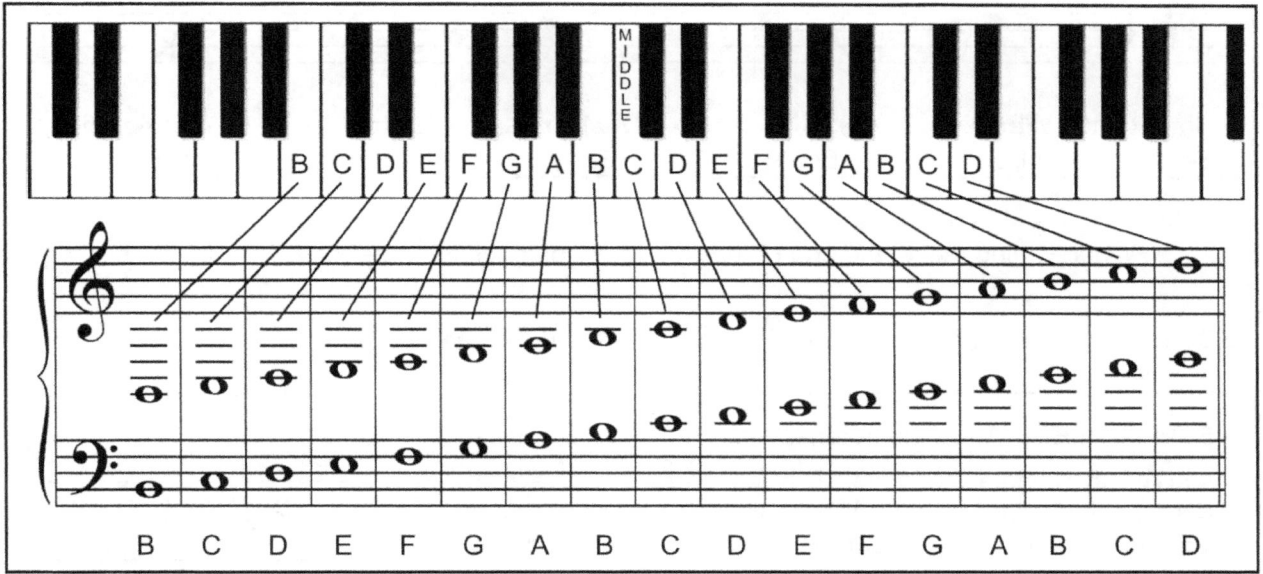

♪ **Note:** When rewriting a note at the same pitch in the alternate clef, a line note will remain a line note and a space note will remain a space note.

1. Rewrite the given note in each measure at the same pitch in the alternate clef. Use ledger lines when necessary. Name the notes.

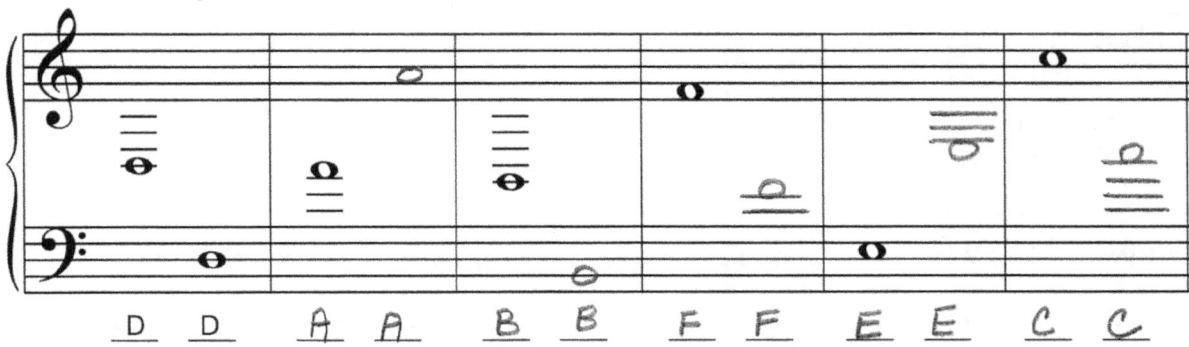

D D   A A   B B   F F   E E   C C

♪ **Note:** When rewriting a melody at the same pitch in the alternate clef, copy the bar lines first.

2. Rewrite the following melody at the same pitch in the Bass Clef.

NOTES, RESTS, TIES and DOTS

Each **NOTE** has a specific time value of sound and each **REST** has a specific time value of silence.

FLAGS: For an eighth note or a sixteenth note, the **FLAG** always goes to the **RIGHT**. When writing these, the end of the flag does not touch the notehead.

RESTS: ▬ hangs from line 4. ▬ sits on line 3. 𝄽 and 𝄿 start in space 3.

STEM RULES: When the notehead is:

ABOVE the middle line, stem DOWN on the left: '𝆏' like 'p' in → *p*izza
ON the middle line, stem DOWN on the left or UP on the right:
BELOW the middle line, stem UP on the right: '𝆑' like 'd' in → *d*onuts

A Stem is approximately one octave in length.

1. Following the example at the top of the page, copy the notes and rests in the Bass Clef. Write the number of beats each note/rest receives.

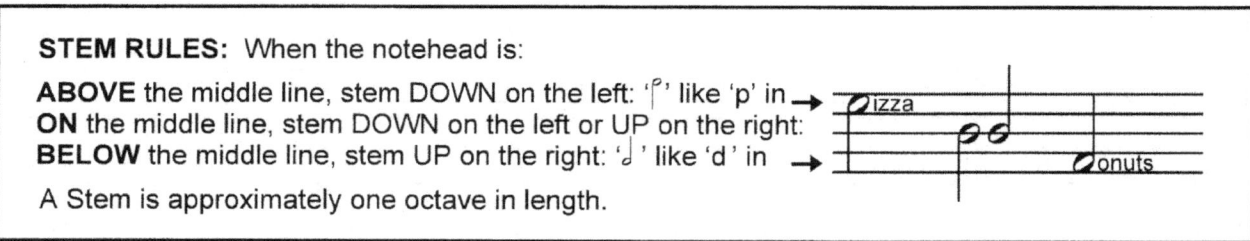

Note/Rest:	**Whole**	**Half**	**Quarter**	**Eighth**	**Sixteenth**
Beats:	**4** Beats	**2** Beats	**1** Beat	**½** Beat	**¼** Beat

A **SINGLE BEAM** is used when two or more ♫ eighth notes are joined together.

A **DOUBLE BEAM** is used when two or more 𝅘𝅥𝅯𝅘𝅥𝅯 sixteenth notes are joined together.

♫ **Note:** The note furthest away from the third line (the middle line) determines the direction of all the stems. Different combinations of note values may be beamed together.

2. Copy the following:

2 beamed eighth notes = __1__ beat   4 beamed sixteenth notes = __1__ beat

16

A **TIE** is a curved line connecting two or more notes of the **SAME PITCH**. The first note is PLAYED and HELD for the combined value of the tied notes. A tie may be used to extend the note value over a bar line.

♪ **Note:** When the stems are down, the tie is written above the notes; when the stems are up, the tie is written below the notes.

3. a) Write the number of beats for each note.   b) Write the total beats for the tied notes.

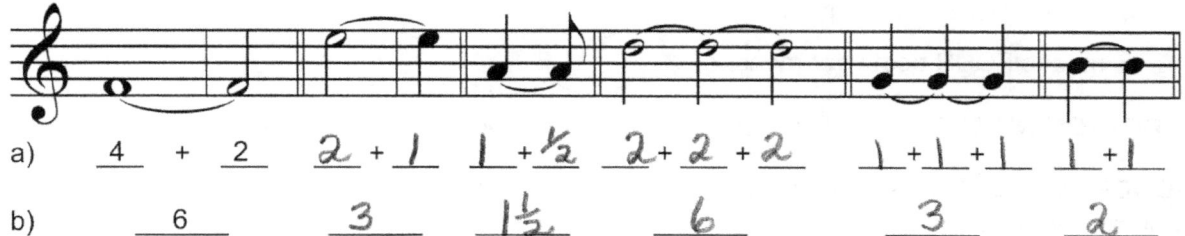

a)   4 + 2   2 + 1   1 + ½   2 + 2 + 2   1 + 1 + 1   1 + 1
b)   6   3   1½   6   3   2

A **DOT** placed after a note adds **"HALF THE VALUE"** of the note. The dot is written BEHIND (after) the note in the same space for a space note, and in the space above for a line note.

♪ **Note:** ♪· dotted eighth note; ♩· dotted quarter note; 𝅗𝅥· dotted half note; o· dotted whole note

4. a) Write the note and the note value of the dot.   b) Write the number of beats for each dotted note.

a)   ♩ + ♪   ♪ + 𝅘𝅥𝅯   o + 𝅗𝅥   𝅗𝅥 + ♩   ♩ + ♪   ♪ + 𝅘𝅥𝅯
b)   1½   ¾   6   3   1½   3/4

5. Write the number of beats for each of the following notes.

Beats: 3   ½   4   ¼   1½   2   1   3/4

Eighth notes and sixteenth notes can be **BEAMED TOGETHER** in combinations that equal **ONE BEAT** (one quarter note). Eighth notes and sixteenth notes can also be combined with **RESTS** to equal one beat (one quarter note).

6. Write the total number of beats in each measure.

Beats: 1   1   1   1   1   1   1   1

TIME SIGNATURES

A **TIME SIGNATURE** is written on the staff after the clef sign.
TWO numbers are used for a TIME SIGNATURE.

In **Simple Time**, the **TOP NUMBER** indicates how many beats are in a measure.

2 means TWO beats per measure

3 means THREE beats per measure

4 means FOUR beats per measure

The **BOTTOM NUMBER** "**4**" indicates that **one quarter note** is equal to **one** beat.

A **SCOOP** (⌣) is a symbol representing one beat. Scoops are a visual aid in grouping notes and/or rests into one beat.

♫ **Note:** A whole rest equals a **whole measure of silence** in Simple Time.

1. Following the examples, add one rest below each bracket to complete the measure.
   Cross off the count as each beat is completed.

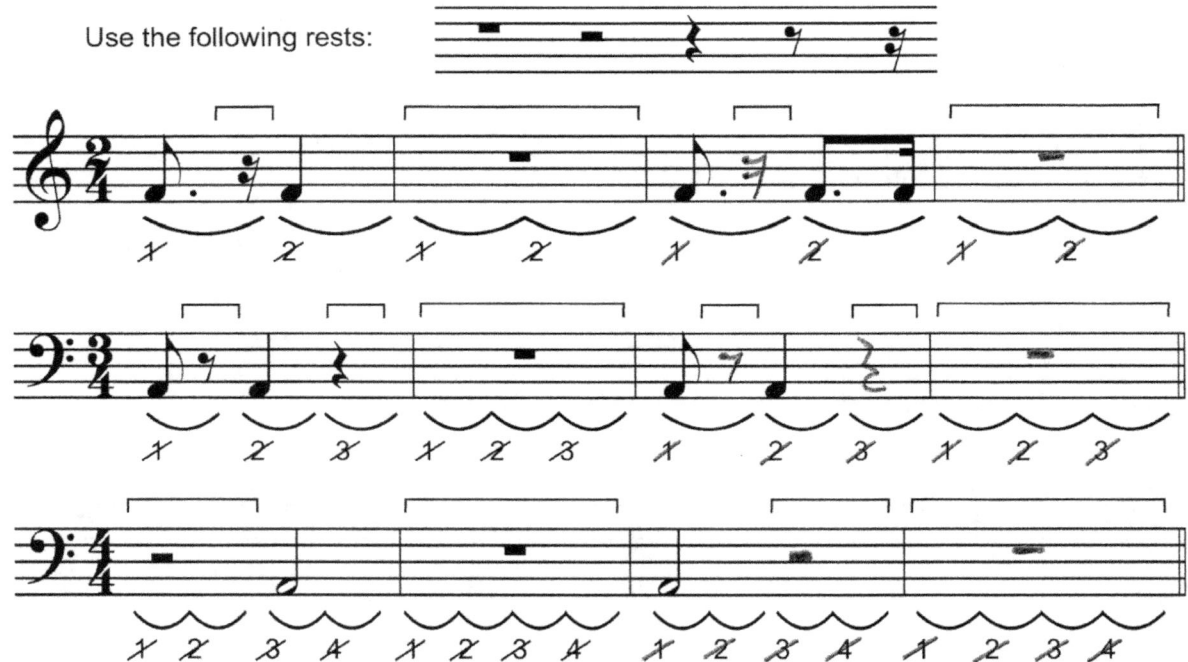

2. Complete the following.

   1 whole note = __2__ half notes

   2 half notes = __4__ quarter notes

   4 quarter notes = __8__ eighth notes

   8 eighth notes = __16__ sixteenth notes

Lesson 1 — Review Test

Total Score: ___ / 100

1. Name the following notes in the **Treble Clef**.

G C F D F E B A G C

2. Name the following notes in the **Bass Clef**.

F E C G D F B B A C

3. Rewrite the given note in each measure at the **SAME PITCH** in the **ALTERNATE CLEF**. Use half notes. Name the notes.

G G   F F   F F   D D   B B

4.
a) Name the following notes on the **Grand Staff**.
b) Draw a line from each note on the staff to the corresponding key on the keyboard.
c) Name the key directly on the keyboard.

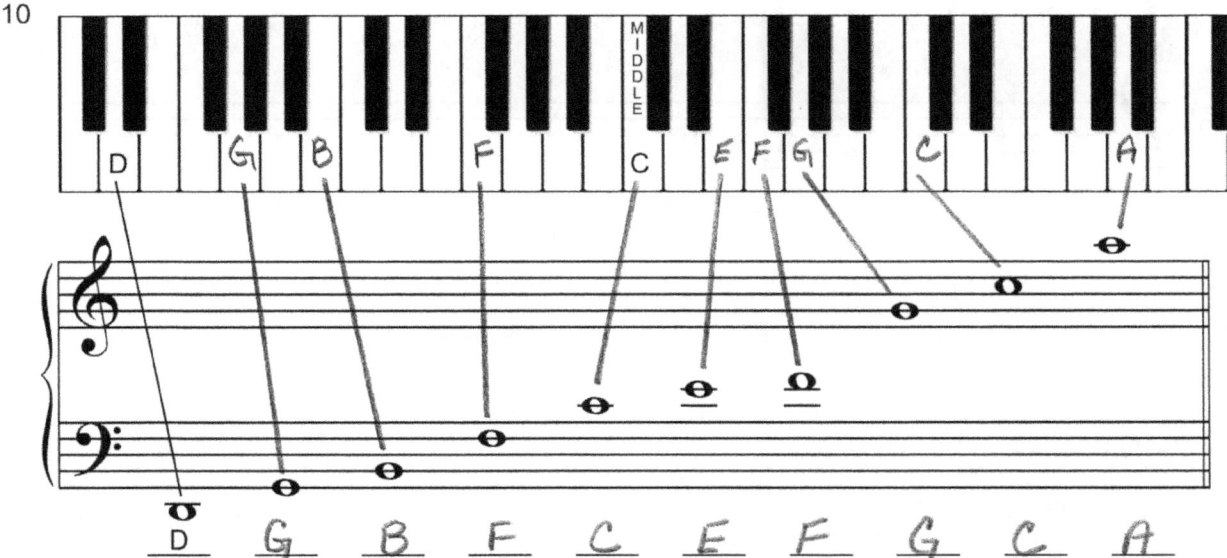

D G B F C E F G C A

5. Write the name and number of beats each note or rest receives.

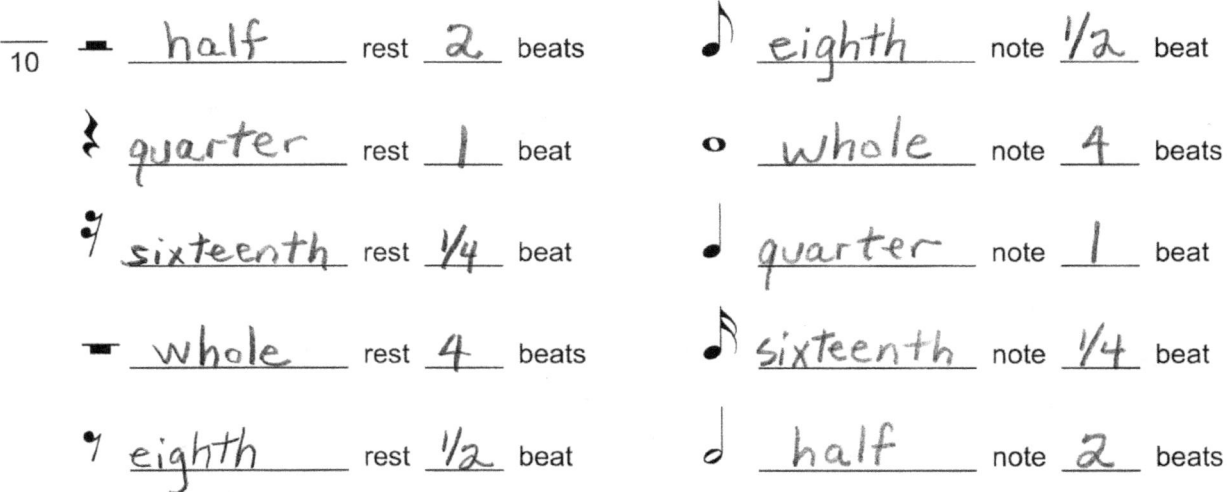

6. Write **ONE NOTE** that is equal to the total value of the notes in each measure.

7. Write **THREE NOTES** of the same value that equal the dotted note in each measure.

8. Write **ONE REST** below each bracket that has the same value as the note in each measure.

9. Rewrite the following melody at the **SAME PITCH** in the Treble Clef.

10. Match each musical term or sign with the English definition. (Not all definitions will be used.)
 (Write the definition letter on the line beside the term.)

Term		Definition
tie	g	a) F Clef
brace	f	b) moderately soft
ledger line	i	c) up on the right or down on the left
Bass Clef	a	d) adds half the value of the note
Treble Clef	k	e) indicates number of beats of silence
mezzo piano, *mp*	b	f) joins the Treble Clef and Bass Clef to create the Grand Staff
a dot after a note	d	g) hold for the combined value of the tied notes
fortissimo, *ff*	j	h) two or more eighth notes joined together
stem direction of a note on line 3	c	i) short line used for notes above or below the staff to extend the range of the staff
rest	e	j) very loud
		k) G Clef

Lesson 2 Accidentals - Sharp #   Flat ♭   Natural ♮   Signs

An **ACCIDENTAL** is a sign placed **IN FRONT** of a note that raises or lowers the pitch.

A **SEMITONE** (or half step) is the shortest distance in pitch between two notes and uses adjacent (closest) keys on the keyboard, black or white.

SHARP #

A **SHARP** sign is written in front of the note and is written after the letter name. A sharp can be a black or white key.

A sharp **RAISES** a note one chromatic semitone (half step).

♪ Note: A **CHROMATIC** semitone (half step) has the **SAME** letter name. Example: F to F#

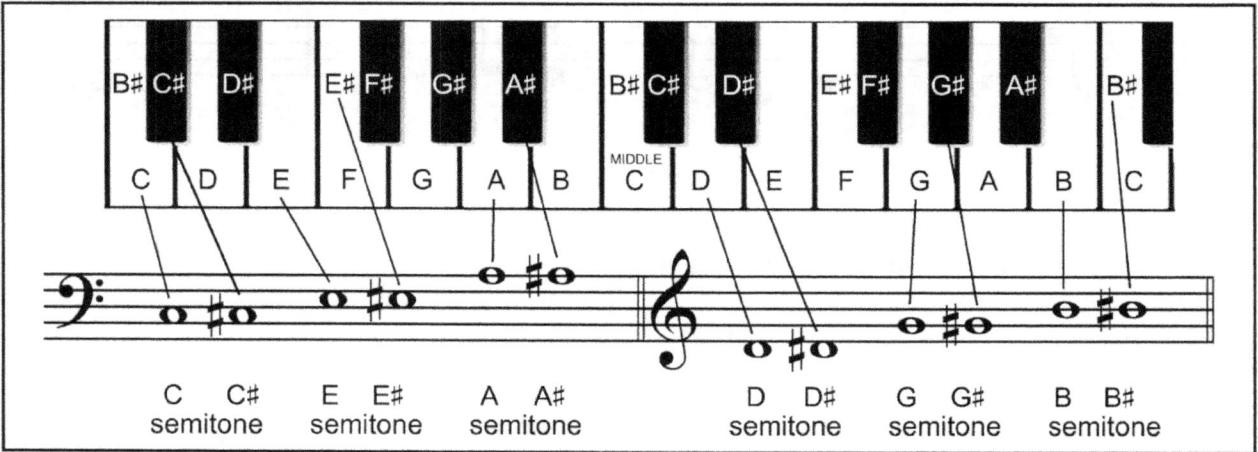

♪ Note: The middle of the sharp sign must be in the same space or on the same line as the note.

1. Draw a line from each note on the staff to the corresponding key on the keyboard. Name the notes.

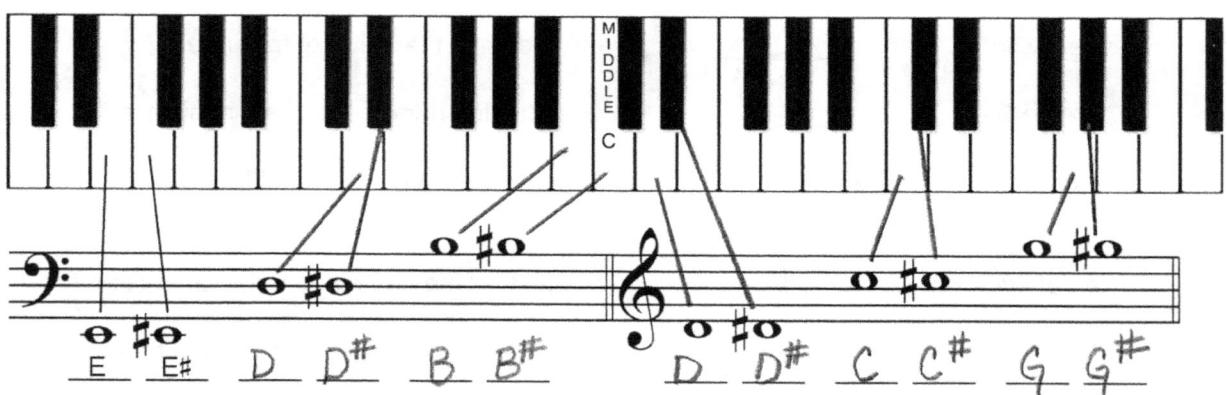

E E#   D D#   B B#   D D#   C C#   G G#

2. Raise the following notes a chromatic semitone (half step) by writing a sharp in front of each note. Name the notes.

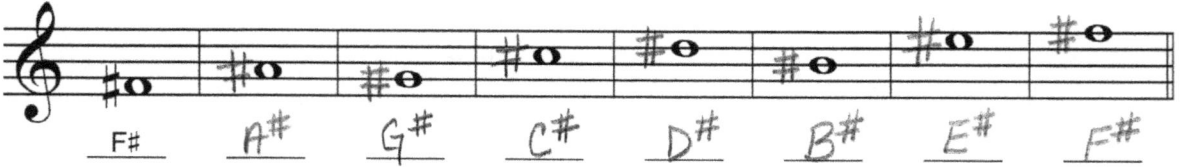

F#   A#   G#   C#   D#   B#   E#   F#

FLAT ♭

A **FLAT** sign is written in front of the note and is written after the letter name. A flat can be a black or white key.

A flat **LOWERS** a note one chromatic semitone (half step).

♪ **Note:** A **CHROMATIC** semitone (half step) has the **SAME** letter name. Example: B to B♭

An accidental in front of a note raises or lowers the pitch.

A sharp raises a note one chromatic semitone (half step).
A flat lowers a note one chromatic semitone (half step).

Each black key has two names and may be called a sharp or a flat. Example: C# or D♭, D# or E♭.

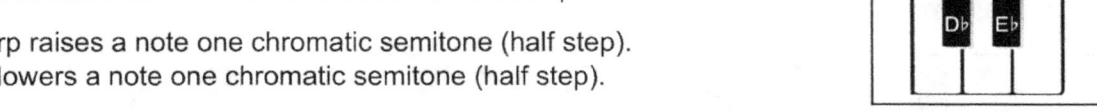

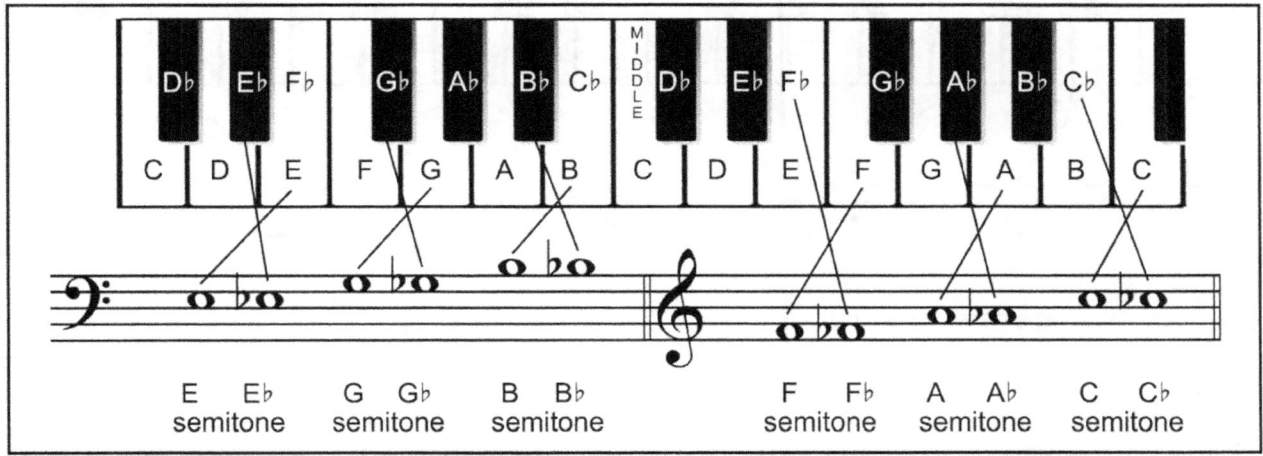

♪ **Note:** The "half heart" of the flat sign must be in the same space or on the same line as the note.

1. Draw a line from each note on the staff to the corresponding key on the keyboard. Name the notes.

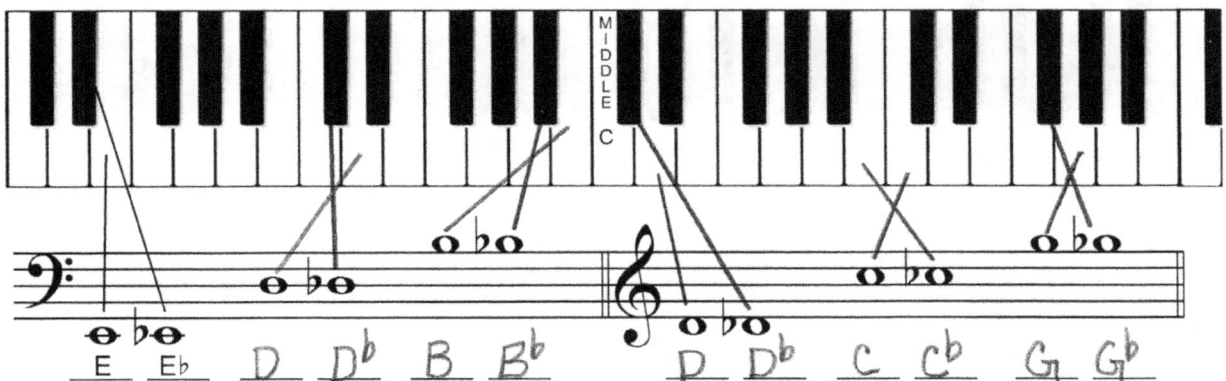

E E♭   D D♭   B B♭   D D♭   C C♭   G G♭

2. Lower the following notes a chromatic semitone (half step) by writing a flat in front of each note. Name the notes.

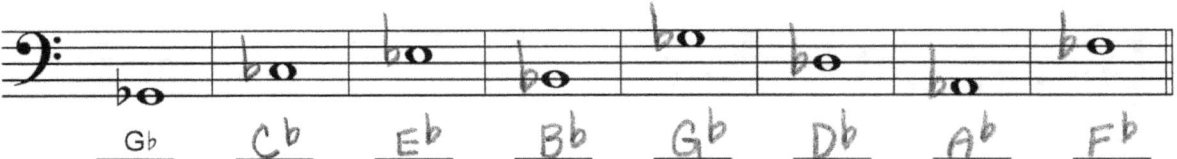

G♭   C♭   E♭   B♭   G♭   D♭   A♭   F♭

23

NATURAL ♮

A **NATURAL** sign **CANCELS** a sharp or flat. A natural sign raises a flat or lowers a sharp one chromatic semitone (half step).

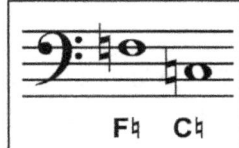

A **NATURAL** sign is written in front of the note and is written after the letter name.
A natural note is ALWAYS a white key.

♪ **Note:** The middle box of the natural sign is written in the same space or on the same line as the note.

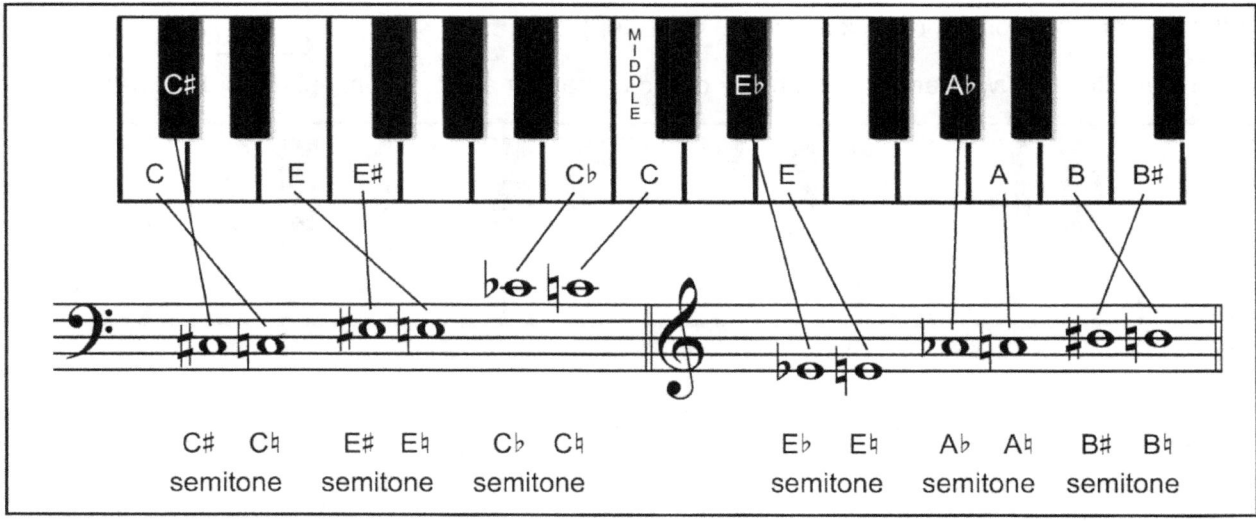

♪ **Note:** The NATURAL sign is written like the letter **L** and the number **7**.   L7 = ♮

1. Draw a line from each note on the staff to the corresponding key on the keyboard. Name the notes.

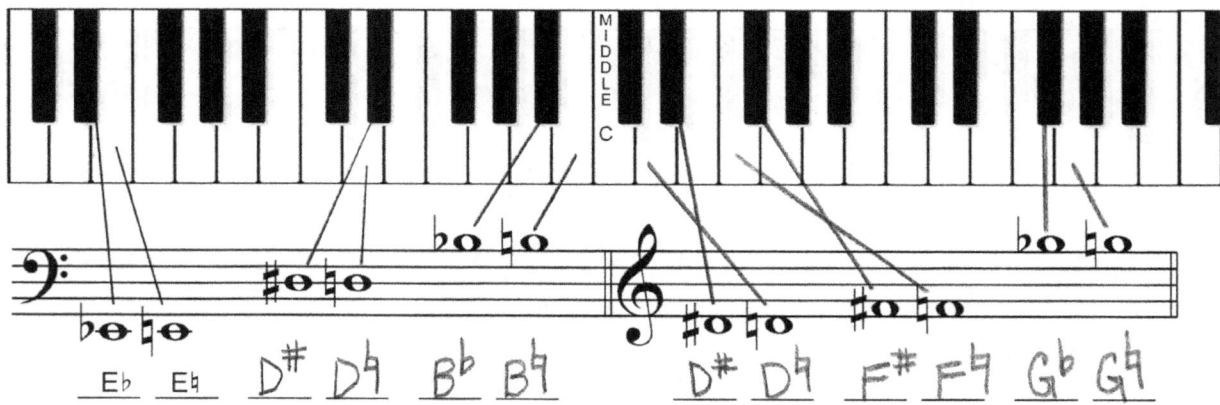

E♭ E♮ D# D♮ B♭ B♮   D# D♮ F# F♮ G♭ G♮

2. Write a natural in front of the 2nd note in each measure. Name the notes.

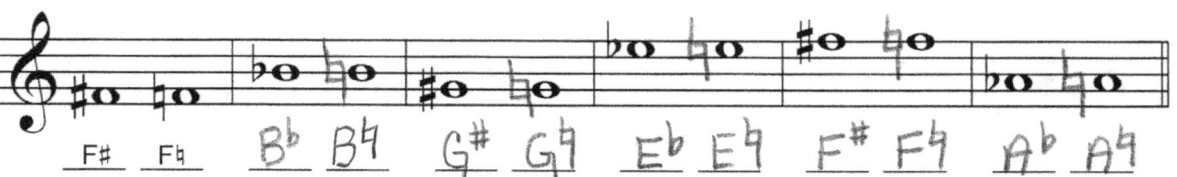

F# F♮   B♭ B♮   G# G♮   E♭ E♮   F# F♮   A♭ A♮

NAMING NOTES with ACCIDENTALS

An **ACCIDENTAL** placed in front of a note applies to any note that is written on that line or in that space until it is cancelled by either another accidental or by a bar line.

♪ **Note:** An **ACCIDENTAL** only applies to the notes on the line or in the space where it is written. It does **NOT** apply to notes that have the same letter name but appear in a higher or lower position on the staff.

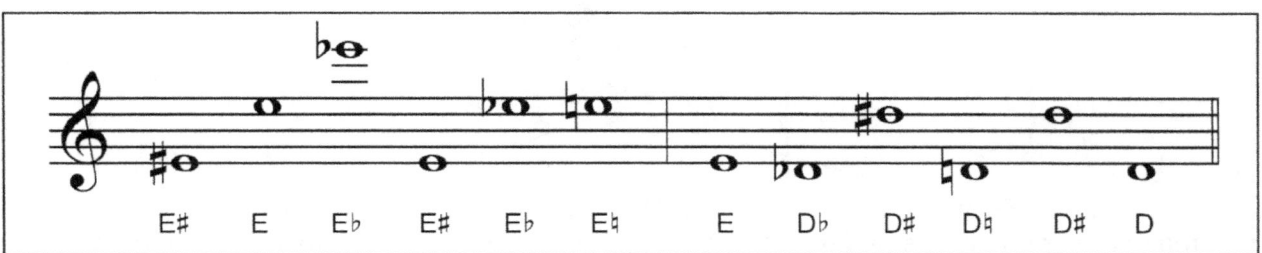

♪ **Note:** A bar line at the end of a measure cancels all accidentals in that measure.

1. Name the following notes in the Treble Clef.

G#   Db   G   G#   Db   D   Ab   D#   A♮   A

2. Name the following notes in the Bass Clef.

Bb   Bb   B#   B♮   B   B   B#   Bb   B#   Bb

3. Raise the following notes a chromatic semitone. Use whole notes. Name the notes.

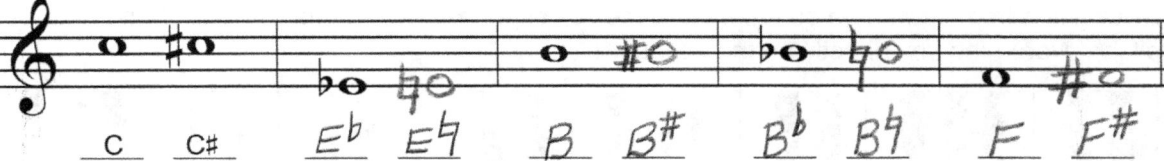

C   C#   Eb   E♮   B   B#   Bb   B♮   F   F#

4. Lower the following notes a chromatic semitone. Use whole notes. Name the notes.

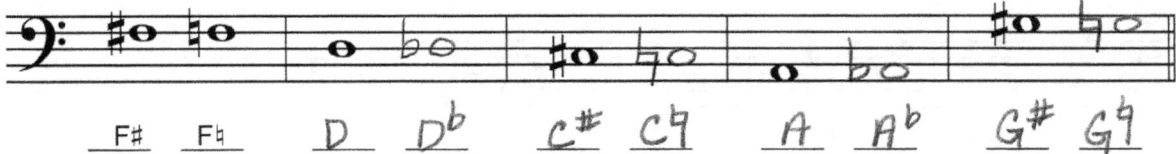

F#   F♮   D   Db   C#   C♮   A   Ab   G#   G♮

25

STYLE in PERFORMANCE, PEDALS and OTTAVA

Terms indicating **STYLE in PERFORMANCE** are used by a composer to guide the performer in the interpretation of the music.

cantabile	-	in a singing style	**grazioso**	-	graceful
dolce	-	sweet, gentle	**maestoso**	-	majestic

On the piano, **PEDALS** change the tone quality.

LEFT PEDAL
una corda or **una corde pedal**
softens (or mellows) the tone
(played with the left foot)

MIDDLE PEDAL
sostenuto pedal sustains
any notes that are held down
when the pedal is depressed

RIGHT PEDAL
damper or **sustain pedal**
prolongs and connects tones
(played with the right foot)

The middle "**sostenuto**" pedal is not found on all pianos. It may also have a different function.

Con pedale, *con ped*. or the sign  indicate to use the damper pedal.
Other markings used to indicate the use of the damper pedal are ⌊____∧____⌋ and ⌊_____⌋.

1. Label the 3 pedals as una corda, sostenuto or damper pedal.

   una corda   _sostenuto_   _damper_

OTTAVA, or 8va, is the interval of an octave.

$8^{va}\mathrm{-----}\rceil$ Indicates to play the notes **one octave higher** than written.

$8^{va}\mathrm{-----}\rfloor$ Indicates to play the notes **one octave lower** than written.

2. Draw a line from each note on the staff to the corresponding key on the keyboard (at the correct pitch). Name the key directly on the keyboard.

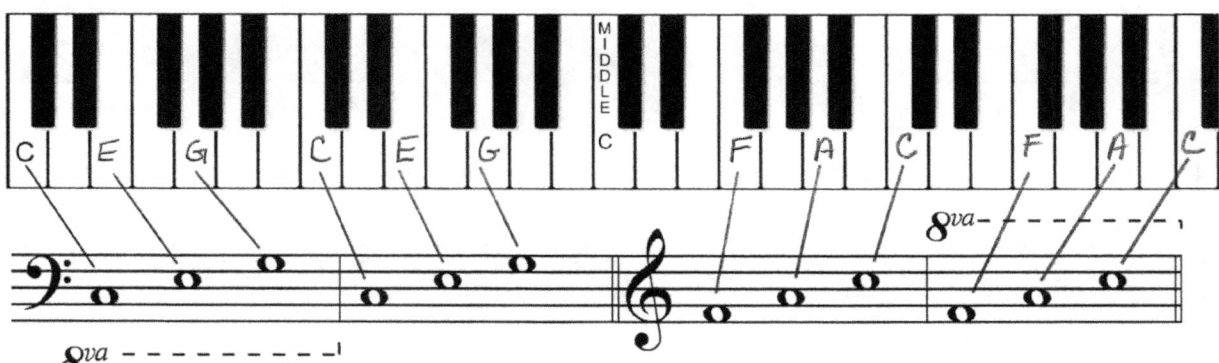

Lesson 2 Review Test

Total Score: ____ / 100

1. Name the following notes in the **Treble Clef**.

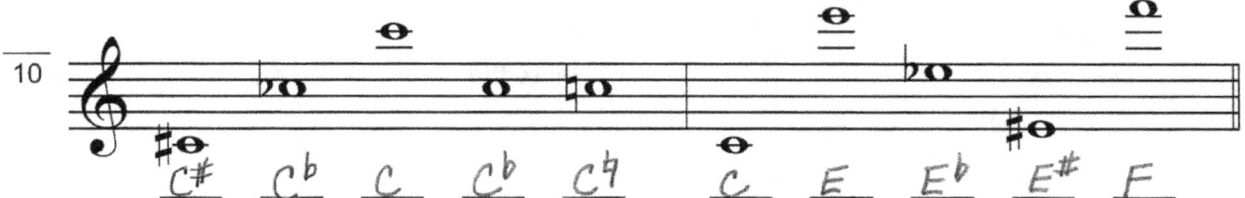

2. Write the following notes in the **Bass Clef**. Use whole notes.

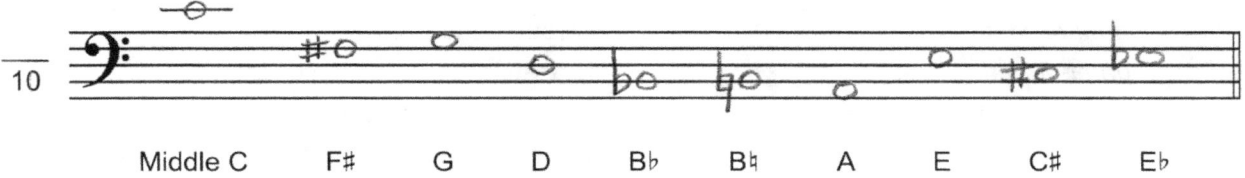

3. Draw a line from each note on the staff to the corresponding key on the keyboard (at the correct pitch). Name the key directly on the keyboard.

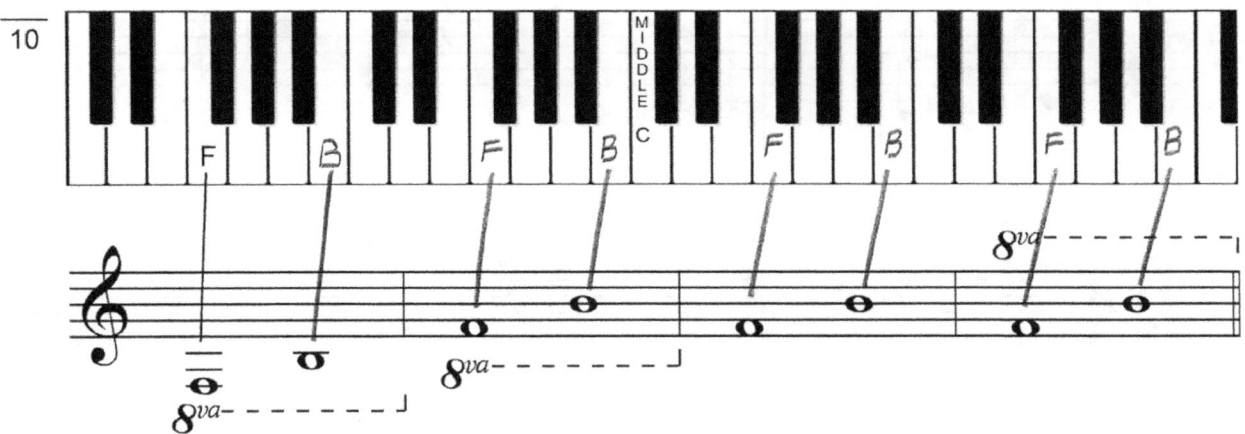

4. **RAISE** the following notes a **CHROMATIC** semitone (half step). Use whole notes.
   Name the notes.

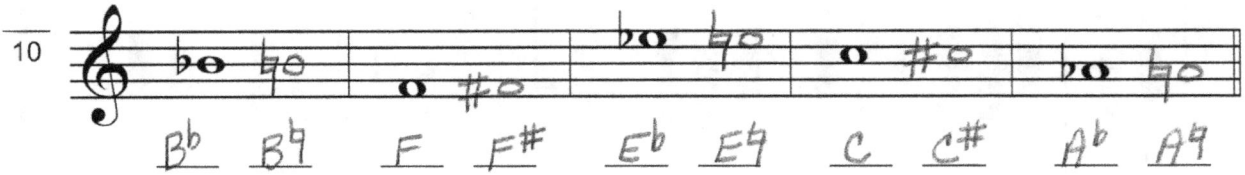

5. **LOWER** the following notes a **CHROMATIC** semitone (half step). Use whole notes.
   Name the notes.

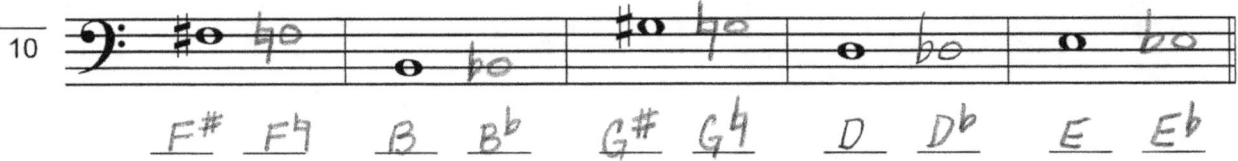

6. Match each musical term or sign with the English definition. (Not all definitions will be used.)

Term		Definition
cantabile	g	a) pedal
semitone	k	b) before the note, after the name
dolce	h	c) majestic
pedale, ped.	a	d) cancels a sharp or flat
grazioso	i	e) prolongs and connects tones
ottava, 8va	j	f) a whole measure of silence
maestoso	c	g) in a singing style
natural sign	d	h) sweet, gentle
damper pedal	e	i) graceful
placement of accidentals	b	j) the interval of an octave
		k) closest distance in pitch between 2 notes (half step)

7. Rewrite the following melody at the **SAME PITCH** in the Bass Clef.

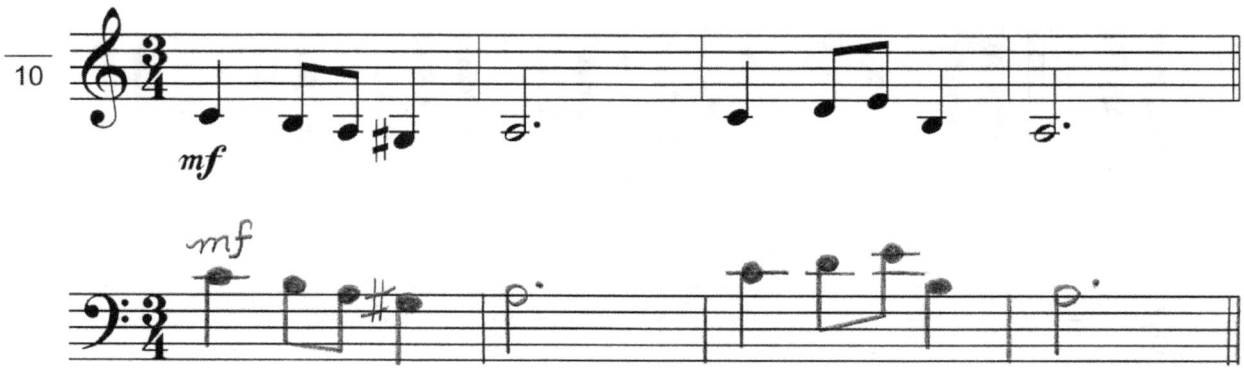

8. Draw a line from each note on the staff to the corresponding key on the keyboard (at the correct pitch). Name the notes.

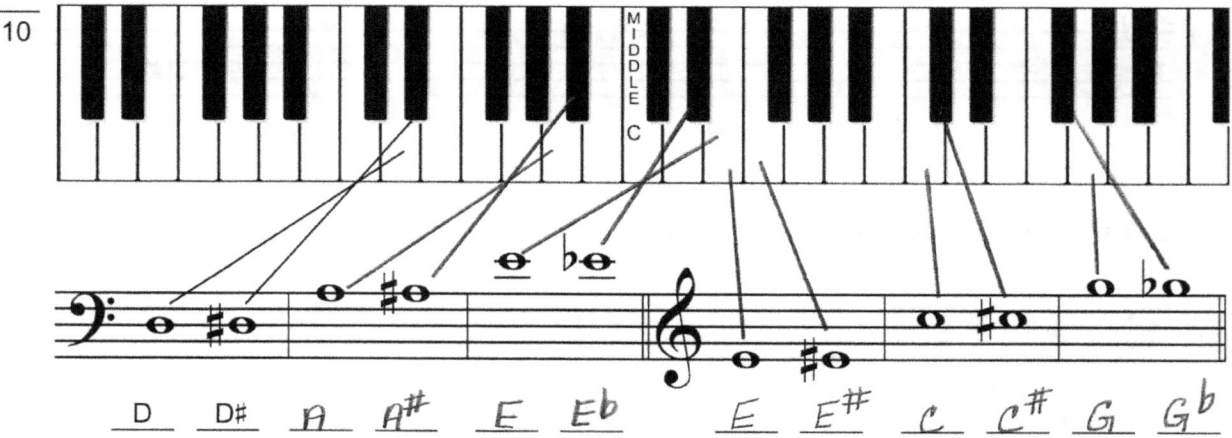

D D# A A# E Eb E E# C C# G Gb

9. Add **ONE REST** below each bracket to complete the measure. Cross off the count as each beat is completed.

Use the following rests:

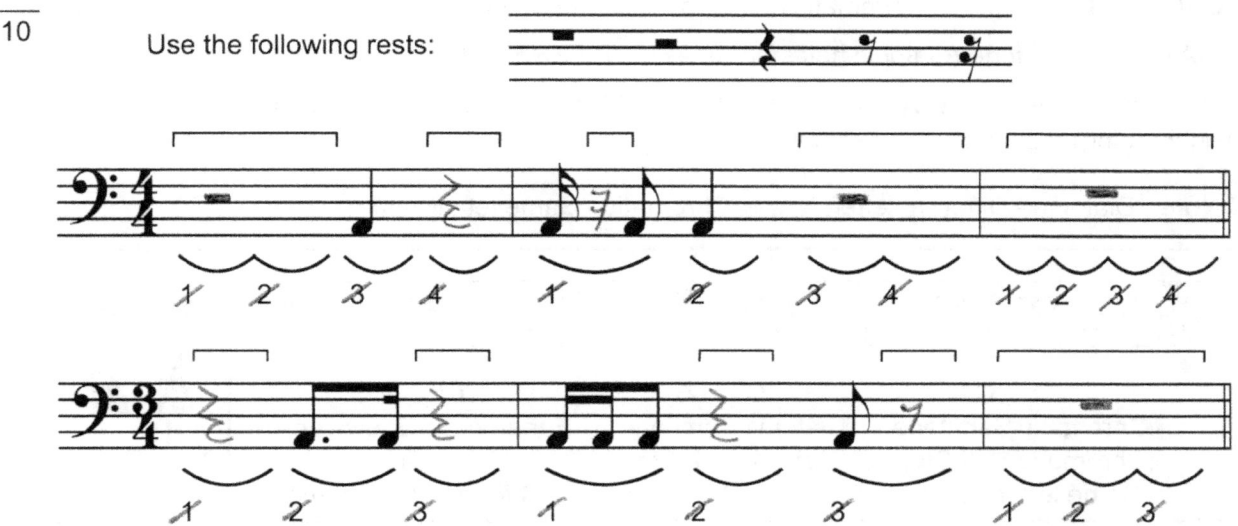

10. Analyze the following piece of music by answering the questions below.

Sneaky

G. St. Germain

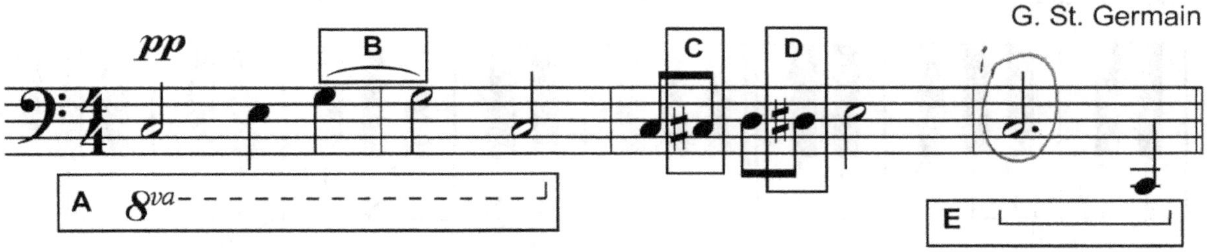

a) Name the title of the piece. _Sneaky_

b) Explain the sign at the letter **A**. _play 8 notes lower than written_

c) Explain the sign at the letter **B**. _Tie - hold for combined value of tied notes_

d) Name the note at the letter **C**. _C#_

e) Name the note at the letter **D**. _D#_

f) Give the meaning of the dynamic sign " **pp** ". _pianissimo - very soft_

g) Name the lowest note in this piece. _C_

h) Explain the sign at the letter **E**. _use the damper pedal_

i) Locate and circle a dotted half note in this piece. Name the note. _C_

j) How many measures are in this piece? _Four_

Lesson 3   Semitones, Enharmonic Equivalents and Whole Tones

A **CHROMATIC** semitone (chromatic half step) uses the **SAME** letter name. Example: C to C#

A **DIATONIC** semitone (diatonic half step) uses a **DIFFERENT** letter name. Example: C to D♭

An **ENHARMONIC EQUIVALENT** is the **SAME PITCH** written with notes using different (neighbouring) letter names. Example: C# and D♭

♩ Note: Diatonic - Different letter name; Chromatic - Same letter name.

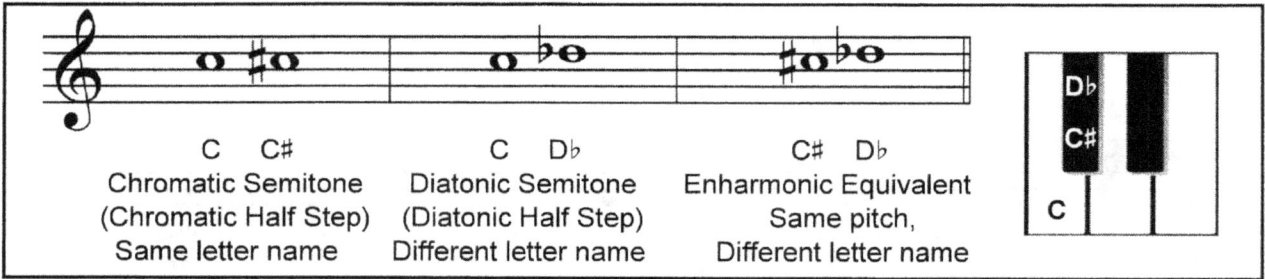

♩ Note: A **CHROMATIC SEMITONE** (chromatic half step) is written as an interval of a first.

1. Raise the following notes a chromatic semitone. Use whole notes. Draw a line from each note on the staff to the corresponding key on the keyboard (at the correct pitch). Name the notes.

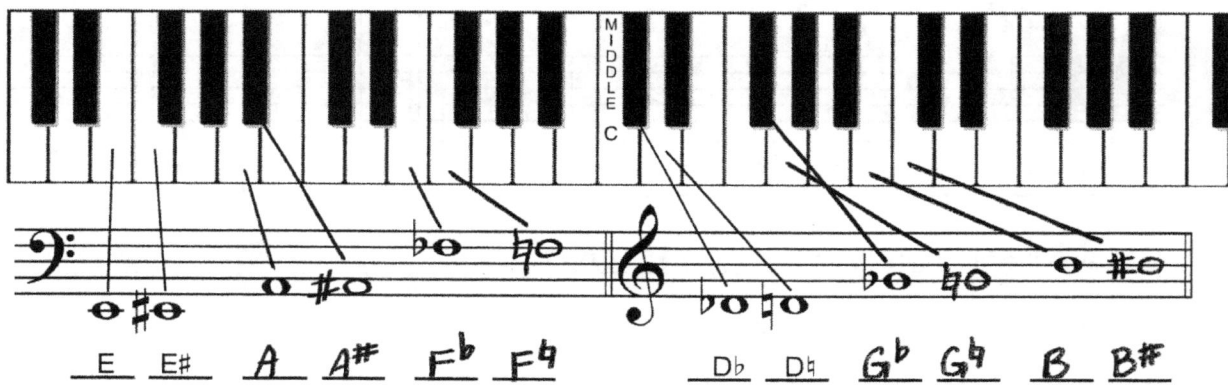

E E#   A A#   F♭ F♮   D♭ D♮   G♭ G♮   B B#

2. Lower the following notes a chromatic semitone. Use whole notes. Draw a line from each note on the staff to the corresponding key on the keyboard (at the correct pitch). Name the notes.

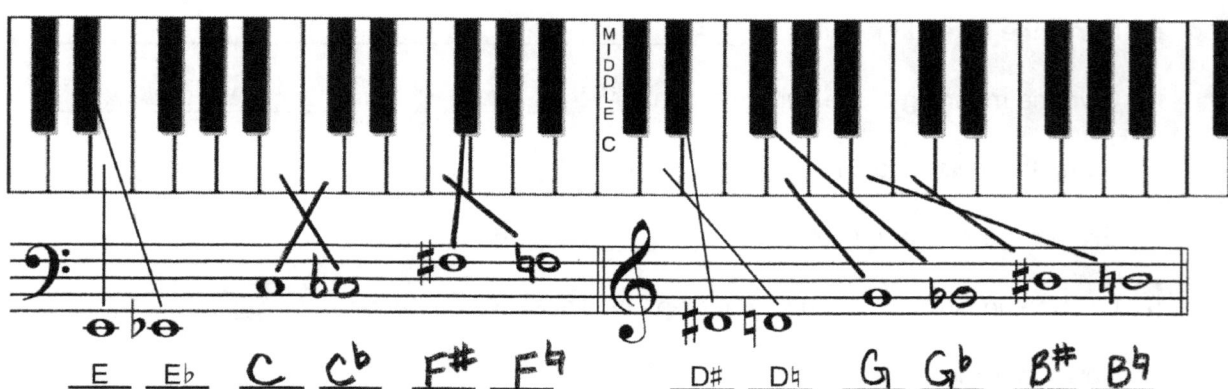

E E♭   C C♭   F# F♮   D# D♮   G G♭   B# B♮

♫ **Note:** A **DIATONIC SEMITONE** (diatonic half step) is written as an interval of a second.

3. Raise the following notes a diatonic semitone. Use whole notes. Draw a line from each note on the staff to the corresponding key on the keyboard (at the correct pitch). Name the notes.

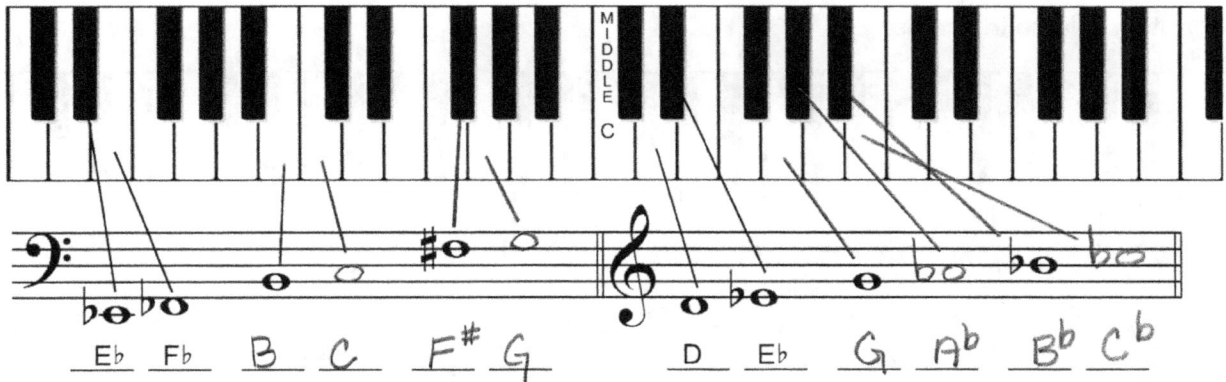

Eb Fb B C F# G   D Eb G Ab Bb Cb

4. Lower the following notes a diatonic semitone. Use whole notes. Draw a line from each note on the staff to the corresponding key on the keyboard (at the correct pitch). Name the notes.

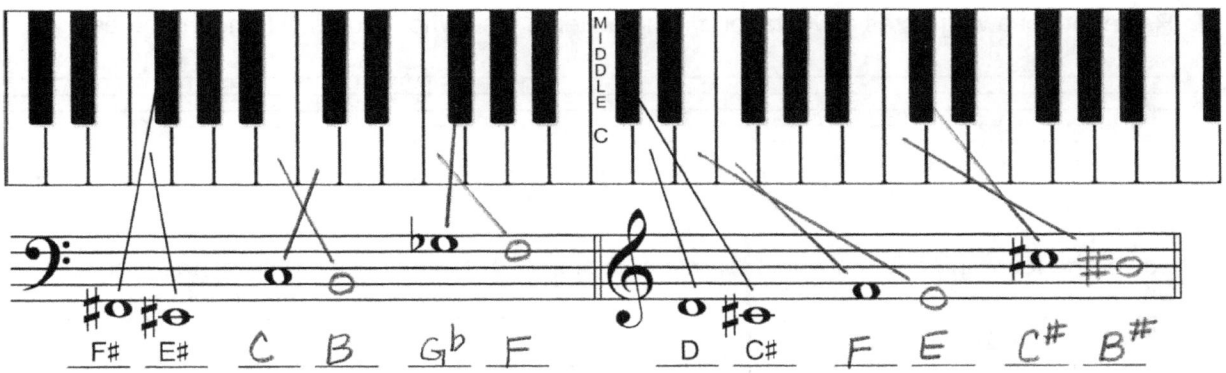

F# E# C B Gb F   D C# F E C# B#

♫ **Note:** An **ENHARMONIC EQUIVALENT** is written as an interval of a second.

5. Write the enharmonic equivalent for each of the following notes. Draw a line from each note on the staff to the corresponding key on the keyboard (at the correct pitch). Name the notes.

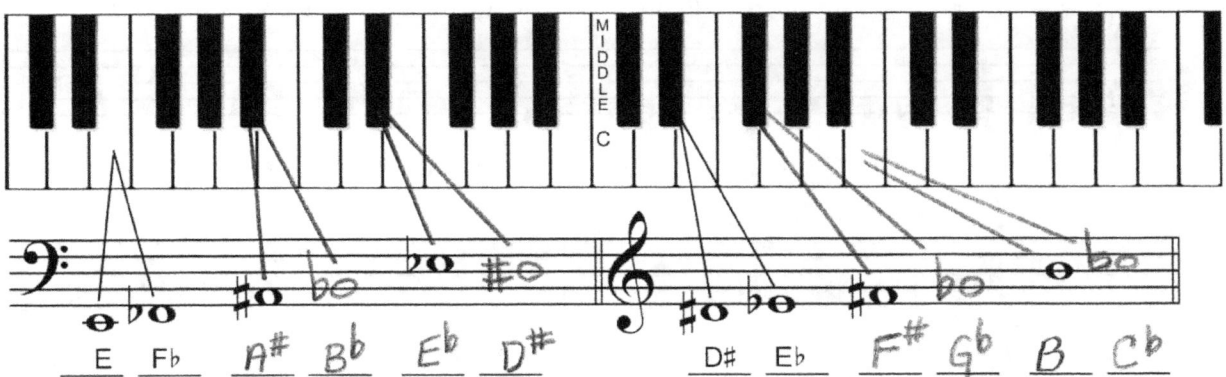

E Fb A# Bb Eb D#   D# Eb F# Gb B Cb

WHOLE TONE (WHOLE STEP or TONE)

A **WHOLE TONE** or **WHOLE STEP** (also referred to as a **TONE**) is equal to **TWO** semitones (half steps) with one key (black or white) between them. Example: C to D, C# to D#, A♭ to B♭, E to F#.

1. Draw a line from each note on the staff to the corresponding key on the keyboard (at the correct pitch). Name the notes.

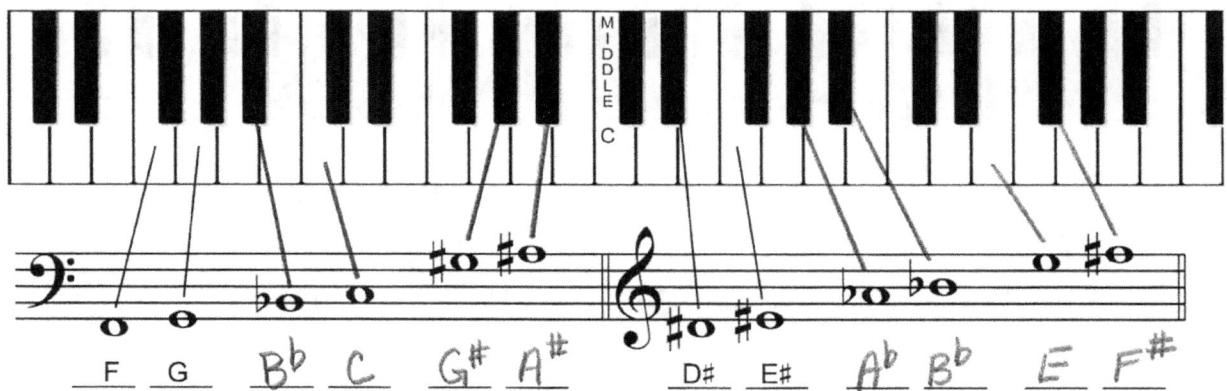

F G B♭ C G# A# D# E# A♭ B♭ E F#

♪ Note: A **Whole Tone** (whole step or tone) is written as an interval of a second.

2. Raise the following notes a whole tone (whole step). Use whole notes. Name the notes.

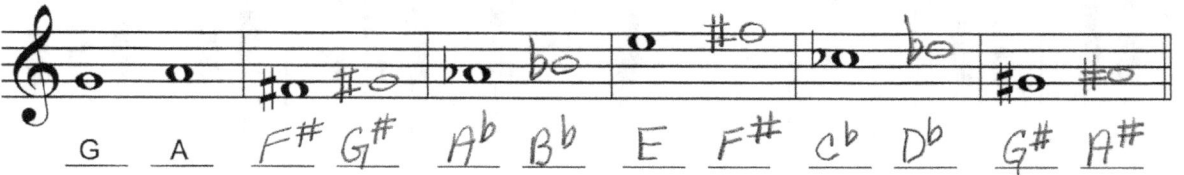

G A F# G# A♭ B♭ E F# C♭ D♭ G# A#

3. Lower the following notes a whole tone (whole step). Use whole notes. Name the notes.

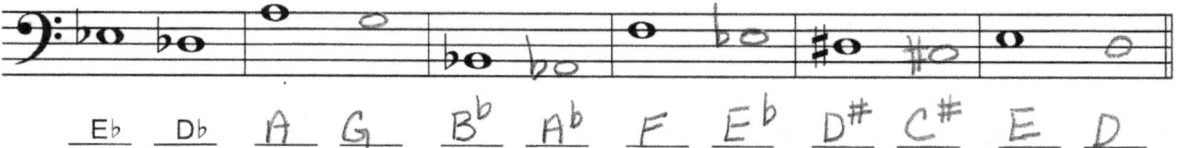

E♭ D♭ A G B♭ A♭ F E♭ D# C# E D

♪ Note: An **Enharmonic Equivalent** is the same pitch written with notes using different letter names.

4. Name each of the following as: d.s. (diatonic semitone), c.s. (chromatic semitone), w.t. (whole tone) or e.e. (enharmonic equivalent).

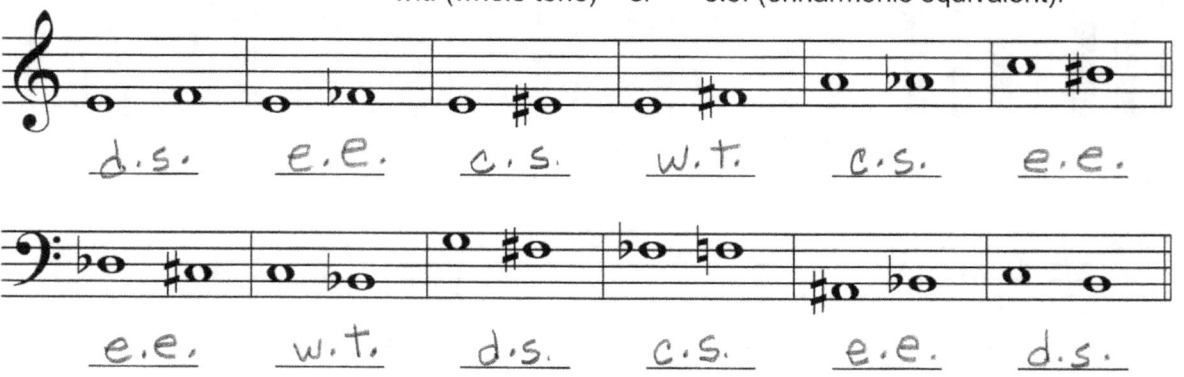

d.s. e.e. c.s. w.t. c.s. e.e.

e.e. w.t. d.s. c.s. e.e. d.s.

TEMPO

TEMPO indicates the speed at which music is performed. The tempo is written at the top left of the music above the Time Signature. Tempo markings are usually indicated by an Italian term.

Tempo	Definition - arranged in order from slowest to fastest.
largo	very slow and broad; a slow and solemn tempo
larghetto	not as slow as *largo*; fairly slow and broad
adagio	slow; slower than *andante*, but not as slow as *largo*
lento	slow
andante	moderately slow; at a walking pace
andantino	a little faster than *andante*
moderato	at a moderate tempo
allegretto	not as fast as *allegro*; fairly fast
allegro	fast
presto	very fast
prestissimo	as fast as possible

1. List the following tempo markings in order from slowest to fastest.

   allegro   *largo*   *andante*   *moderato*   *adagio*

   <u>largo</u>   <u>adagio</u>   <u>andante</u>   <u>moderato</u>   <u>allegro</u>

CHANGES in TEMPO

accelerando, accel.	becoming quicker
a tempo	return to the original tempo
fermata, 𝄐	a pause - hold the note or rest longer than its written value
rallentando, rall.	slowing down
ritardando, rit.	slowing down gradually
Tempo primo, Tempo I	return to the original tempo

♪ **Note:** ***Tempo primo, Tempo I*** or ***a tempo*** indicates that the tempo of the piece is returned to the original tempo after a ritardando, rallentando or accelerando.

2. Fill in the blanks.

   a) When the music is slowing down gradually, it is indicated by a
      <u>rallentando, rall.</u> or <u>ritardando, rit.</u>.

   b) When the music is becoming quicker, it is indicated by an <u>accelerando, accel.</u>.

   c) When the music is to return to the original tempo, it is indicated by a
      <u>Tempo primo, Tempo I</u> or <u>a tempo</u>.

   d) When there is a pause to hold the note or rest longer than its value, it is indicated by a
      <u>fermata 𝄐</u>.

ARTICULATION

ARTICULATION refers to the way that a note can be played. **Articulation Marks** are used in music to indicate different sounds.

Term	Definition	Articulation Mark
staccato	sharply detached	
tenuto	held, sustained (hold for the full value of the note)	
marcato, marc.	marked or stressed	
accent	a stressed note	
legato	smooth	
slur	play notes legato (smoothly)	

♫ **Note:** An *accent*, *slur*, *staccato* and *tenuto* are all placed close to the notehead and away from the stems.

1. Write the articulation mark in the correct place (either above or below the notes).

    accent   slur   slur   staccato   tenuto

Mano Sinistra *(M.S.)* is used in music to indicate the **LEFT** hand.
Mano Destra *(M.D.)* is used in music to indicate the **RIGHT** hand.

♫ **Note:** A *fermata* is always written above the staff.

2. Copy the music in the Treble Clef below.

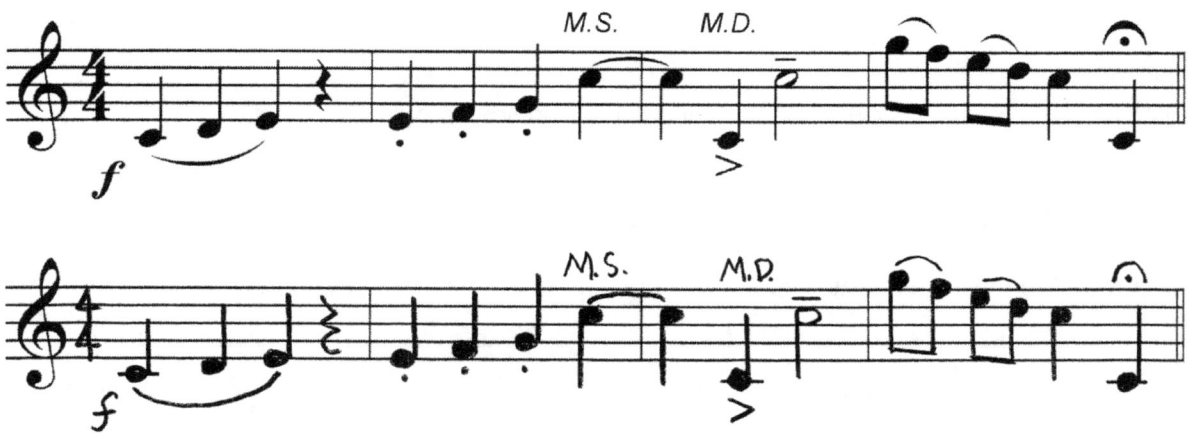

Lesson 3 — Review Test

Total Score: ____ / 100

1. Name the following notes in the **Bass Clef**.

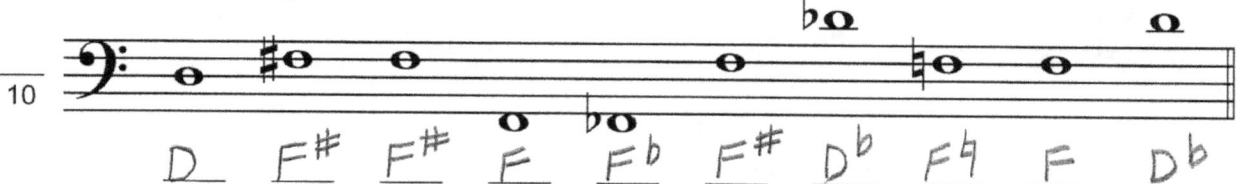

2. Write the following notes **ABOVE** the **Treble Clef**. Use ledger lines. Use half notes.

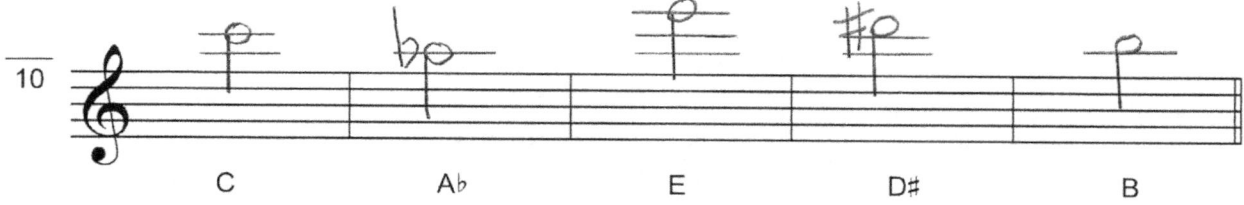

3. **RAISE** the following notes a **WHOLE TONE**. Use whole notes. Draw a line from each note on the staff to the corresponding key on the keyboard (at the correct pitch). Name the notes.

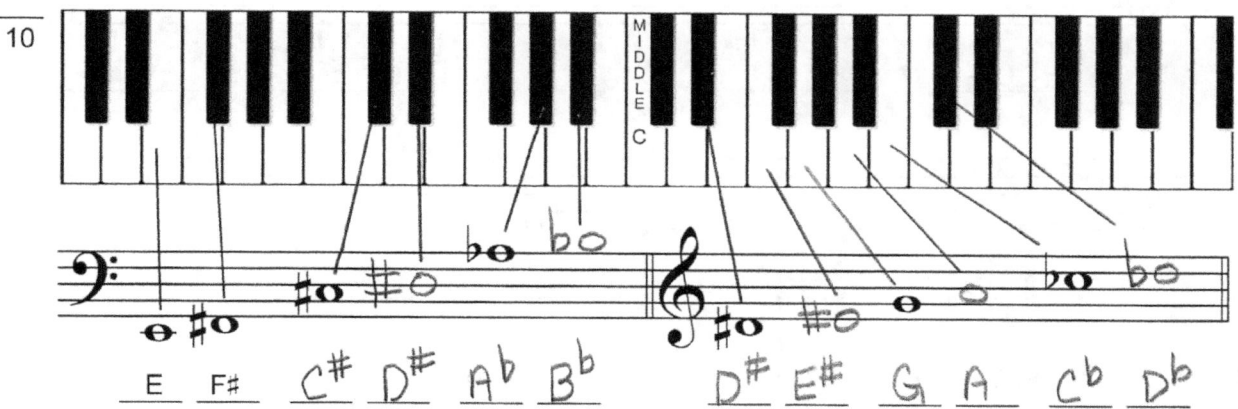

4. **LOWER** the following notes a **DIATONIC** semitone (half step). Use whole notes. Name the notes.

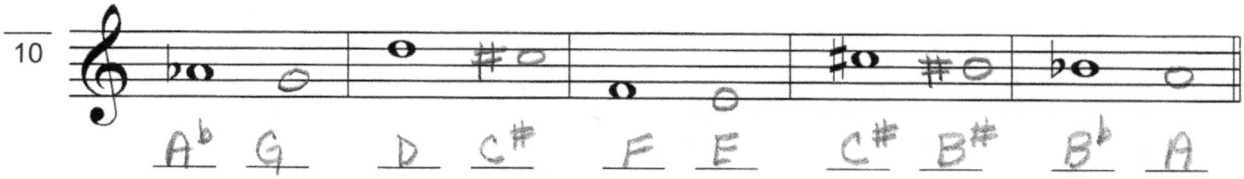

5. **RAISE** the following notes a **CHROMATIC** semitone (half step). Use whole notes. Name the notes.

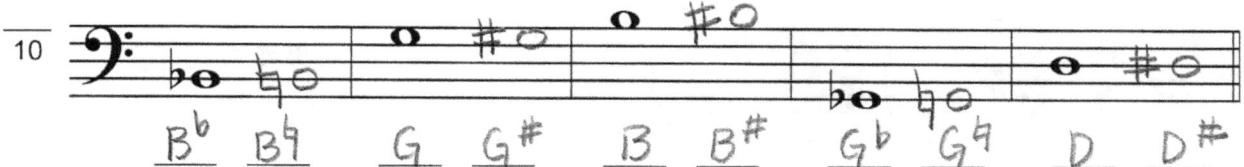

6. Rewrite the following melody at the **SAME PITCH** in the Treble Clef.

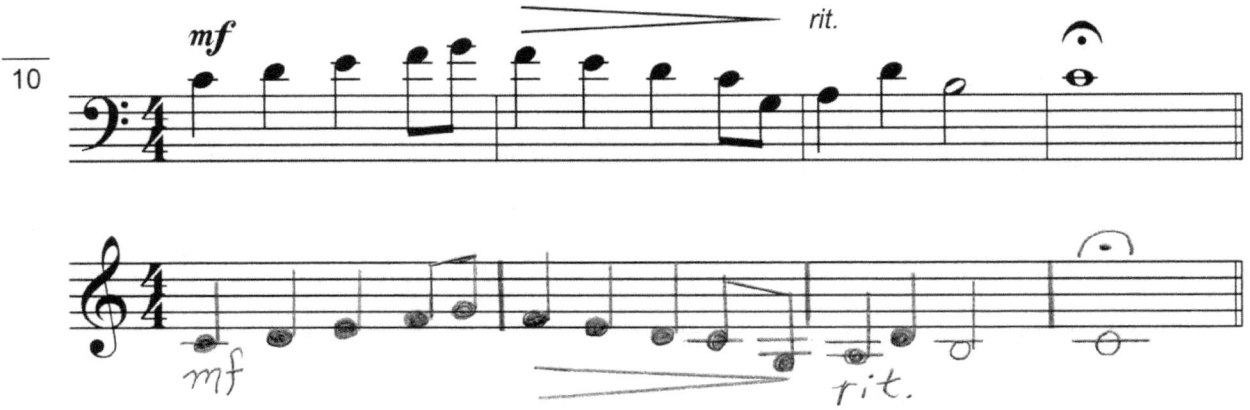

7. Name each of the following as: **d.s.** (diatonic semitone), **c.s.** (chromatic semitone), **w.t.** (whole tone) or **e.e.** (enharmonic equivalent).

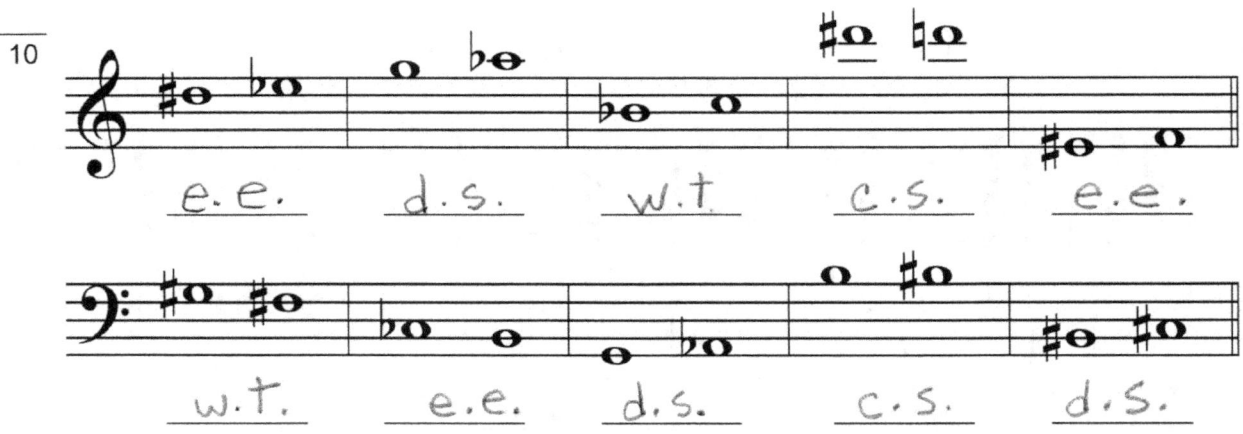

8. Add **ONE REST** below each bracket to complete the measure. Cross off the count as each beat is completed.

9. Match each musical term or sign with the English definition. (Not all definitions will be used.)

Term		Definition
marcato, marc.	e	a) at a moderate tempo
legato	g	b) becoming quicker
adagio	d	c) right hand
accelerando	b	d) slow, but not as slow as *largo*
Mano Destra, M.D.	c	e) marked or stressed
presto	i	f) slowing down gradually
moderato	a	g) smooth
Tempo primo, Tempo I	j	h) left hand
Mano Sinistra, M.S.	h	i) very fast
ritardando, rit.	f	j) return to the original tempo
		k) as fast as possible

10. Analyze the following piece of music by answering the questions below.

Cookies and Milk

a) Name the title of this piece. __Cookies and Milk__

b) Explain the sign at the letter **A**. __staccato - sharply detached__

c) Explain the sign at the letter **B**. __accent - stressed note__

d) How many beats does the rest at the letter **C** receive? __three__

e) Explain the sign at the letter **D**. __slur - play legato (smooth)__

f) Explain the sign at the letter **E**. __fermata - hold longer than its written value.__

g) How many beats does the note at the letter **F** receive? __three__

h) Locate and circle a diatonic semitone in this piece. Label it as d.s.

i) Locate and circle a whole tone in this piece. Label it as w.t.

j) Explain the meaning of **Allegro**. __fast__

Lesson 4   Major Scales and the Circle of Fifths - Major Keys

MAJOR SCALES

A **MAJOR SCALE** is a series of 8 degrees (notes) in alphabetical order using a specific Major Scale Pattern of **(T) Tones** (whole tones or whole steps) and **(ST) Semitones** (half steps).
A **circumflex** " ^ " or **caret** sign (hat) above a number ($\hat{3}$) indicates the degree number of the scale.

Major Scale Pattern: $\hat{1}$ tone $\hat{2}$ tone $\hat{3}$ semitone $\hat{4}$ tone $\hat{5}$ tone $\hat{6}$ tone $\hat{7}$ semitone $\hat{8}$ ($\hat{1}$)

In a Major scale, semitones are between degrees (notes) $\hat{3}$ - $\hat{4}$ and degrees (notes) $\hat{7}$ - $\hat{8}$ ($\hat{1}$).
Semitones are indicated by a slur.

♪ **Note:** This pattern of tones and semitones will create a Major Scale beginning on any note.

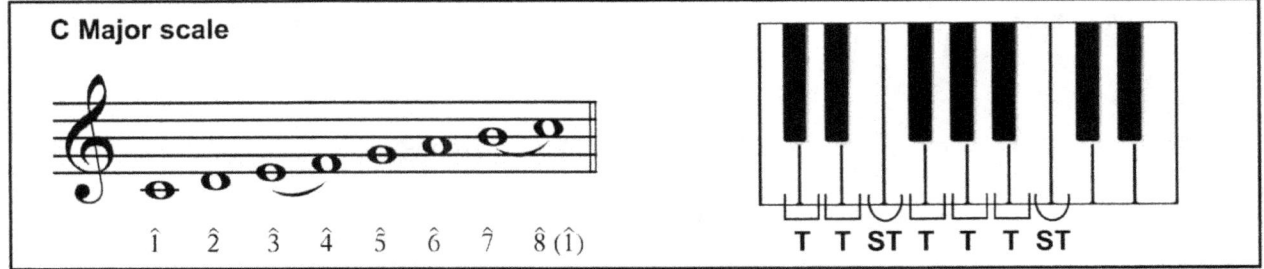

1. Copy the C Major scale. Number the scale degrees. Mark the semitones with a slur.

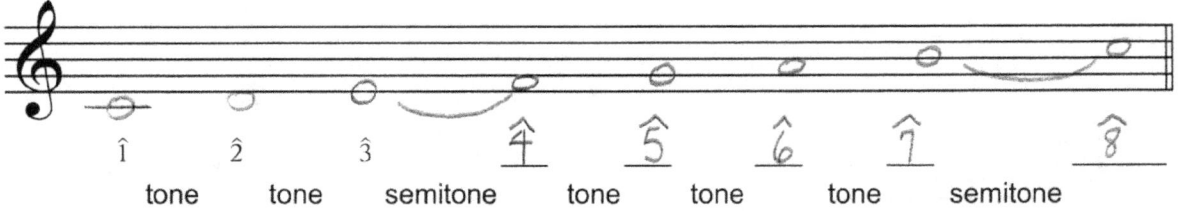

The first degree or note of the scale is called the **Tonic (I)** or **Key Note**. The Roman Numeral "**I**" is used for the Tonic. In the C Major scale, the Tonic note (I) is C.

♪ **Note:** When writing a scale **ASCENDING** (going up) and **DESCENDING** (going down), a **center bar line** may be used after the highest Tonic note.

2. Write the C Major scale ascending and descending. Mark the semitones with a slur.
    Label the Tonic (I) notes. Add a center bar line after the highest Tonic note C. Use whole notes.

MAJOR SCALE PATTERN

When writing the **MAJOR SCALE PATTERN** beginning on notes other than C, accidentals will be required ascending and descending to keep the Major Scale Pattern of tones (whole steps) and semitones (half steps).

G Major scale begins on the Tonic G and follows the Major Scale Pattern. G Major has 1 sharp, F♯.

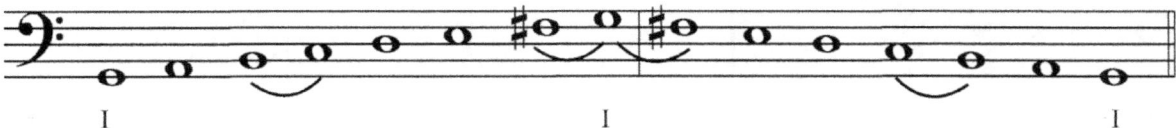

1. Write the G Major scale ascending and descending. Use an accidental for the F♯. Mark the semitones with a slur. Label the Tonic (I) notes. Add a center bar line. Use whole notes.

F Major scale begins on the Tonic F and follows the Major Scale Pattern. F Major has 1 flat, B♭.

2. Write the F Major scale ascending and descending. Use an accidental for the B♭. Mark the semitones with a slur. Label the Tonic (I) notes. Add a center bar line. Use whole notes.

D Major scale begins on the Tonic D and follows the Major Scale Pattern. D Major has 2 sharps, F♯ and C♯.

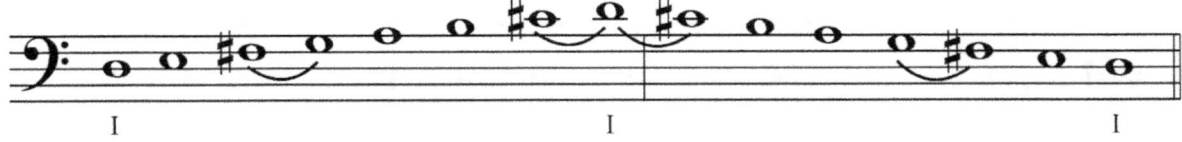

3. Write the D Major scale ascending and descending. Use accidentals for the F♯ and C♯. Mark the semitones with a slur. Label the Tonic (I) notes. Add a center bar line. Use whole notes.

MAJOR SCALE PATTERNS and ACCIDENTALS

MAJOR SCALE PATTERNS are used to identify the **ACCIDENTALS** found in each Major scale.

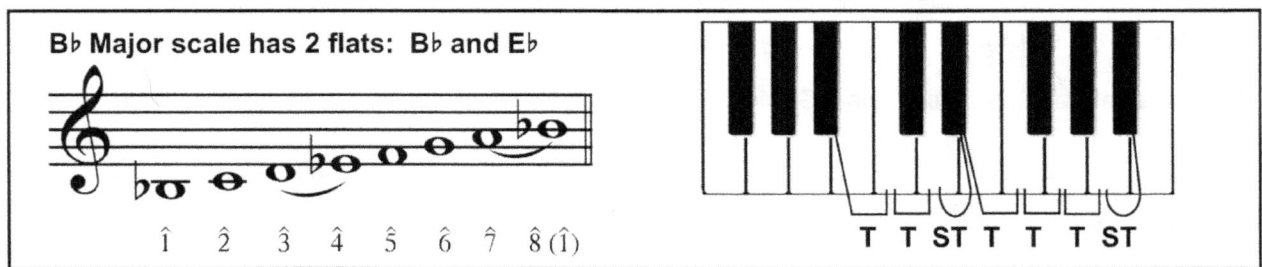

1. Write the B♭ Major scale ascending and descending. Use accidentals for the B♭ and E♭. Mark the semitones with a slur. Label the Tonic (I) notes. Add a center bar line. Use whole notes.

MAJOR SCALES using **ACCIDENTALS** may be written with or without a center bar line.

♪ **Note:** When writing a scale using accidentals **WITH** a center bar line, the accidentals must be repeated in the descending scale. When writing a scale using accidentals **WITHOUT** a center bar line, accidentals are **ONLY** written in the ascending scale.

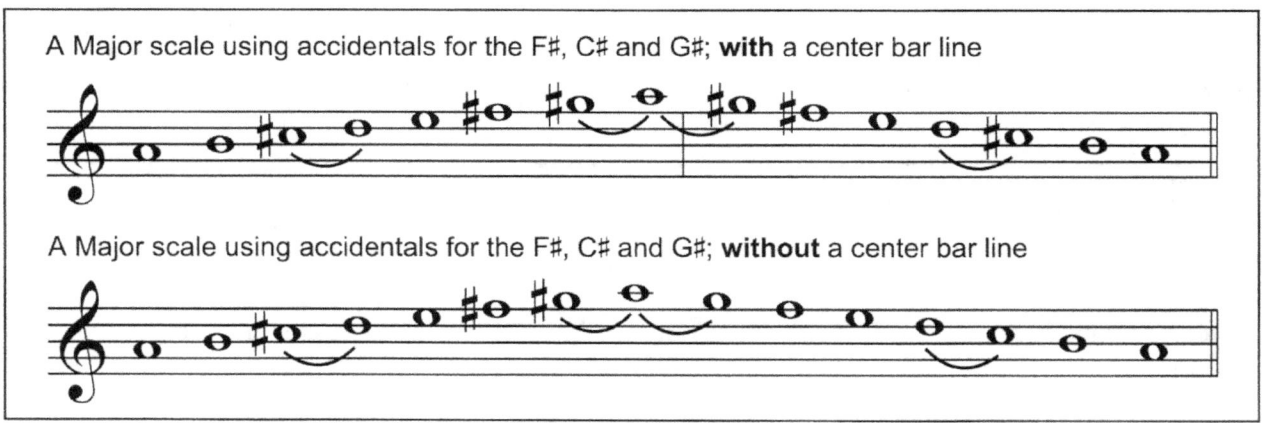

♪ **Note:** Always write scales in the **SAME WAY**, either **WITH** or **WITHOUT** a center bar line.

2. Write the A Major scale ascending and descending. Use accidentals for the F♯, C♯ and G♯. Mark the semitones with a slur. Label the Tonic (I) notes. Use whole notes.

MAJOR SCALES using ACCIDENTALS

MAJOR SCALES using **ACCIDENTALS** may be written with or without a center bar line.

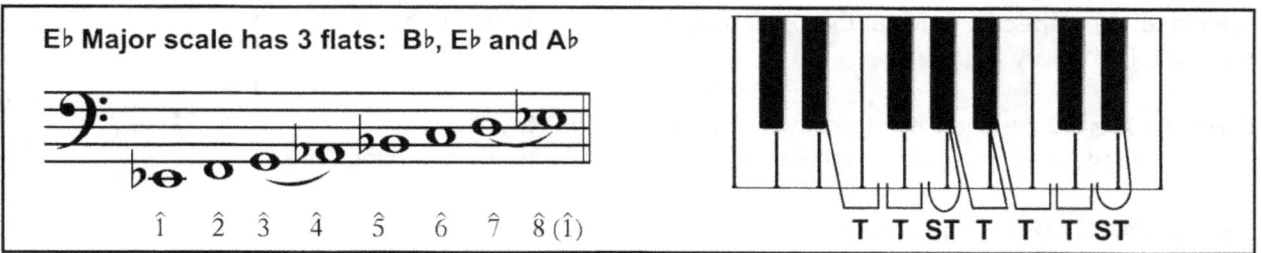

1. Write the E♭ Major scale ascending and descending. Use accidentals for the B♭, E♭ and A♭. Mark the semitones with a slur. Label the Tonic (I) notes. Use whole notes.

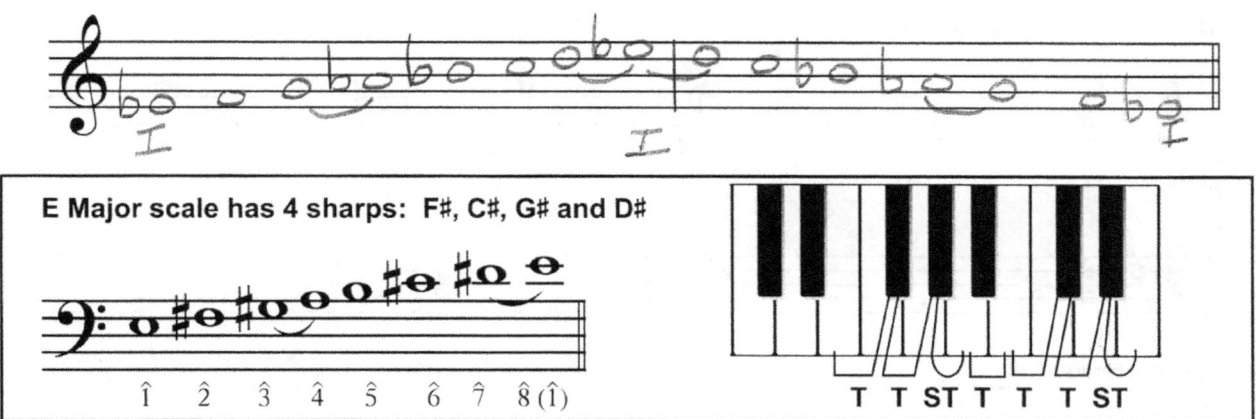

2. Write the E Major scale ascending and descending. Use accidentals for the F♯, C♯, G♯ and D♯. Mark the semitones with a slur. Label the Tonic (I) notes. Use whole notes.

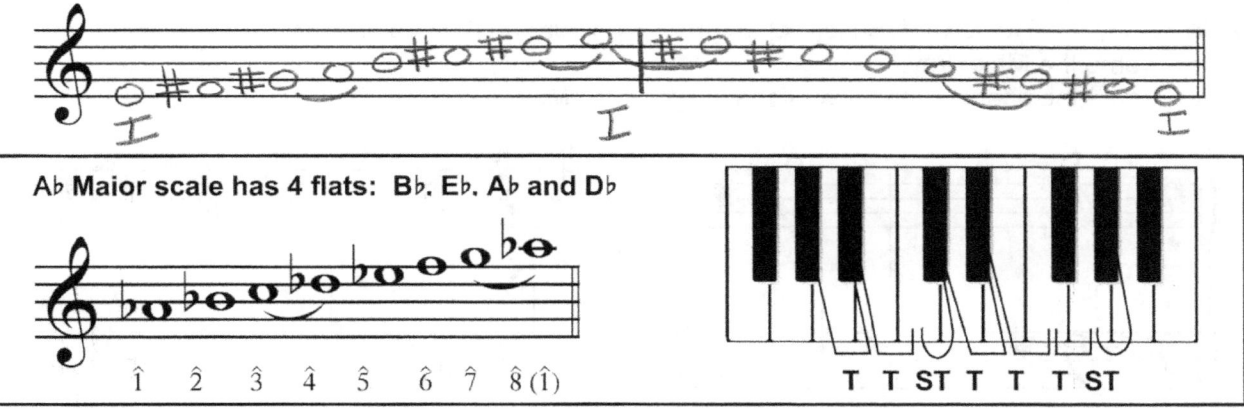

3. Write the A♭ Major scale ascending and descending. Use accidentals for the B♭, E♭, A♭ and D♭. Mark the semitones with a slur. Label the Tonic (I) notes. Use whole notes.

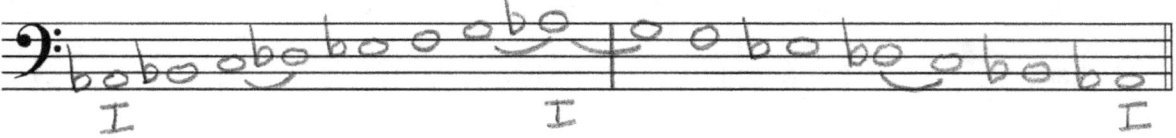

KEY SIGNATURES

The **KEY SIGNATURE** is a group of sharps or flats that indicates the key. Instead of using accidentals, the sharps or flats from the Major Scale Patterns are placed in a specific order at the beginning of the staff, directly after the clef sign, in the Key Signature.

♪ **Note:** The **KEY** is the main tonality of the music. The Key Signature identifies 2 possible tonalities - the Major key or its relative minor key.

KEY SIGNATURES with SHARPS

The order of **SHARPS** is: F#   C#   G#   D#

1. a) Copy the Treble Clef, Bass Clef and Key Signature on the Grand Staff.
   b) Name the order of sharps.

Order of Sharps: __F#   C#   G#   D#__   __F# C# G# D#__   __F# C# G# D#__

♪ **Note:** A **SINGLE** bar line cancels an accidental but **NOT** the Key Signature.
A **DOUBLE** bar line (2 thin bar lines together) cancels the Key Signature.

2. a) Copy the Treble Clef, Bass Clef and Key Signature on the Grand Staff.
   b) Name the Major key.
   c) Name the sharps in the Key Signature for each Major key.

Key: G Major __G Major__   D Major __D Major__   A Major __A Major__   E Major __E Major__

Key Signature:
   1 sharp: F#   2 sharps: F# C#   3 sharps: F# C# G#   4 sharps: F# C# G# D#
   1 sharp: __F#__   2 sharps: __F# C#__   3 sharps: __F# C# G#__   4 sharps: __F# C# G# D#__

KEY SIGNATURES with FLATS

The order of FLATS is: B♭   E♭   A♭   D♭

1. a) Copy the Treble Clef, Bass Clef and Key Signature on the Grand Staff.
   b) Name the order of flats.

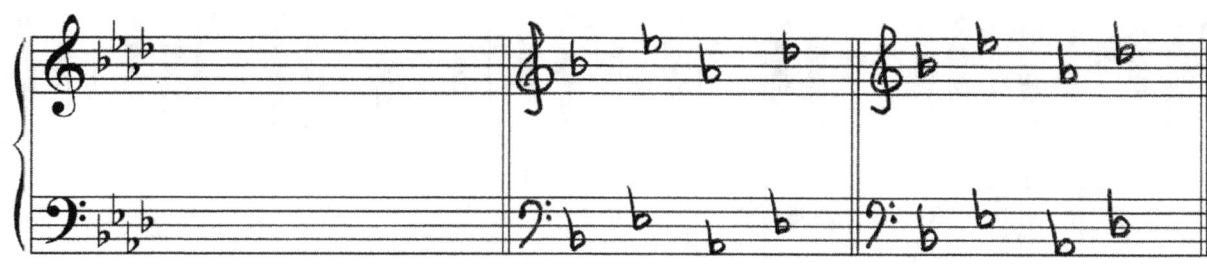

Order of Flats: B♭   E♭   A♭   D♭   B♭ E♭ A♭ D♭   B♭ E♭ A♭ D♭

2. a) Copy the Treble Clef, Bass Clef and Key Signature on the Grand Staff.
   b) Name the Major key.
   c) Name the flats in the Key Signature for each Major key.

Key: F Major _F Major_   B♭ Major _B♭ Major_   E♭ Major _E♭ Major_   A♭ Major _A♭ Major_

Key Signature:
   1 flat: B♭   2 flats: B♭ E♭   3 flats: B♭ E♭ A♭   4 flats: B♭ E♭ A♭ D♭

   1 flat: _B♭_   2 flats: _B♭ E♭_   3 flats: _B♭ E♭ A♭_   4 flats: _B♭ E♭ A♭ D♭_

♪ **Note:** C Major Key Signature has no sharps and no flats. The abbreviation "Maj" is used for Major. In Music, when a Key Signature changes to C Major, natural signs are used to cancel the outgoing Key Signature in the first measure. In Theory Exercises at this level, it is optional.

3. Name the Major key for each of the following Key Signatures.

Key: _G_ Maj   _E♭_ Maj   _F_ Maj   _A_ Maj   _B♭_ Maj   _C_ Maj   _A♭_ Maj   _D_ Maj   _E_ Maj

CIRCLE OF FIFTHS

The **CIRCLE of FIFTHS** is a map of the Major and minor Key Signatures. It identifies the number of flats and sharps found in each key. The distance from one key to the next key around the Circle of Fifths is a fifth. Each fifth is 5 letter names and 7 semitones.

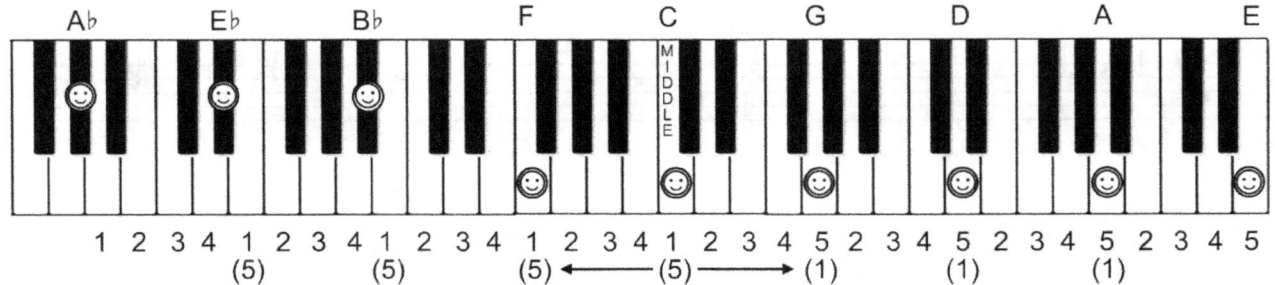

When moving UP from C the fifth note is counted again as (1).   1 2 3 4 5 (1) 2 3 4 5 (1)
When moving DOWN from C the first note is counted again as (5).   5 4 3 2 1 (5) 4 3 2 1 (5)

Circle of Fifths

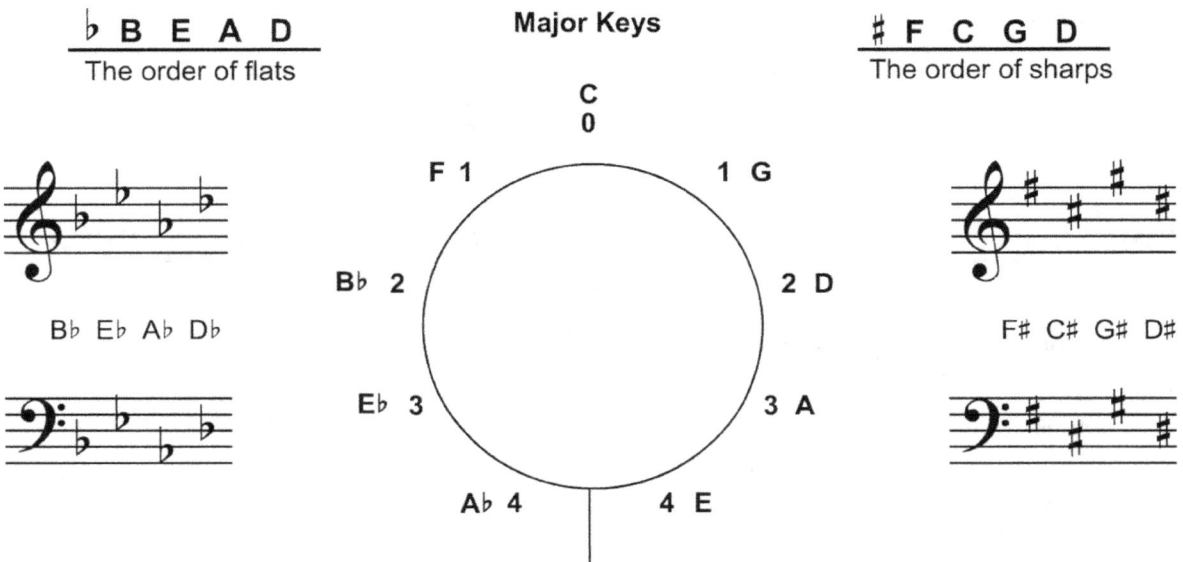

♪ **Note:** The Circle of Fifths identifies the number of flats or sharps in each key.
      The order of flats and the order of sharps identify the flats or sharps used.

1. Write the Key Signature for the following Major keys.

C Major - <u>No Flats and No Sharps</u>

F Major Bb
B♭ Major Bb Eb
E♭ Major Bb Eb Ab
A♭ Major Bb Eb Ab Db

G Major F#
D Major F# C#
A Major F# C# G#
E Major F# C# G# D#

CIRCLE OF FIFTHS - MAJOR KEYS

The sentence "**Father Charles Goes Down And Ends Battle**" is used to draw the Circle of Fifths. The musical alphabet distance between the first letter in each word of this sentence is a fifth.

```
      F       C       G       D       A       E     B
      1 2 3 4 5 2 3 4 5 2 3 4 5 2 3 4 5 2 3 4 5 2 3 4 5
         (1)     (1)     (1)     (1)     (1)
```

1. Start at the number "1" on the flat side with **F** (Father). Move clockwise (to the right) up a fifth each time. Trace the given letters to complete the Circle of Fifths.

Father **C**harles **G**oes **D**own **A**nd **E**nds (**A**nd♭ **E**nds♭) **B**attle♭

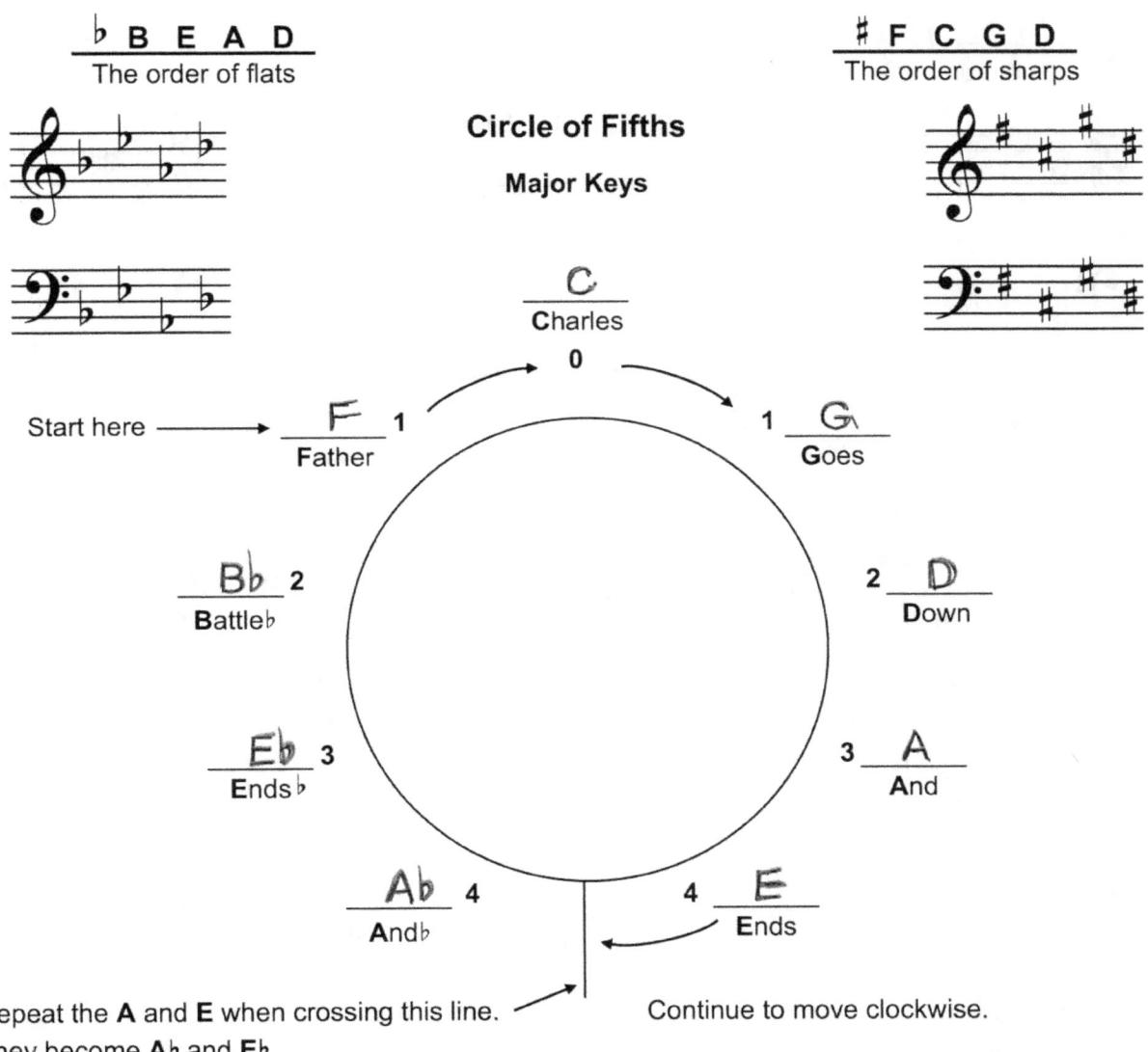

2. Copy the following sentence for writing out the Major keys.

Father **C**harles **G**oes **D**own **A**nd **E**nds (**A**nd♭ **E**nds♭) **B**attle♭

Father Charles Goes Down And Ends (And♭ Ends♭) Battle♭

COMPLETE the CIRCLE of FIFTHS - MAJOR KEYS

♪ **Note: MAJOR** keys go **OUTSIDE** the circle beside the numbers.

1. Complete the Circle of Fifths:
   a) Write the order of flats. Draw the Flat Key Signature in both the Treble Clef and Bass Clef.
   b) Write the order of sharps. Draw the Sharp Key Signature in both the Treble Clef and Bass Clef.
   c) Write the Major keys around the outside of the circle. Use UPPER case letters for Major keys. Start at the number "1" on the flat side with F. Move clockwise up a fifth each time.

Use the Major key sentence: **F**ather **C**harles **G**oes **D**own **A**nd **E**nds (**A**nd♭ **E**nds♭) **B**attle♭.

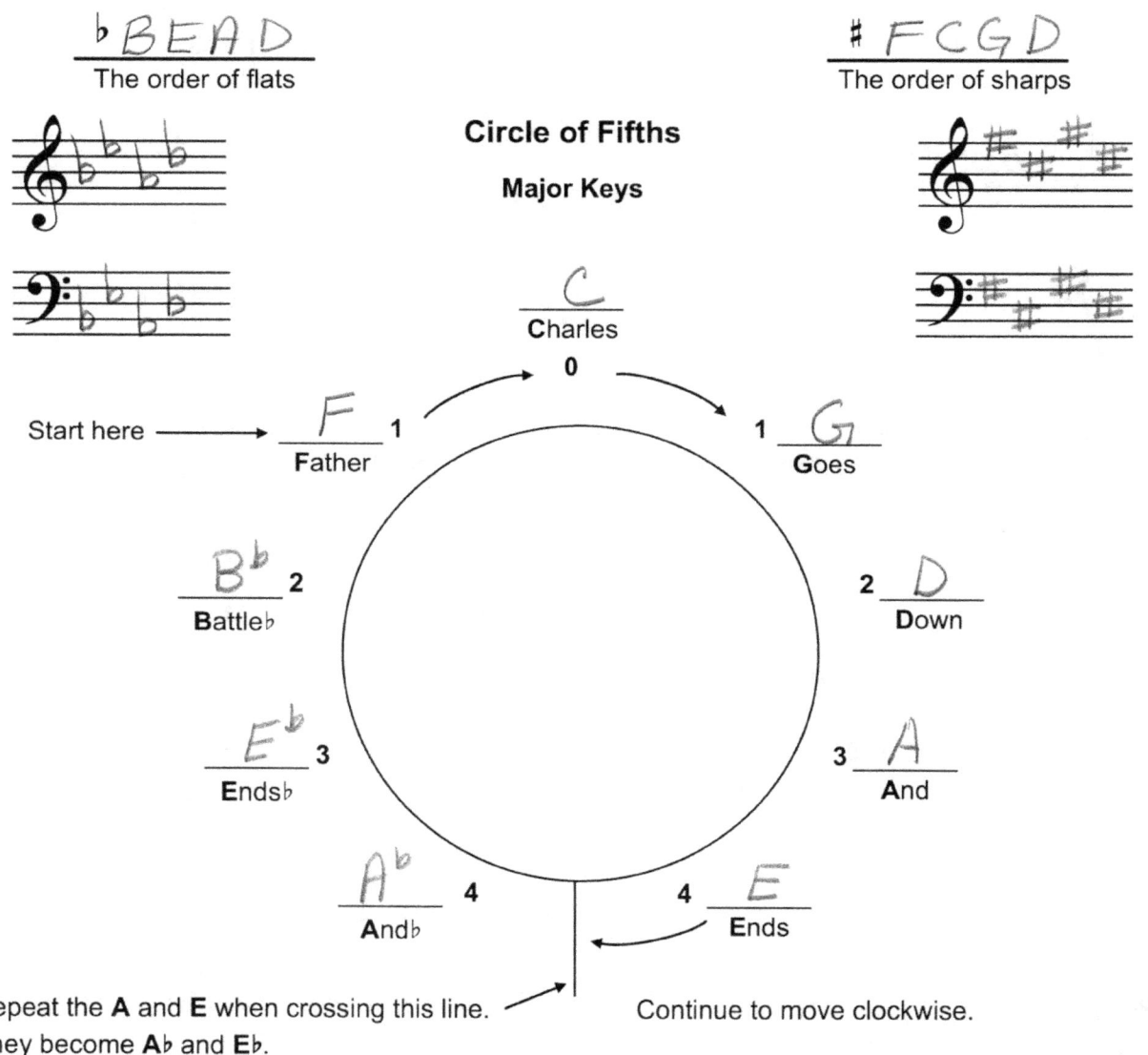

2. Write the Major key sentence.

Father Charles Goes Down And Ends (And♭ Ends♭) Battle♭

WRITING THE CIRCLE of FIFTHS

MAJOR KEY SENTENCE:

Father **C**harles **G**oes **D**own **A**nd **E**nds (**A**nd♭ **E**nds♭) **B**attle♭

1. Complete the Circle of Fifths:
   a) Write the flat sign and the order of flats on the top left line.
   b) Write the sharp sign and the order of sharps on the top right line.
   c) Start at the top of the circle with 0. Add the numbers 1, 2, 3, 4 around the outside of the circle on the sharp side. Continue with the numbers 4, 3, 2, 1 around the flat side.
   d) Write the Major keys on the outside of the circle. Use UPPER case letters. Start at the number "1" on the flat side with F (Father).

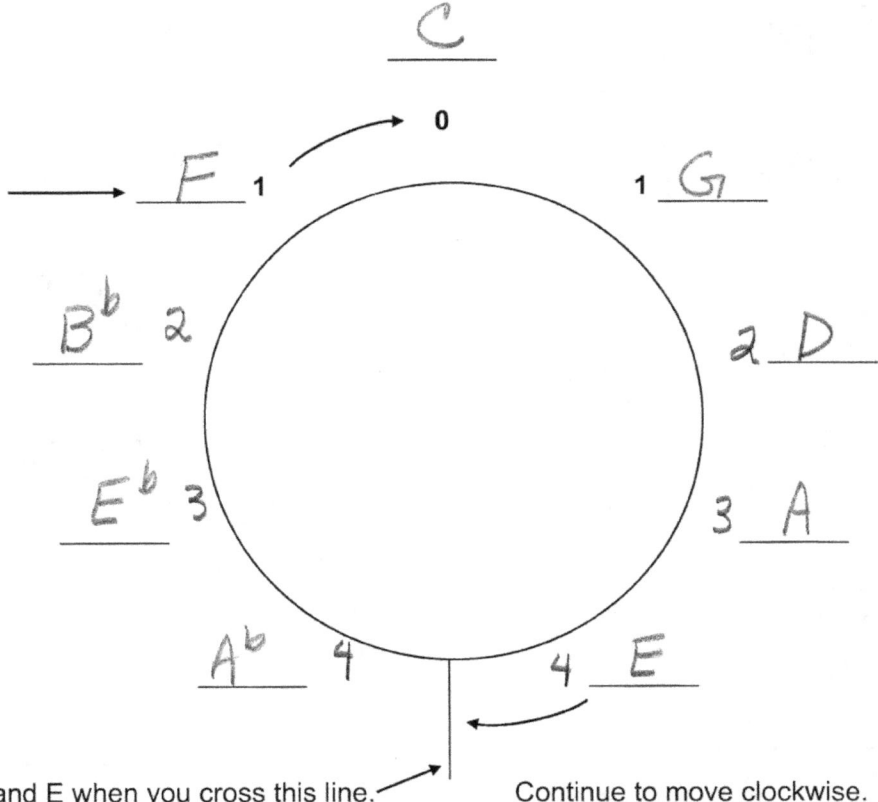

♭ BEAD
The order of flats

♯ FCGD
The order of sharps

C — 0
F 1   1 G
B♭ 2   2 D
E♭ 3   3 A
A♭ 4   4 E

Repeat the A and E when you cross this line. They become A♭ and E♭.

Continue to move clockwise.

Practice writing the **CIRCLE OF FIFTHS** on a blank piece of paper.
Write it out many times until memorized.
Always write it in the **SAME** order.

KEY SIGNATURES AROUND the CIRCLE of FIFTHS

This **Circle of Fifths** contains the Major keys up to and including 4 flats and 4 sharps. The Circle of Fifths will continue to map out Major keys that have up to 7 flats and 7 sharps.

♪ **Note:** The complete order of **FLATS** is:

Bb Eb Ab Db Gb Cb Fb
Battle **E**nds **A**nd **D**own **G**oes **C**harles **F**ather

♪ **Note:** The complete order of **SHARPS** is:

F# C# G# D# A# E# B#
Father **C**harles **G**oes **D**own **A**nd **E**nds **B**attle

1. Following the example for F Major, copy the Treble Clef, the Bass Clef and the Key Signature. Name the Major key.

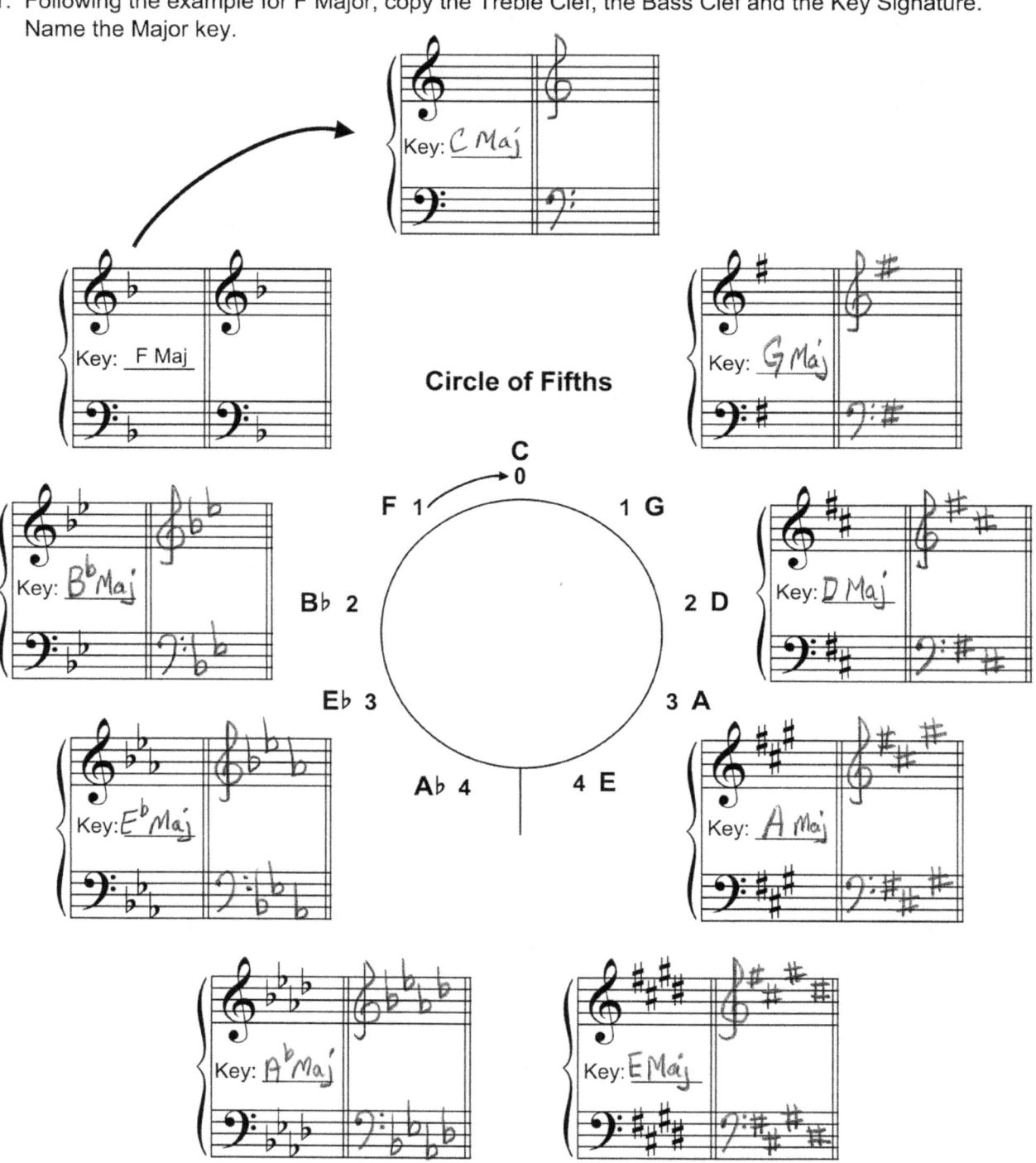

REPEAT SIGNS

A **REPEAT** sign is written as two **DOTS** (one in space 2 and one in space 3) in front of a double bar line (thin and thick bar lines).
A REPEAT sign indicates that the music is repeated from the beginning of the piece.

When there are **TWO** repeat signs, the music is repeated within the double bar lines.

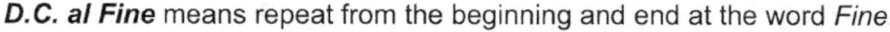

da capo, D.C. means repeat from the beginning.
dal segno, D.S. means repeat from the sign (𝄋).
Fine means "the end" of the piece of music.

D.C. al Fine means repeat from the beginning and end at the word *Fine*.
D.S. al Fine means repeat from the sign (𝄋) and end at the word *Fine*.

♪ **Note:** The sharps or flats in the Key Signature affect **ALL** the notes with the same letter name on the staff and on ledger lines.

1. For each of the following:
   a) Name the Major key.
   b) Name the notes in measures 2 and 3.
   c) Name the sharps or flats in the Key Signature.
   d) When all repeat signs are followed, how many measures are played?

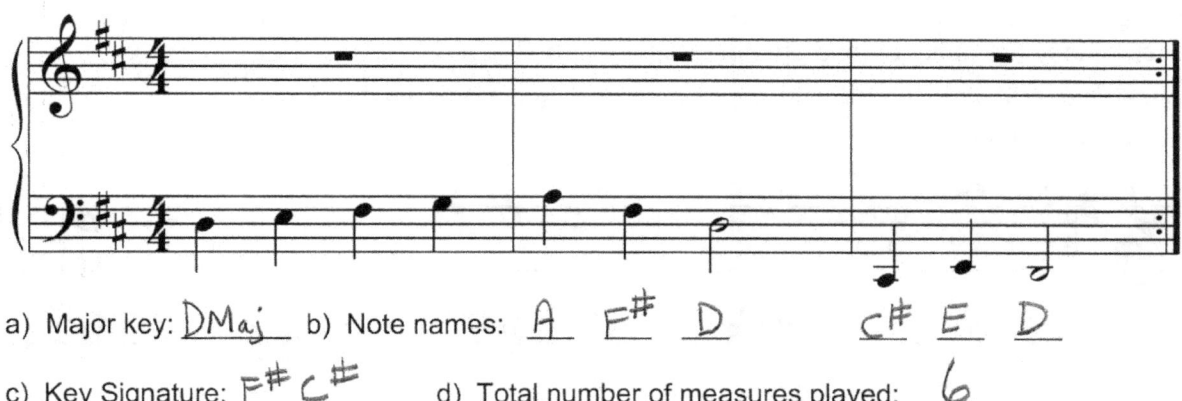

a) Major key: DMaj   b) Note names: A F# D   C# E D
c) Key Signature: F# C#   d) Total number of measures played: 6

♪ **Note:** 4/4 Time is also known as **COMMON TIME**. The symbol for Common Time is 𝄴.

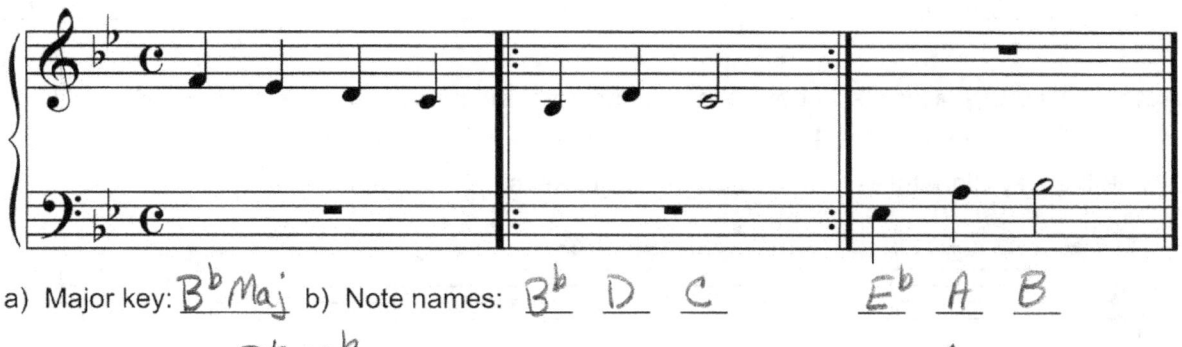

a) Major key: B♭Maj   b) Note names: B♭ D C   E♭ A B
c) Key Signature: B♭ E♭   d) Total number of measures played: 4

MAJOR KEY SIGNATURES - SHARPS

To name the **MAJOR KEY** with **SHARPS**, go to the **LAST** sharp of the Key Signature and go up one diatonic semitone (half step). That note is the name of the Major key.

Example: Key Signature is F# C#: the last sharp is C#. From C#, go up one diatonic semitone to D. That names the Major key as D Major.

♫ **Note:** The abbreviation for Major is "**Maj**". Example: C Major or C Maj

1. Name the Major key for the following Key Signatures.

♫ **Note:** The Tonic note is the FIRST note of the key.

In Music, when a Key Signature changes to C Major, natural signs are used to cancel the outgoing Key Signature in the first measure. In Theory Exercises where a Key Signature is changed with each measure, they are optional (and are not a requirement).

2. Name the Major key for the following Key Signatures. Write the Tonic note of each key. Use whole notes.

♫ **Note:** A **Key Signature** is written at the beginning of the music after the clef and affects **ALL** the notes on the staff (and on ledger lines) with the same letter name.

3. Write the Key Signatures for the following Major keys. Name the notes.

MAJOR SCALES using a KEY SIGNATURE - SHARPS

When writing a **MAJOR SCALE** using a **Key Signature**, the notes begin **AFTER** the Key Signature.

Correct

Incorrect

E Major scale using a Key Signature, with a center bar line

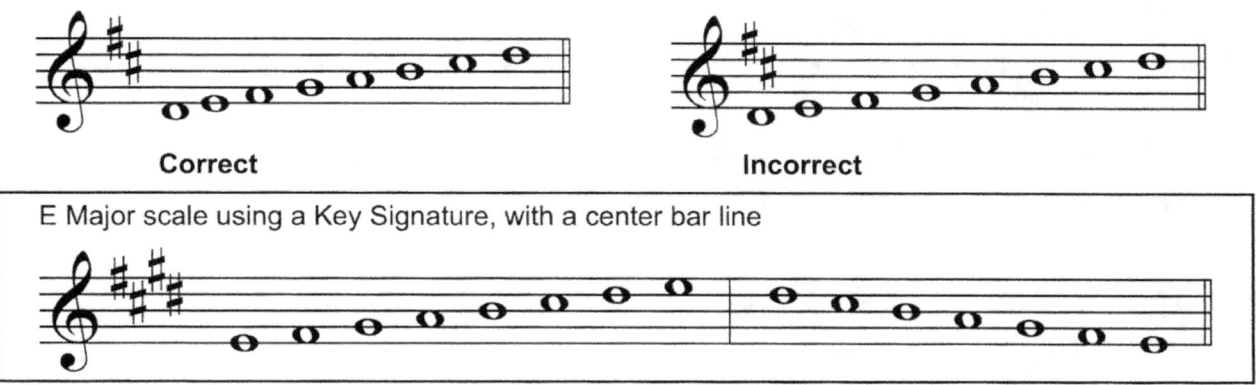

♫ **Note:** Always write scales in the **SAME WAY**, either **WITH** or **WITHOUT** a center bar line.

1. Write the following scales, ascending and descending, using a Key Signature. Use whole notes.

   a) D Major in the Treble Clef
   b) G Major in the Bass Clef
   c) C Major in the Treble Clef
   d) E Major in the Bass Clef
   e) A Major in the Treble Clef

a)

b)

c)

d)

e)

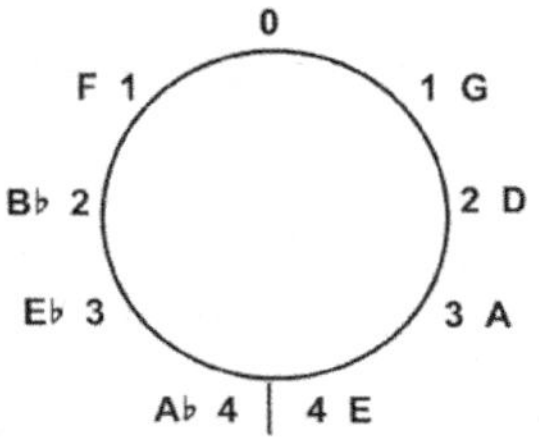

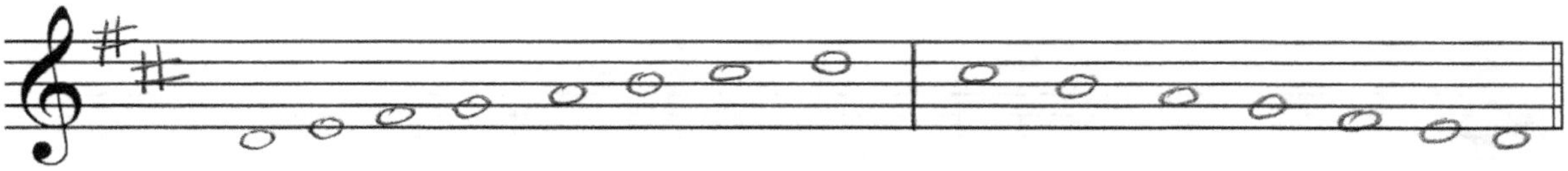

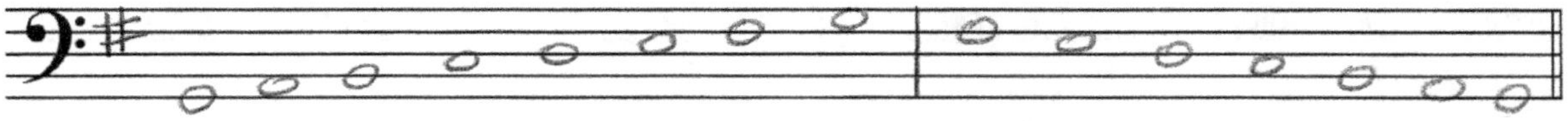

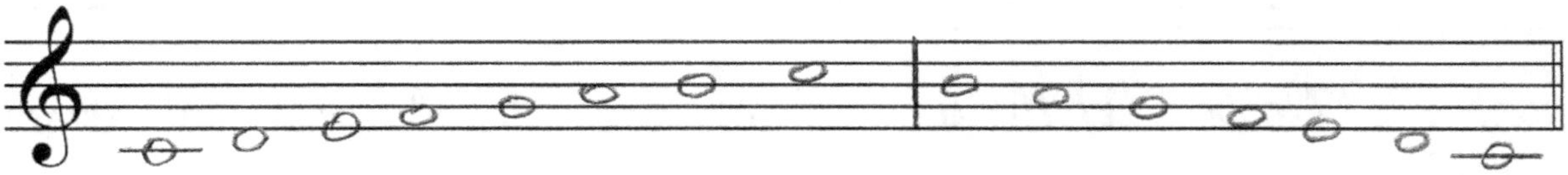

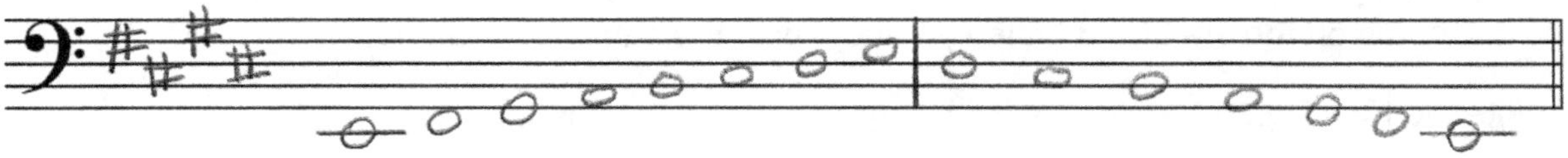

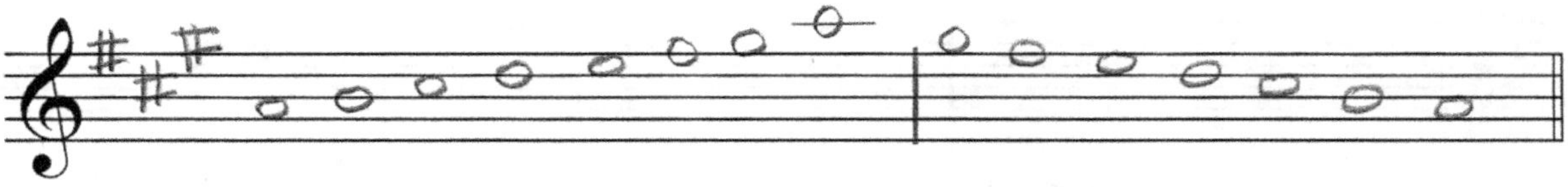

MAJOR KEY SIGNATURES - FLATS

To name the **MAJOR KEY** with **FLATS**, go to the **SECOND LAST** flat of the Key Signature. That note is the name of the Major key.

Example: Key Signature is B♭ E♭ A♭: the second last flat is E♭. That names the Major key as E♭ Major.

♪ **Note:** The exception to the rule is **F Major***, with only B♭.

1. Name the Major key for the following Key Signatures.

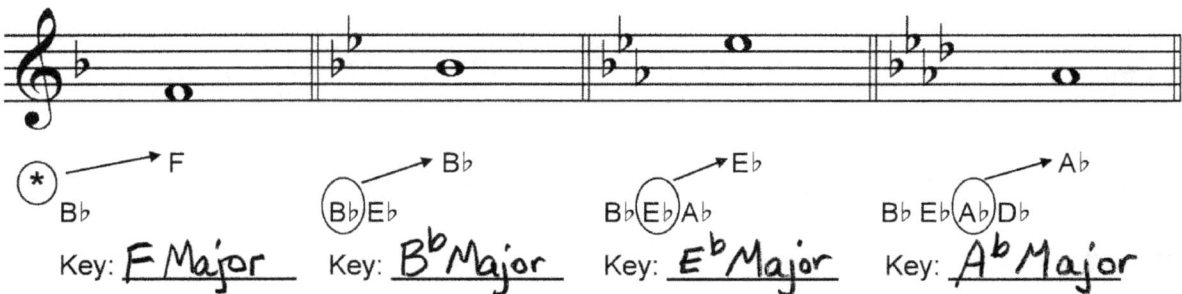

♪ **Note:** The Tonic note is the FIRST note of the key.

In Music, when a Key Signature changes to C Major, natural signs are used to cancel the outgoing Key Signature in the first measure. In Theory Exercises where a Key Signature is changed with each measure, they are optional (and are not a requirement).

2. Name the Major key for the following Key Signatures. Write the Tonic note of each key. Use whole notes.

♪ **Note:** A **Key Signature** is written at the beginning of the music after the clef and affects **ALL** the notes on the staff (and on ledger lines) with the same letter name.

3. Write the Key Signatures for the following Major keys. Name the notes.

MAJOR SCALES using a KEY SIGNATURE - FLATS

When writing a **MAJOR SCALE** using a **Key Signature**, the notes begin **AFTER** the Key Signature.

        Correct   **Incorrect**

A flat Major using a Key Signature, without a center bar line

♪ **Note:** Always write scales in the **SAME WAY**, either **WITH** or **WITHOUT** a center bar line.

1. Write the following scales, ascending and descending, using a Key Signature. Use whole notes.

   a) B flat Major in the Treble Clef
   b) C Major in the Bass Clef
   c) F Major in the Treble Clef
   d) A flat Major in the Bass Clef
   e) E flat Major in the Treble Clef

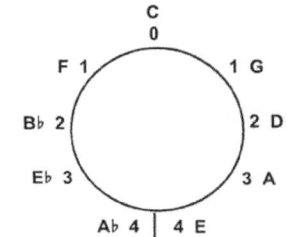

a)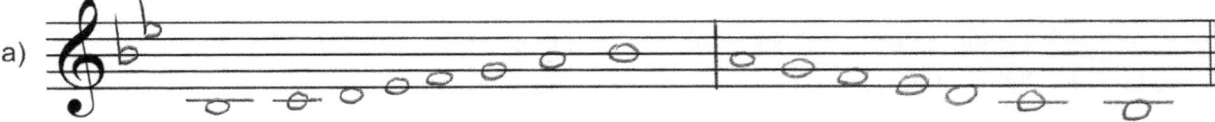

b)

c)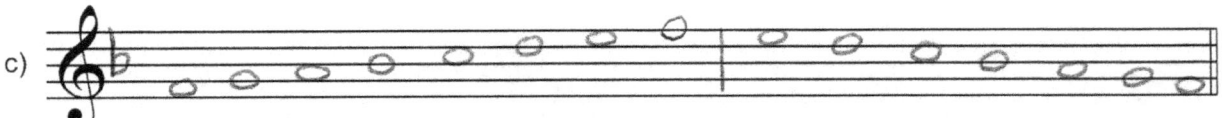

d)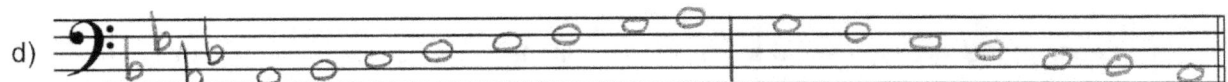

e)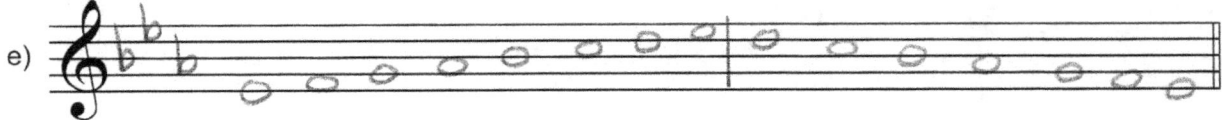

Lesson 4 — Review Test

Total Score: ____ / 100

1. Write the following notes **ABOVE** the **Treble Clef**. Use ledger lines. Use dotted half notes.

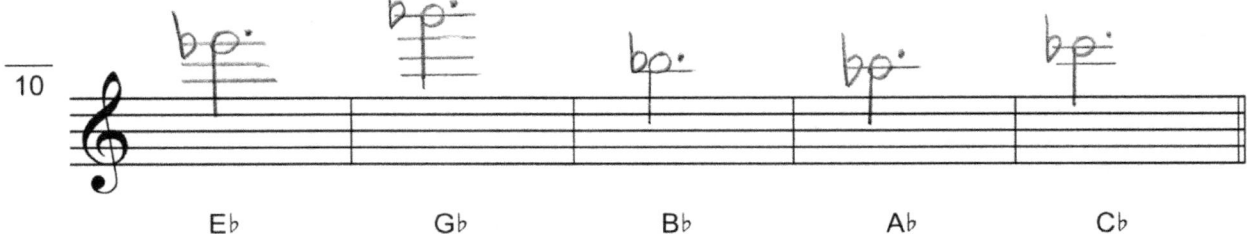

Eb   Gb   Bb   Ab   Cb

2. Rewrite the following notes at the **SAME PITCH** in the **Bass Clef**. Use half notes. Name the notes.

E E E E F# F# F# F# A A A A

3. Write the following notes in the Bass Clef. Use the correct **KEY SIGNATURE**. Use single eighth notes.

a) the TONIC note of B flat Major
b) the TONIC note of G Major
c) the TONIC note of C Major
d) the TONIC note of A flat Major
e) the TONIC note of E Major

4. Name each of the following as: **d.s.** (diatonic semitone), **c.s.** (chromatic semitone), **w.t.** (whole tone) or **e.e.** (enharmonic equivalent).

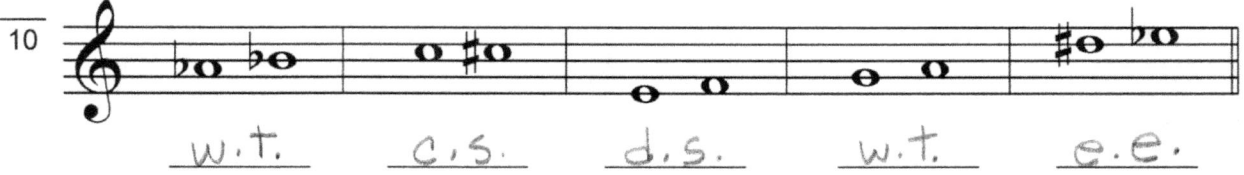

w.t.   c.s.   d.s.   w.t.   e.e.

5. Complete the **CIRCLE OF FIFTHS**:
   a) Write the order of flats and sharps.
   b) Write the Major keys on the **OUTSIDE** of the circle.

10

♭ BEAD
The order of flats

C
0

♯ FCGD
The order of sharps

F 1

1 G

B♭ 2

2 D

E♭ 3

3 A

A♭ 4

4 E

6. Write the following scales, ascending and descending, using a **KEY SIGNATURE**. Use whole notes.

   a) A flat Major in the Treble Clef

   10
   b) F Major in the Bass Clef
   c) E Major in the Treble Clef
   d) B flat Major in the Bass Clef
   e) C Major in the Treble Clef

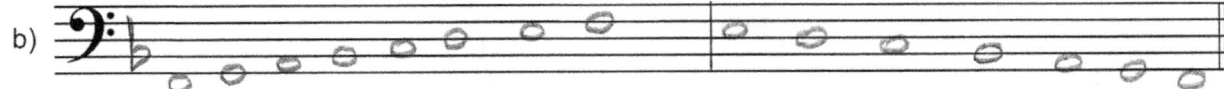

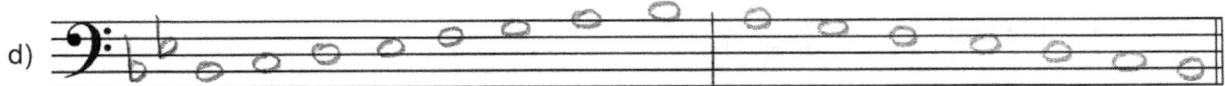

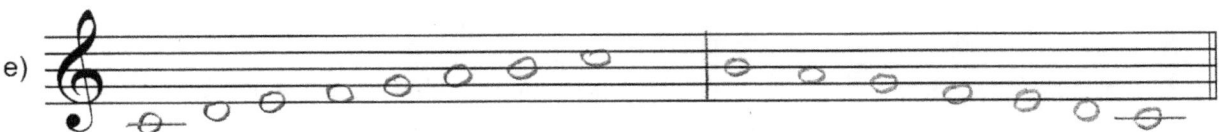

7. Add the correct clef and any necessary **ACCIDENTALS** to form the following scales.

   a) D Major
   b) E flat Major
   c) A Major
   d) G Major
   e) C Major

   _10_

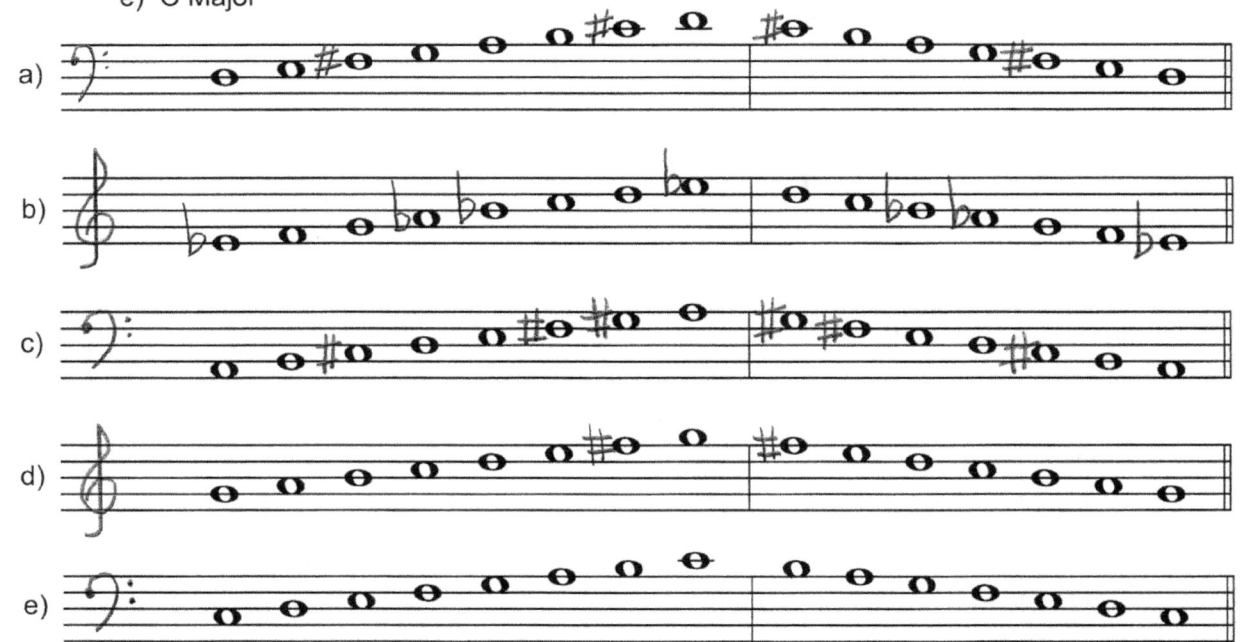

8. Match each musical term or sign with the English definition. (Not all definitions will be used.)

   _10_

Term		Definition
D.S. al Fine	c	a) tone tone semitone tone tone tone semitone
D.C. al Fine	b	b) repeat from the beginning and end at *Fine*
Key Signature	k	c) repeat from the sign and end at *Fine*
grazioso	h	d) B E A D
accidental	i	e) F C G D
Major scale pattern	a	f) from the sign
order of sharps	e	g) from the beginning
order of flats	d	h) graceful
dal segno, D.S.	f	i) sharp, flat or natural sign in front of a note
da capo, D.C.	g	j) with pedal
		k) sharps or flats written at the beginning of the music directly after the clef

9. Add **ONE REST** below each bracket to complete the measure. Cross off the count as each beat is completed.

10. Analyze the following piece of music by answering the questions below.

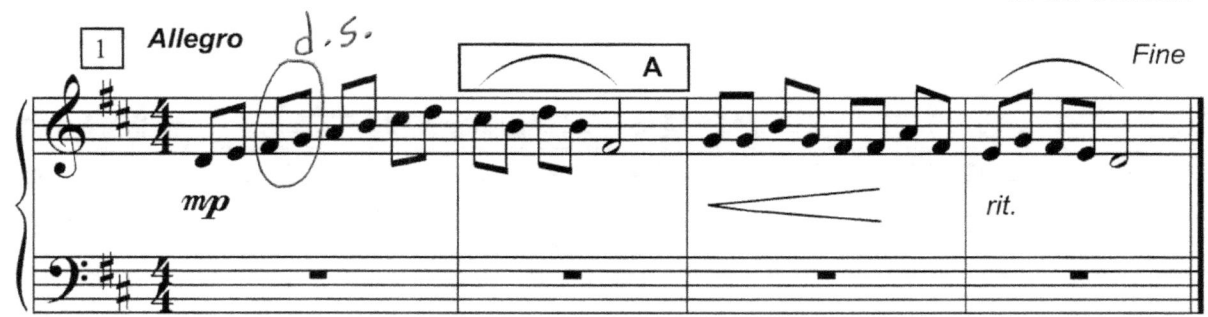

a) Name the key of this piece. ___D Major___

b) Name the Tonic note of this piece. ___D___

c) Explain the sign at the letter **A**. ___slur - play legato (smooth)___

d) Write the measure number in the box at the letter **B**.

e) Name the scale at the letter **C**. ___D Major scale___

f) Explain the term at the letter **D**. ___repeat from the beginning and end at Fine___

g) When all signs are followed, how many measures are played? ___12___

h) Name the note at the letter **E**. ___G#___

i) Locate and circle a diatonic semitone in this piece. Label it as d.s.

j) Explain the meaning of *Fine*. ___the end___

Lesson 5   Intervals - Perfect, Major and Minor

HARMONIC and MELODIC INTERVALS

An **INTERVAL** is the distance in pitch between TWO notes. Numbers (1, 2, 3, etc.) are used to identify the size of the interval. To identify the interval, count each line and each space from the lowest note to the highest note. The lowest note is always counted as 1.

Example: C - D is an interval of a SECOND (2), C - E is an interval of a THIRD (3).

HARMONIC INTERVALS

A **HARMONIC** interval is written one note **ABOVE** the other, both played at the same time (together). **H** is for Harmony.

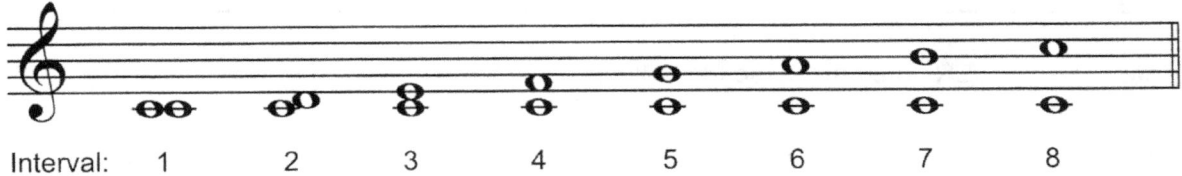

Interval: 1   2   3   4   5   6   7   8

1. Name each of the following harmonic intervals.

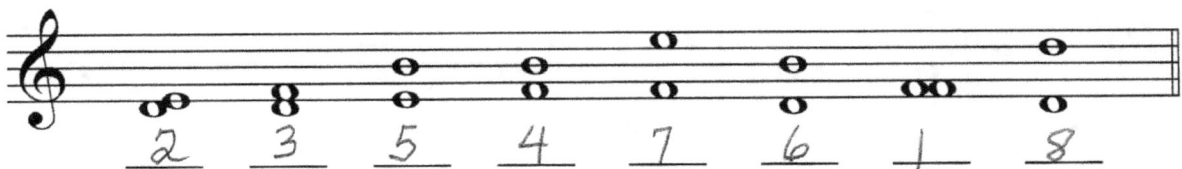

    2   3   5   4   7   6   1   8

MELODIC INTERVALS

A **MELODIC** interval is written one note **BESIDE** the other, played one note after the other (separately). **M** is for Melody.

♪ **Note:** A melodic interval may be written ascending (going up) or descending (going down).

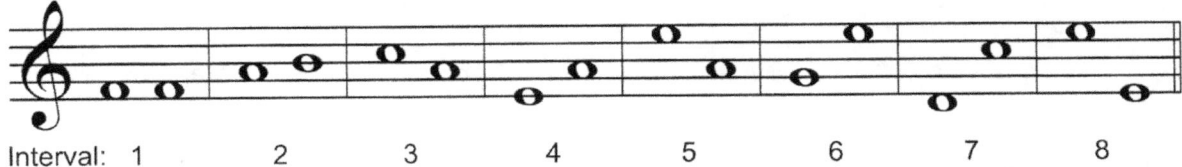

Interval: 1   2   3   4   5   6   7   8

2. Name each of the following melodic intervals.

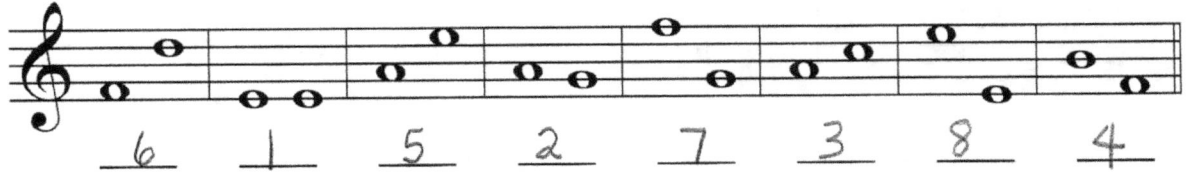

    6   1   5   2   7   3   8   4

PERFECT and MAJOR INTERVALS

PERFECT INTERVALS are 1, 4, 5 and 8.

The abbreviation for Perfect is "**Per**".
MAJOR INTERVALS are 2, 3, 6 and 7.
The abbreviation for Major is "**Maj**".

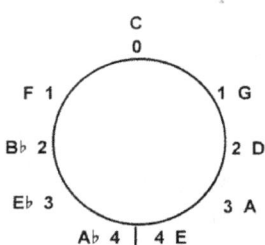

The **LOWER** note of the interval is the **TONIC** of the Major key.
If D is the lowest note, intervals are written based on the notes of the D Major scale.

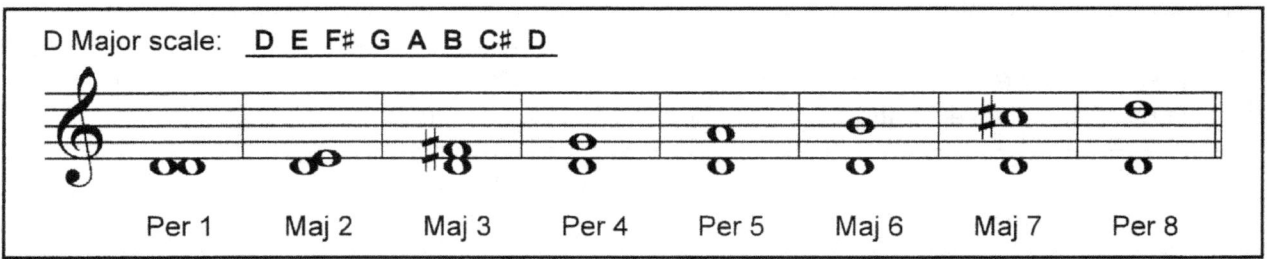

♪ **Note:** The LOWER note names the Major key.

1. Write melodic intervals above each given note D (Key of D Major). Use accidentals. Use whole notes.

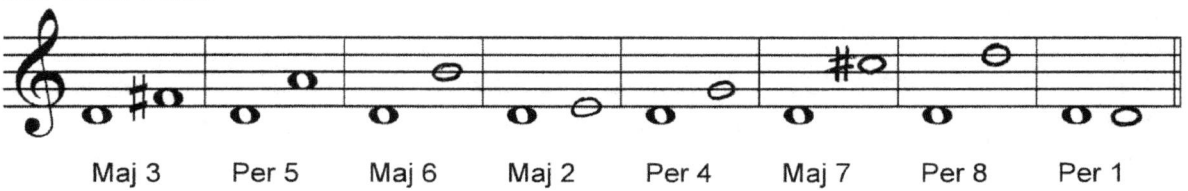

E Major scale: **E F# G# A B C# D# E**

2. Write harmonic intervals above each given note E (Key of E Major). Use accidentals. Use whole notes.

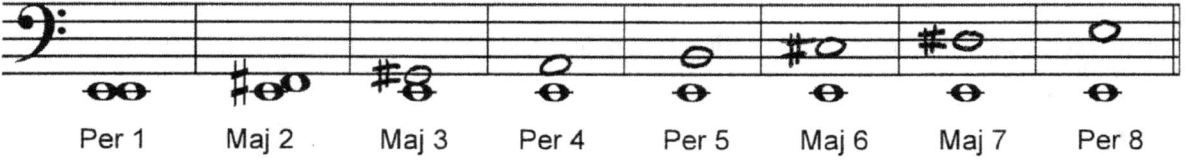

3. Write melodic intervals above each given note E (Key of E Major). Use accidentals. Use whole notes.

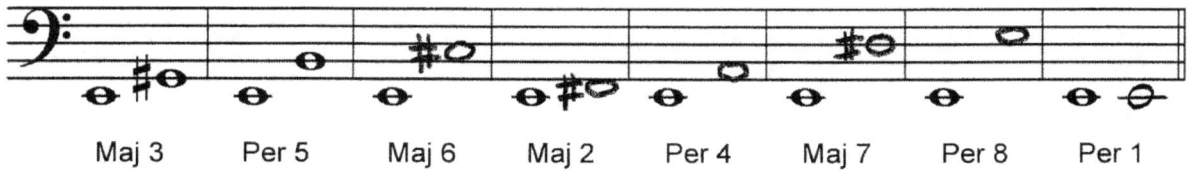

HARMONIC and MELODIC INTERVALS

For **HARMONIC** intervals of a 1, 2, 3, 4, 5 and 6: when **BOTH** notes have accidentals, the accidental is written closest to the higher note and further away from the lower note.

For **HARMONIC** intervals of a 7 and 8: when **BOTH** notes have accidentals, the accidentals are written lined up vertically (above each other).

♪ **Note:** When writing a harmonic interval, and there is no room for correct placement of accidentals, it is acceptable to place the accidental further away from the upper note.

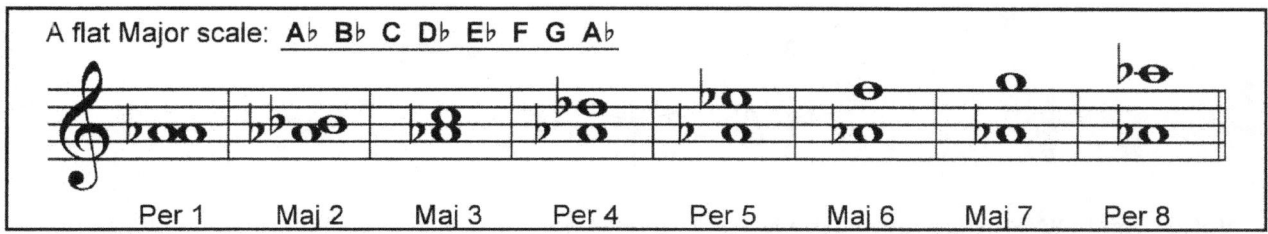

1. Write harmonic intervals above each given note A♭. Use accidentals. Use whole notes.

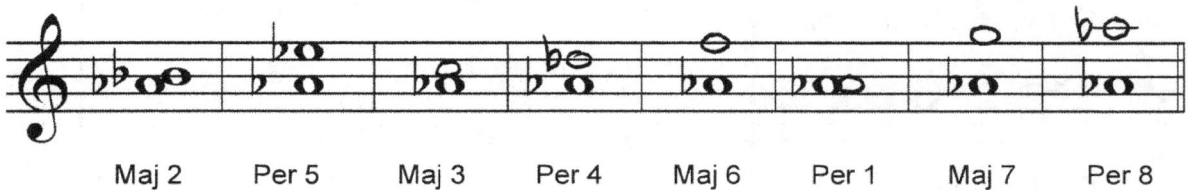

♪ **Note:** The LOWER note names the Major key.

2. Write the note names of the G Major scale. Name the melodic intervals.

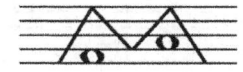

G Major scale: G A B C D E F# G

3. Write the note names of the B flat Major scale. Name the harmonic intervals.

B flat Major scale: B♭ C D E♭ F G A B♭

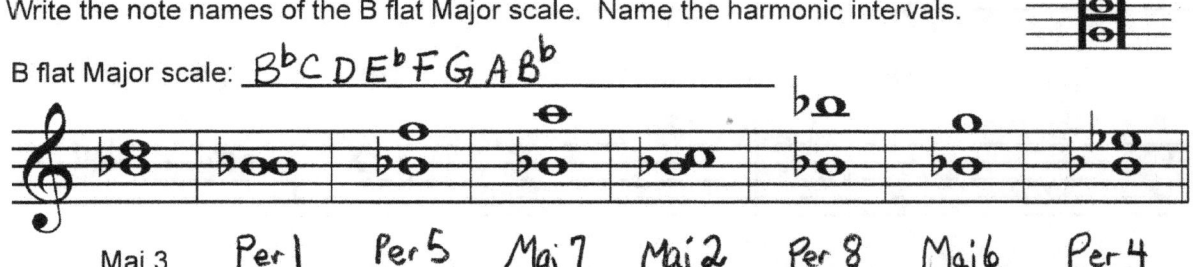

IDENTIFYING and WRITING HARMONIC INTERVALS

1. Complete the Circle of Fifths:
   a) Write the order of flats and sharps.
   b) Write the Major keys on the outside of the circle.

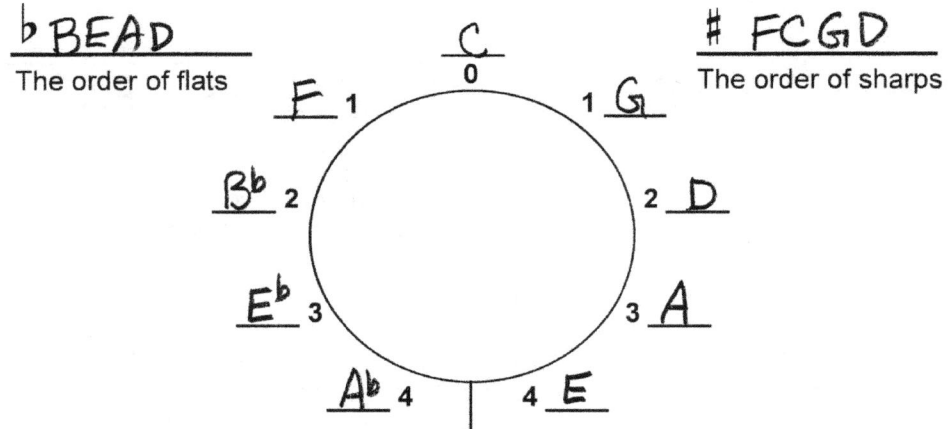

♪ Note: The LOWER note names the Major key. Use the Circle of Fifths to identify the sharps or flats in the Key Signature for each Major key.

2. Name the following harmonic intervals.

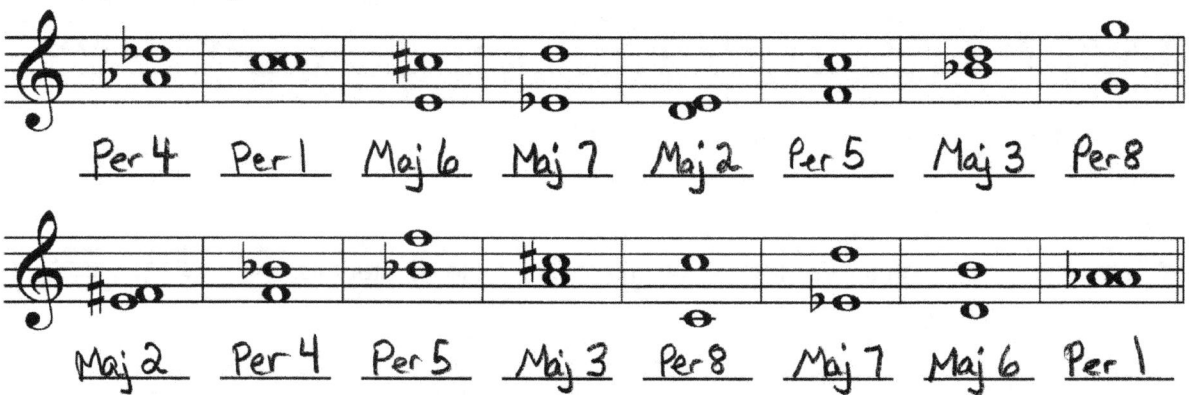

3. Write harmonic intervals above the given notes. Use accidentals. Use whole notes.

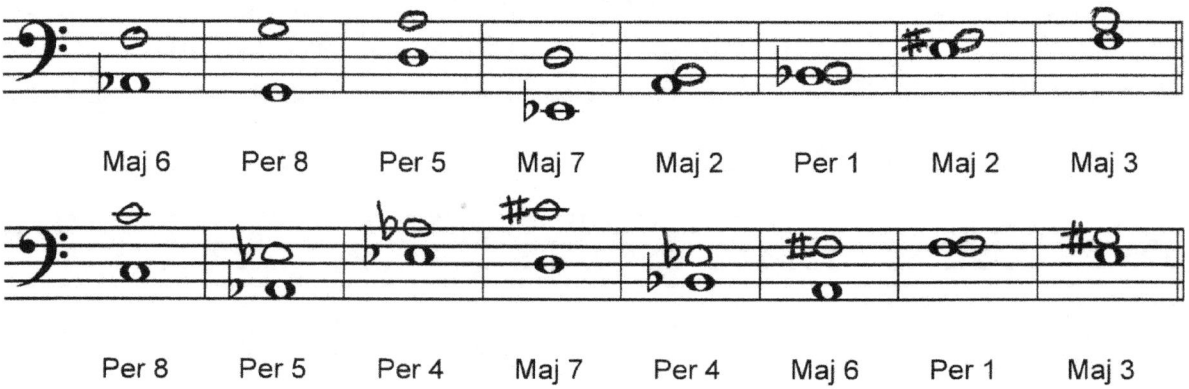

MAJOR and MINOR INTERVALS

A **MINOR** interval is **ONE** chromatic semitone (half step) **SMALLER** than a Major interval. Only the intervals **2, 3, 6** and **7** can become minor. The abbreviation for minor is "**min**".

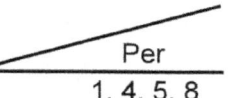

♪ **Note:** The intervals of 1, 4, 5 and 8 are **PERFECT**. The interval of a Perfect 1 is also known as a **Perfect Unison**. The interval of a Perfect 8 is also known as a **Perfect Octave** (8ve).

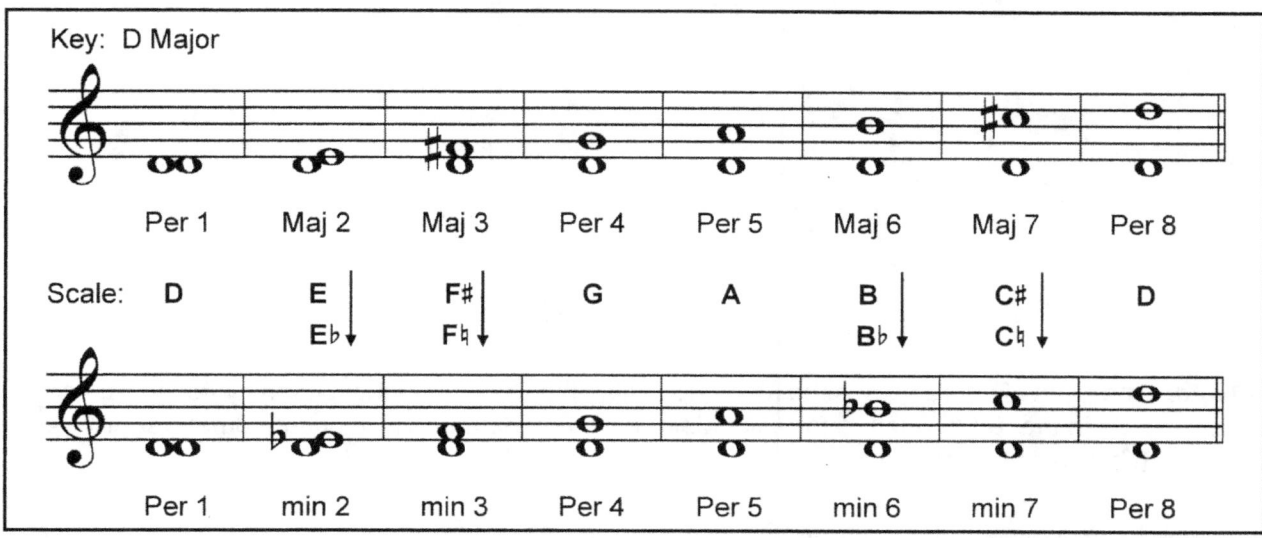

1. Write the note names of the A Major scale. Write the harmonic intervals above the given notes.

A Major scale: A B C# D E F# G# A

♪ **Note:** A Major 2, 3, 6 and 7 becomes minor by lowering the top note one chromatic semitone.

2. Change the following Major intervals into minor intervals by lowering the top note one chromatic semitone (chromatic half step). Name the intervals.

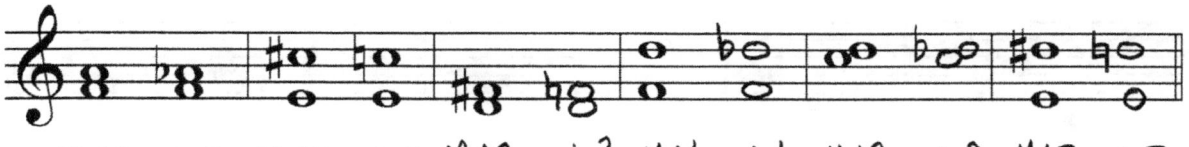

Maj 3   min 3   Maj 6   min 6   Maj3   min3   Maj6   min6   Maj2   min2   Maj7   min7

IDENTIFYING and WRITING MELODIC INTERVALS

1. Complete the Circle of Fifths:
    a) Write the order of flats and sharps.
    b) Write the Major keys on the outside of the circle.

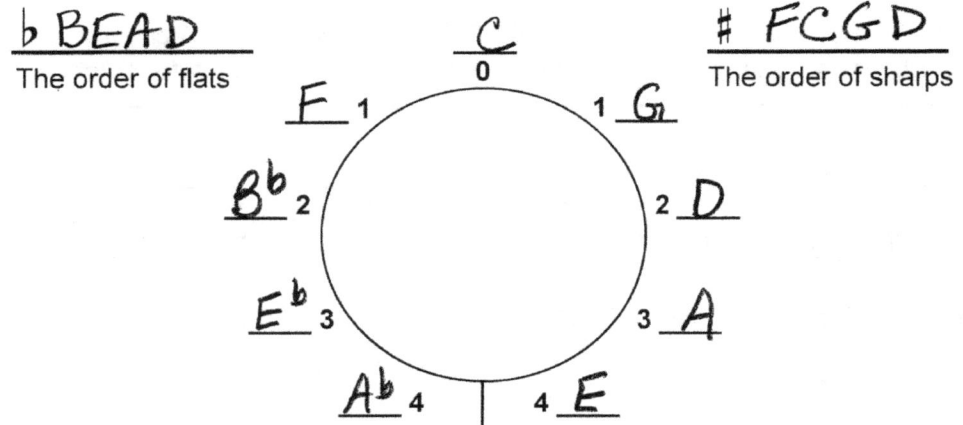

♪ **Note:** The LOWER note names the Major key. Use the Circle of Fifths to identify the sharps or flats in the Key Signature for each Major key. A minor interval is one chromatic semitone (chromatic half step) smaller than a Major interval.

2. Name the following melodic intervals.

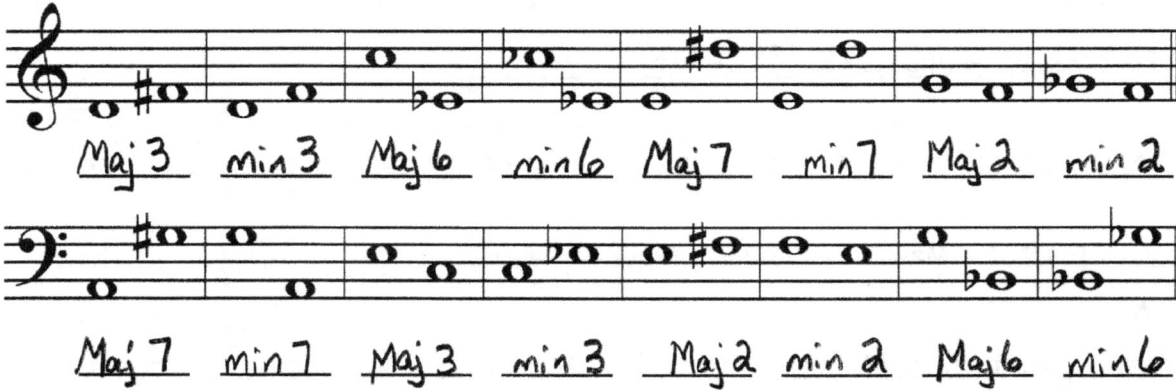

3. Write melodic intervals above the given notes. Use accidentals. Use whole notes.

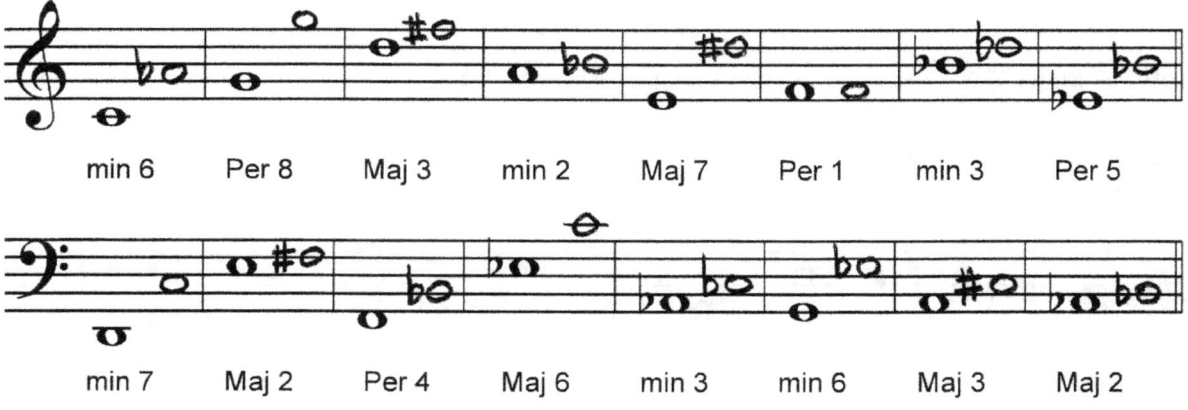

NAMING INTERVALS with a KEY SIGNATURE

When **NAMING INTERVALS** with a **KEY SIGNATURE**, count the distance between the two notes to determine the interval number (1, 2, 3, etc.). Observe the Key Signature and any accidentals in the measure that may affect the given notes. The **LOWER** note of the interval determines the **Major key** used to name the interval.

♫ **Note:** The Key Signature of the melody will affect ALL the notes on the staff (and on ledger lines).

1. Following the examples, name the intervals by completing the following:

Key Signature: __F# C#__

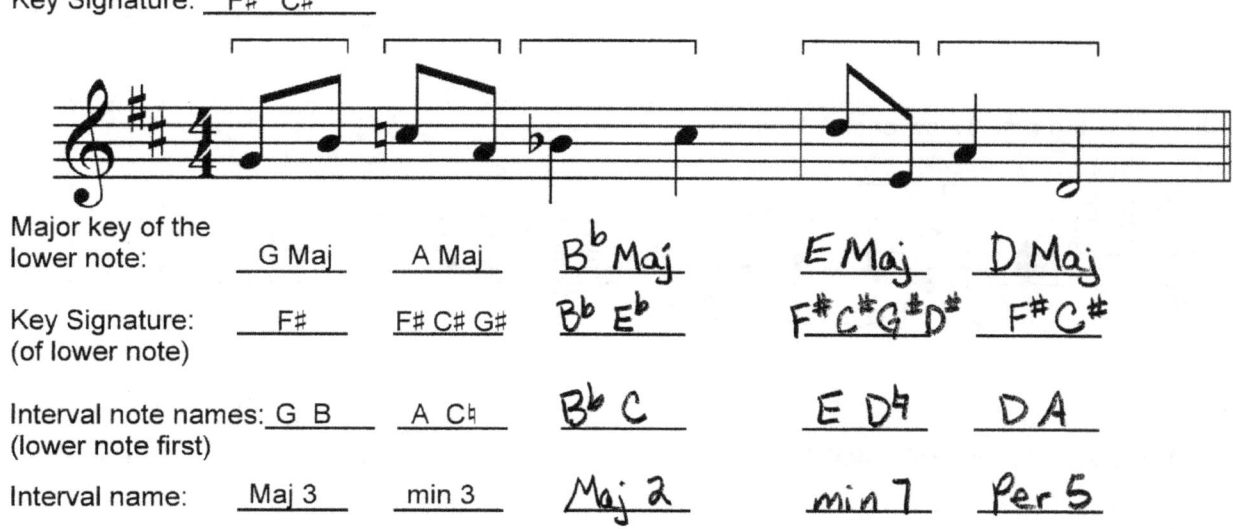

2. a) Name the sharps or flats in the Key Signature.
   b) Name the melodic intervals below each bracket.

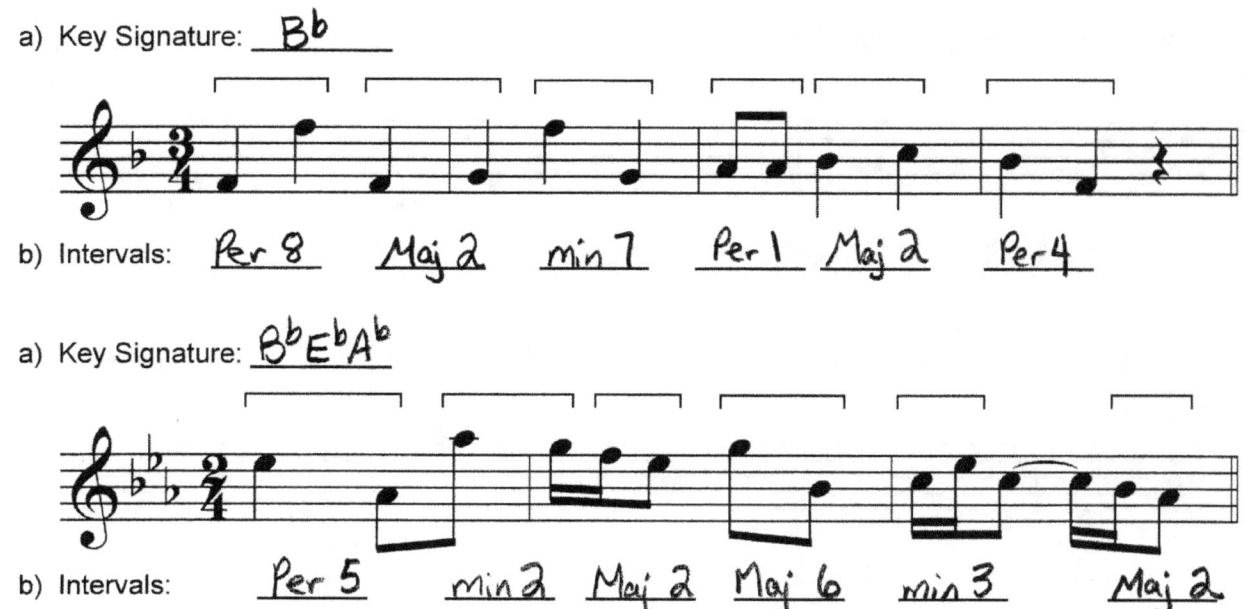

Lesson 5 — Review Test

Total Score: ____ / 100

1. a) Write the following notes **BELOW** the **Treble Clef**. Use ledger lines. Use whole notes.

Ab   E♮   G#   Bb   F

b) Name the note below each bracket.

E   F#   C#   G#   D#

2. a) Write the following **HARMONIC** intervals ABOVE each of the given notes. Use whole notes.

minor 3   Major 2   Perfect 4   minor 6   Major 7

b) Write the following **MELODIC** intervals ABOVE each of the given notes. Use whole notes.

Perfect 5   minor 7   Major 3   Perfect 8   minor 2

3. Name the following Major keys. Write the **TONIC** note for each Major key. Use half notes.

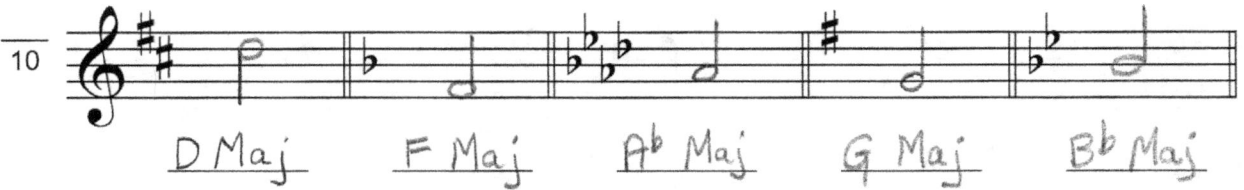

D Maj   F Maj   Ab Maj   G Maj   Bb Maj

4. Complete the **CIRCIRCLE OF FIFTHS**:
   a) Write the order of flats and sharps.
   b) Write the Major keys on the **OUTSIDE** of the circle.

___10___

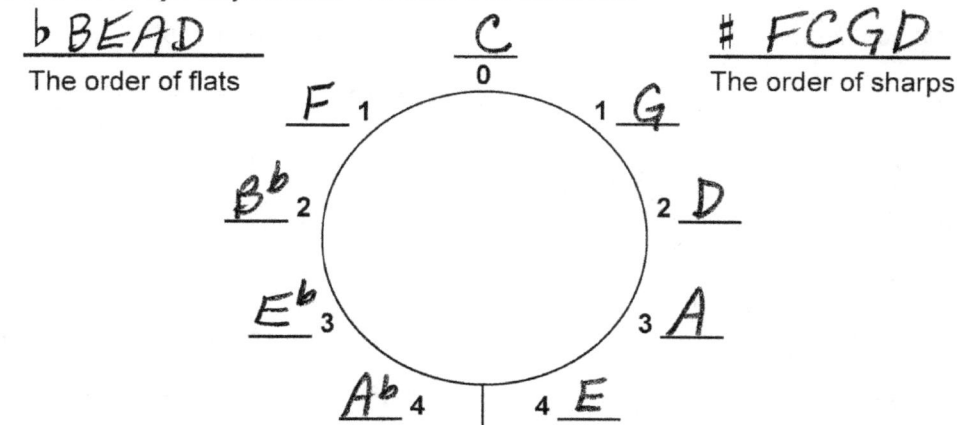

b BEAD — The order of flats
FCGD — The order of sharps

c) Write the A flat Major scale, ascending and descending. Use a KEY SIGNATURE. Use whole notes.

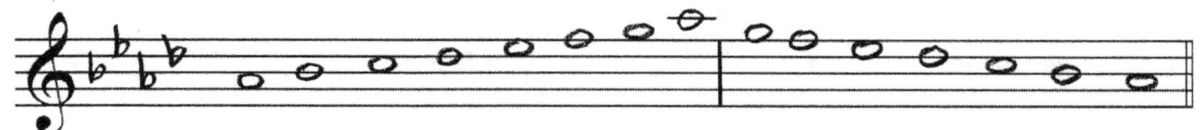

d) Write the E Major scale, ascending and descending. Use ACCIDENTALS. Use whole notes.

5. Name the melodic intervals below the brackets.

___10___

min 2, Maj 6, Per 5

Per 4, Per 5, Maj 2

Per 1, Maj 2, Per 8, Maj 7

6. Match each musical term or sign with the English definition. (Not all definitions will be used.)

Term — **Definition**

- harmonic interval — h
- presto — j
- melodic interval — g
- maestoso — e
- mano destra, M.D. — k
- Perfect interval — d
- Major interval — b
- minor interval — f
- slur — a
- andantino — c

a) play the notes legato (smoothly)
b) intervals 2, 3, 6, 7 within the Major scale
c) a little faster than *andante*
d) intervals 1, 4, 5, 8
e) majestic
f) one semitone smaller than a Major interval
g) two notes, one beside the other (separate)
h) two notes, one on top of the other (together)
i) left hand
j) very fast
k) right hand

7. Add **ONE REST** below each bracket to complete the measure. Cross off the count as each beat is completed.

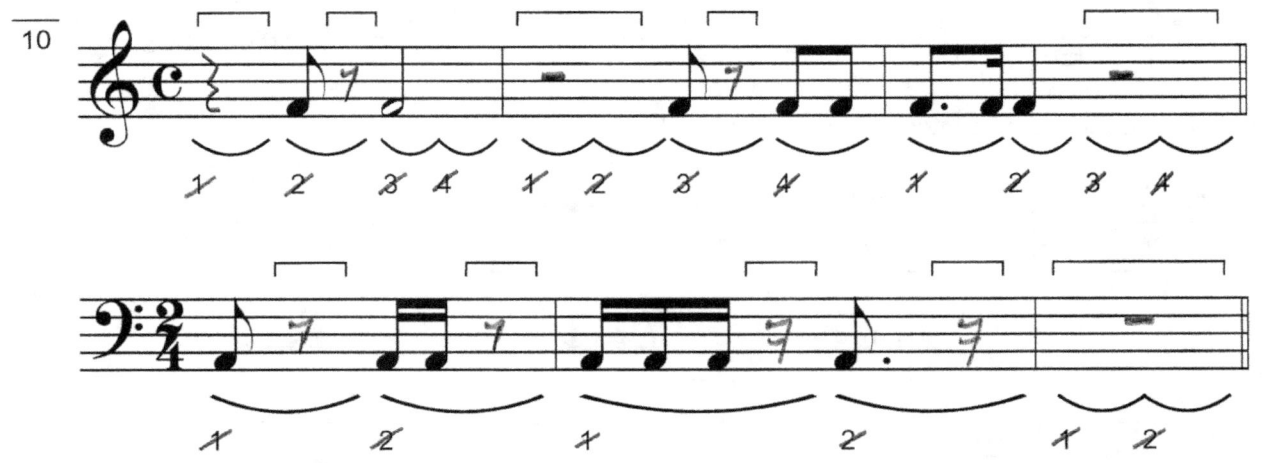

8. Name each of the following as: **d.s.** (diatonic semitone), **c.s.** (chromatic semitone), **w.t.** (whole tone) or **e.e.** (enharmonic equivalent).

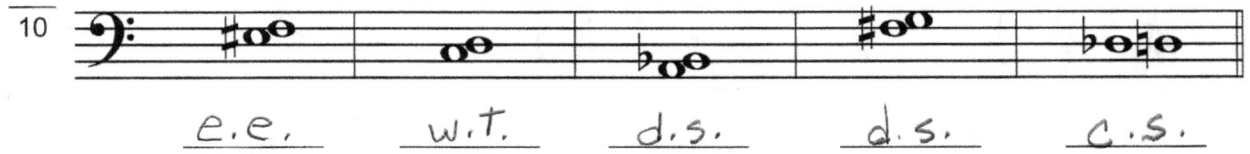

e.e.   w.t.   d.s.   d.s.   c.s.

9. Name the key of the following melody. Rewrite it at the **SAME PITCH** in the **Treble Clef**.

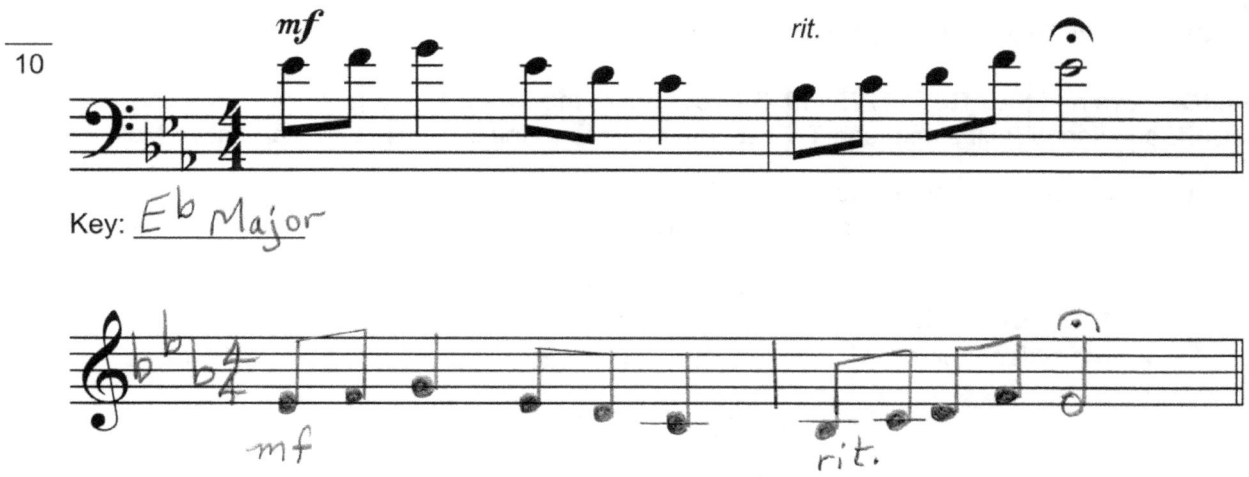

Key: E♭ Major

10. Analyze the following piece of music by answering the questions below.

Twirling
S. McKibbon

a) Name the title of this piece. **Twirling**

b) Explain the meaning of **Allegretto**. **fairly fast (a little slower than allegro)**

c) How many beats does the rest at the letter **A** receive? **Two**

d) Explain the sign at the letter **B**. **natural sign - cancels the F# to F♮**

e) Explain the sign at the letter **C**. **accent - a stressed note**

f) Add the missing rest (below the bracket) in the Treble Clef in measure 4.

g) Explain the meaning of *accel.* **becoming quicker**

h) Locate and circle a chromatic semitone in this piece. Label it as c.s.

i) Locate and circle a diatonic semitone in this piece. Label it as d.s.

j) When the repeat signs are followed, how many measures are played? **Six**

Lesson 6 Circle of Fifths - Minor Keys and Minor Scales

CIRCLE OF FIFTHS - MINOR KEYS

MAJOR keys and their **RELATIVE MINOR** keys share the **SAME** Key Signature. The minor key is THREE semitones (half steps) and THREE letter names (a minor third) below its relative Major.

♪ **Note:** The Major keys are written on the OUTSIDE of the Circle of Fifths using **UPPER** case letters. The minor keys are written on the INSIDE of the Circle of Fifths using **lower** case letters.

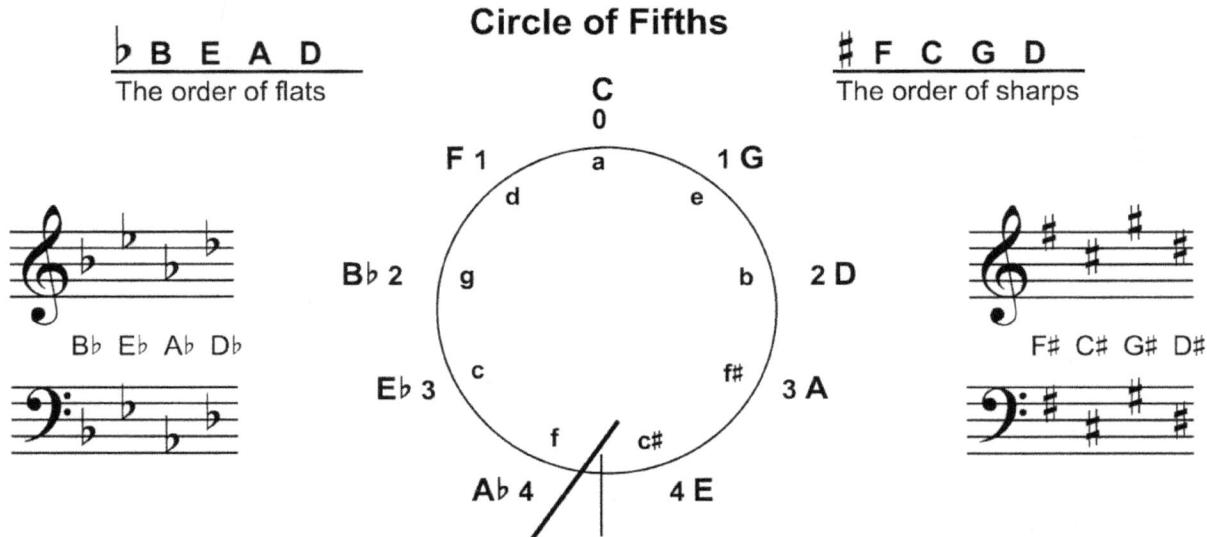

♪ **Note:** From the Major key to its relative minor, go **DOWN** 3 semitones (a minor third). From the minor key to its relative Major, go **UP** 3 semitones (a minor third).

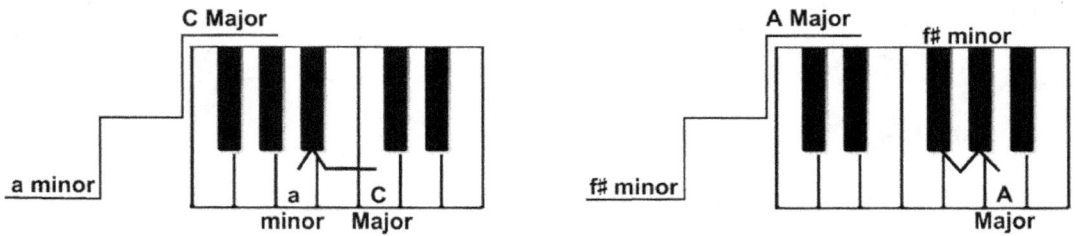

1. a) For each Major key, name its relative minor. b) Write the Key Signature for each.

Major key	relative minor key	Key Signature
C Major	a minor	no sharps / no flats
G Major	e minor	F#
D Major	b minor	F# C#
A Major	f# minor	F# C# G#
E Major	c# minor	F# C# G# D#
F Major	d minor	Bb
Bb Major	g minor	Bb Eb
Eb Major	c minor	Bb Eb Ab
Ab Major	f minor	Bb Eb Ab Db

COMPLETE the CIRCLE of FIFTHS - MINOR KEYS

♪ **Note:** Relative **MINOR** keys go **INSIDE** the circle.

1. Complete the Circle of Fifths:
   a) Write the order of flats and the order of sharps.
   b) Write the Major keys on the outside of the circle, starting with F Major on the flat side.
      Use the Major key sentence: **Father Charles Goes Down And Ends (And♭ Ends♭) Battle♭.**
   c) Start with the 1st letter of the alphabet "A"; draw a line under the A♭ going into the circle.
      This is the landmark line for beginning to write the relative minor keys.
   d) Write the relative minor keys on the inside of the circle, starting with f minor
      (relative minor of A♭ Major).
      Use the minor key sentence: **father charles goes down and ends battle (father# charles#).**

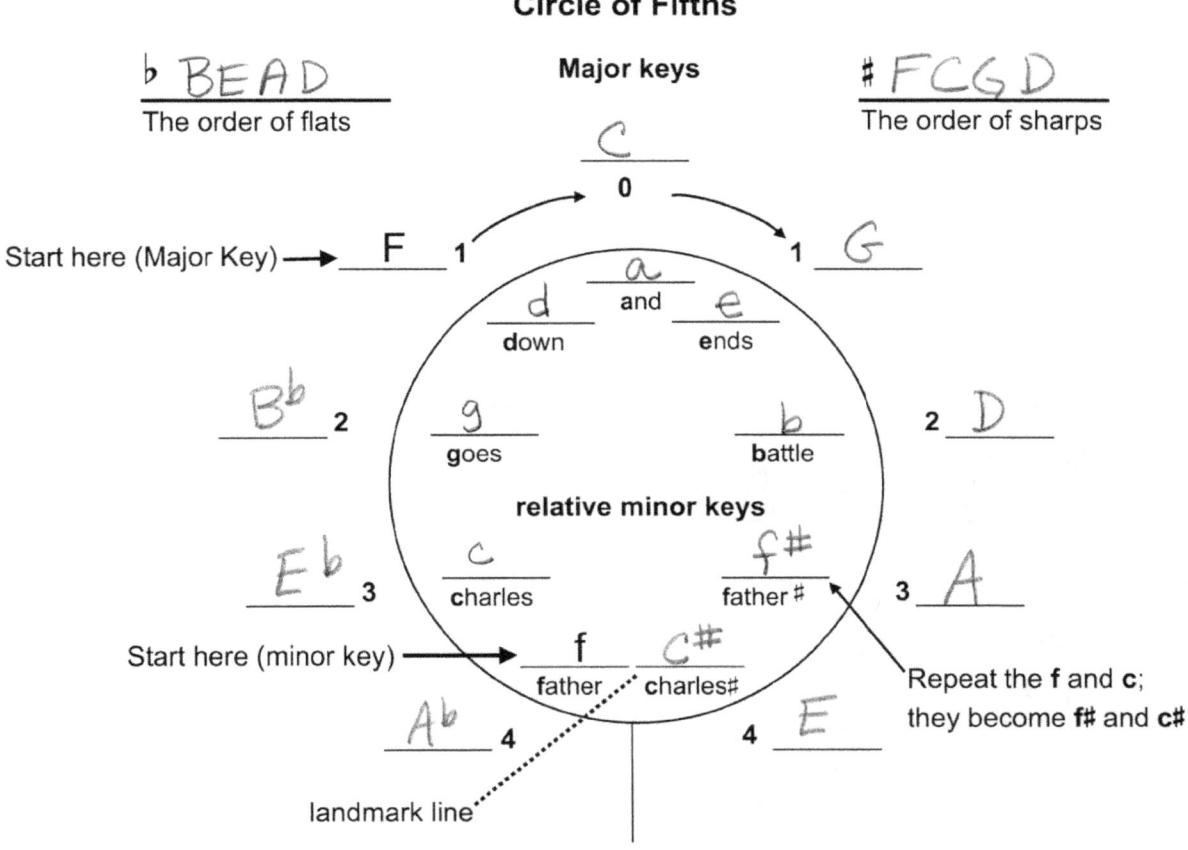

♪ **Note:** Moving around the Circle of Fifths, the distance between a Major key to a Major key or a minor key to a minor key is a Perfect fifth (five letter names).

2. Write the minor key sentence.

father Charles goes down and ends battle (father# Charles#)

COMPLETING the CIRCLE of FIFTHS with MAJOR and MINOR KEYS

1. Complete the Circle of Fifths:
   a) Write the order of flats and the order of sharps.
   b) Write the Major keys on the outside of the circle, starting with F Major on the flat side.
      Use the Major key sentence: **Father Charles Goes Down And Ends (And♭ Ends♭) Battle♭**.
   c) Write the relative minor keys on the inside of the circle, starting with f minor
      (relative minor of A♭ Major).
      Use the minor key sentence: father charles goes down and ends battle (father# charles#).

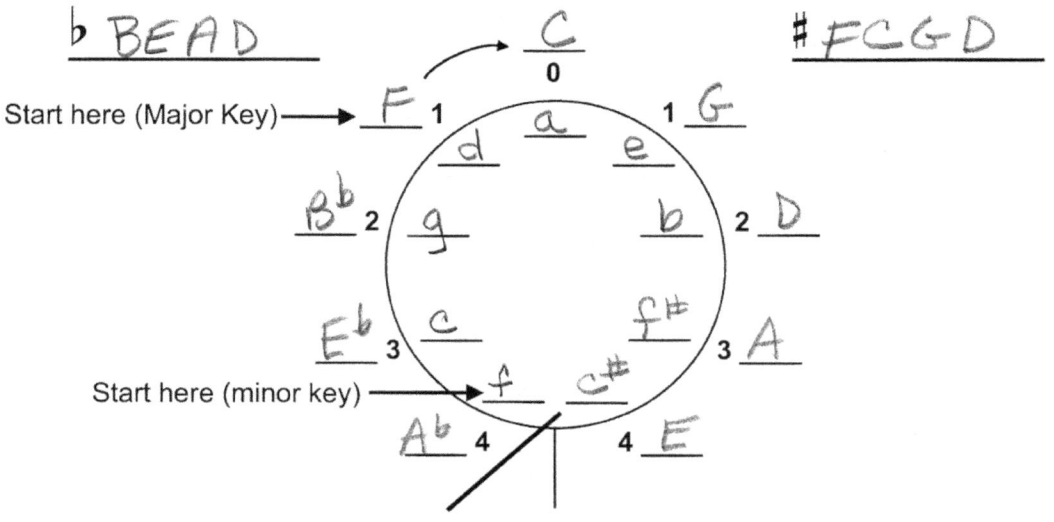

2. Name the Major key and its relative minor key for each of the following Key Signatures.

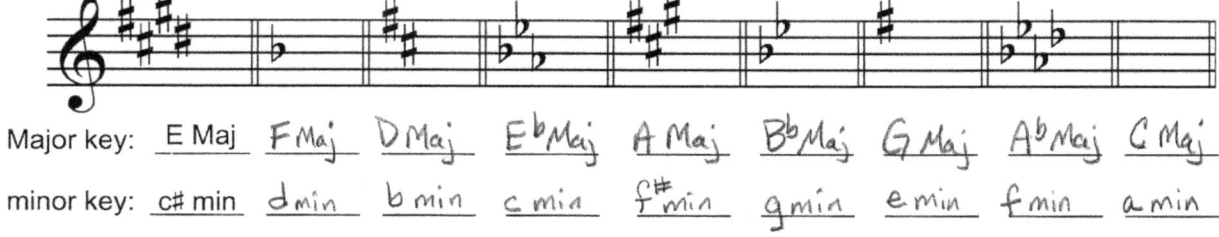

Major key:	E Maj	F Maj	D Maj	E♭ Maj	A Maj	B♭ Maj	G Maj	A♭ Maj	C Maj
minor key:	c# min	d min	b min	c min	f# min	g min	e min	f min	a min

♪ **NOTE:** The Tonic note is the first note of the minor key. Example: C# is the Tonic note of c# minor.

3. Write the Key Signature and the Tonic note for the following minor keys. Use whole notes.

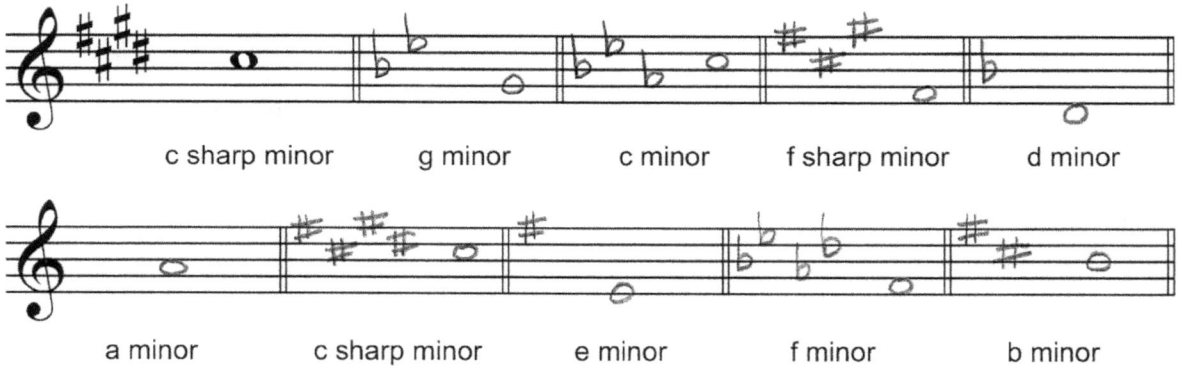

c sharp minor   g minor   c minor   f sharp minor   d minor

a minor   c sharp minor   e minor   f minor   b minor

USING the CIRCLE of FIFTHS to IDENTIFY MAJOR and MINOR KEYS

1. Complete the Circle of Fifths:
   a) Write the order of flats and the order of sharps.
   b) Write the Major keys on the outside of the circle.
   c) Write the relative minor keys on the inside of the circle.

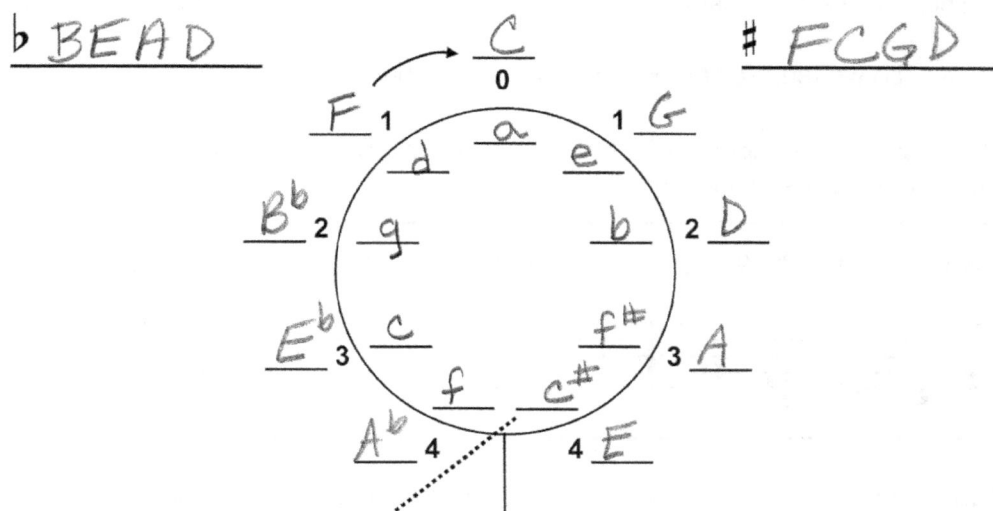

♪ **NOTE:** Use the Circle of Fifths to identify the Key Signatures for the Major and relative minor keys.

2. Name the Major key and its relative minor key for each of the following Key Signatures.

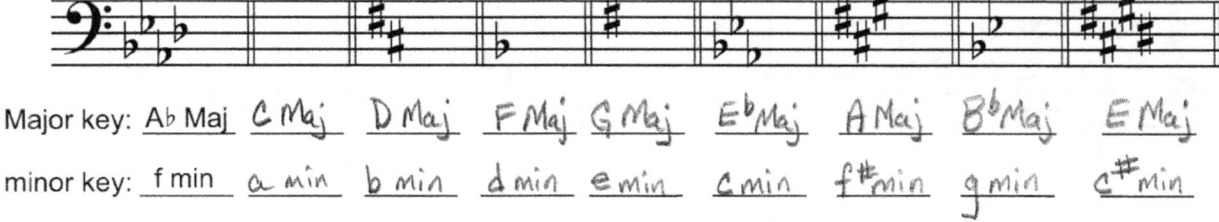

Major key: Ab Maj, C Maj, D Maj, F Maj, G Maj, Eb Maj, A Maj, Bb Maj, E Maj
minor key: f min, a min, b min, d min, e min, c min, f# min, g min, c# min

♪ **NOTE:** Use the Circle of Fifths to identify the number of sharps or flats in each Key Signature.

3. Write the Key Signature and the Tonic note for the following minor keys. Use whole notes.

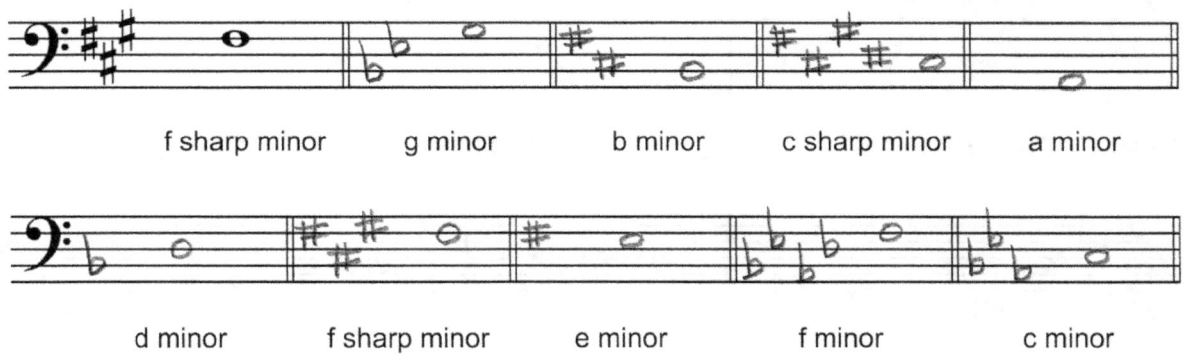

f sharp minor, g minor, b minor, c sharp minor, a minor

d minor, f sharp minor, e minor, f minor, c minor

NATURAL MINOR SCALES

A **NATURAL MINOR** scale has the **SAME** Key Signature as its relative Major.

♪ **Note:** As the word **NATURAL** indicates, **NOTHING** is added.

N

Minor scales may be written using a KEY SIGNATURE or using ACCIDENTALS. The accidentals used in the minor scale are the same sharps or flats found in the Key Signature of its relative Major.

Minor scales may be written **WITH** or **WITHOUT** a center bar line.

♪ **Note:** When using a Key Signature, a natural minor scale written WITH or WITHOUT a center bar line will not require any accidentals.

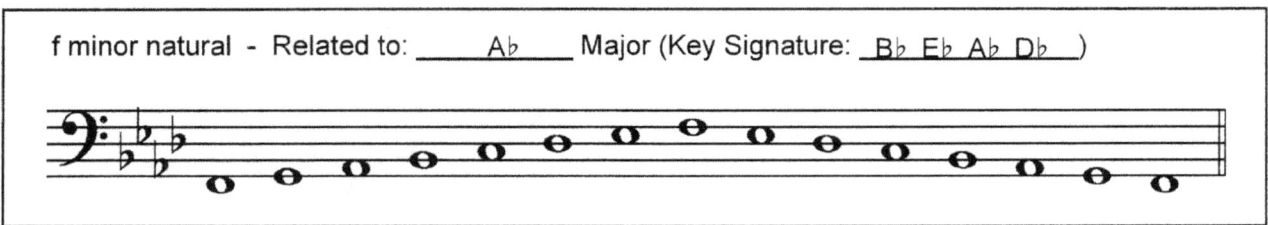
f minor natural - Related to: __Ab__ Major (Key Signature: _Bb Eb Ab Db_)

♪ **Note:** Always write scales in the **SAME WAY**, either **WITH** or **WITHOUT** a center bar line.

1. a) Name the relative Major key. Name the sharps or flats in the Key Signature.
   b) Write the natural minor scale, ascending and descending. Use a Key Signature. Use whole notes.

   e minor natural - Related to: __G__ Major (Key Signature: __F#__)

   c# minor natural - Related to: __E__ Major (Key Signature: _F# C# G# D#_)

   c minor natural - Related to: __Eb__ Major (Key Signature: _Bb Eb Ab_)

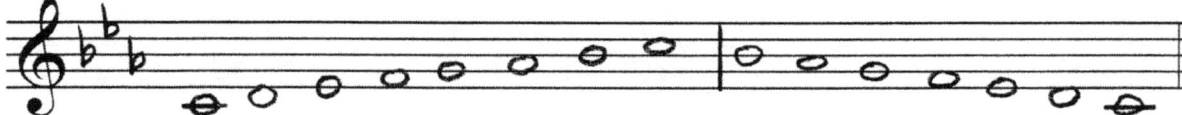

NATURAL MINOR SCALES - TONES (WHOLE STEP) and SEMITONES (HALF STEP)

Natural Minor Scale Pattern:
  $\hat{1}$ tone $\hat{2}$ semitone $\hat{3}$ tone $\hat{4}$ tone $\hat{5}$ semitone $\hat{6}$ tone $\hat{7}$ tone $\hat{8}(\hat{1})$

In a **NATURAL MINOR** scale, semitones (half steps) are between degrees (notes) $\hat{2}$ - $\hat{3}$ and $\hat{5}$ - $\hat{6}$.

♪ **Note:** When using accidentals, a natural minor scale written **WITH** a center bar line will repeat the accidentals in the descending scale.

c sharp minor natural - Related to: ____E____ Major (Key Signature: __F# C# G# D#__)

♪ **Note:** When using accidentals, a natural minor scale written **WITHOUT** a center bar line will only use accidentals in the ascending scale.

f minor natural - Related to: ____Ab____ Major (Key Signature: __Bb Eb Ab Db__)

♪ **Note:** "Semitone Slurs" are curved lines used to indicate the location of a semitone (half step). They do not have the same function as the slurs used in music that indicate to play smoothly.

1. a) Name the relative Major key. Name the sharps or flats in the Key Signature.
   b) Write the natural minor scale, ascending and descending. Use accidentals. Use whole notes.
   c) Mark the semitones (half steps) with a slur.

g minor natural - Related to: __Bb__ Major (Key Signature: __Bb Eb__)

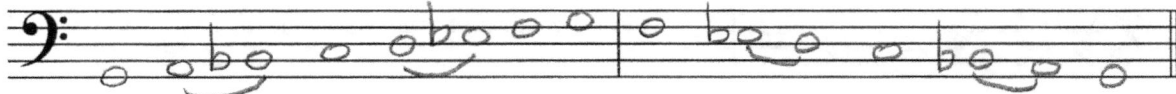

f# minor natural - Related to: __A__ Major (Key Signature: __F# C# G#__)

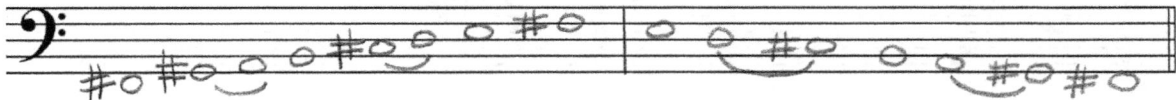

HARMONIC MINOR SCALES

A **HARMONIC MINOR** scale has the **SAME** Key Signature as its relative Major. In the harmonic minor scale the **7th** note is **RAISED** one chromatic semitone ascending and descending.

When using a Key Signature, the raised 7th note is written with an accidental.

♫ **Note:** When using a Key Signature, a harmonic minor scale written **WITH** a center bar line will use an accidental in the ascending and descending scale.

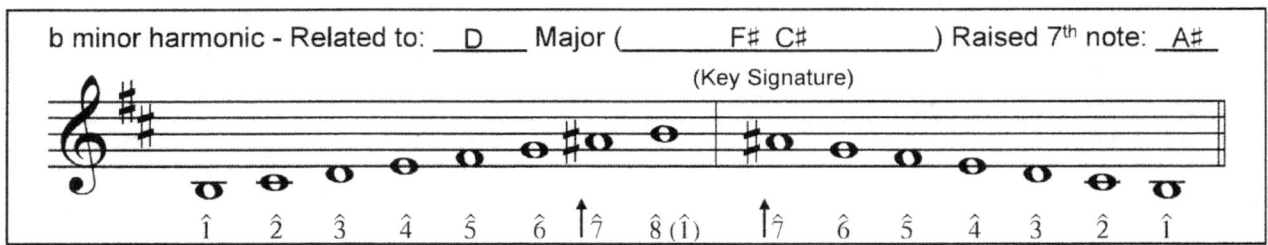

♫ **Note:** When using a Key Signature, a harmonic minor scale written **WITHOUT** a center bar line will only use an accidental in the ascending scale.

1. a) Name the relative Major key, the Key Signature and the raised 7th note of the harmonic minor.
   b) Write the harmonic minor scale, ascending and descending. Use a Key Signature and any necessary accidentals. Use whole notes.

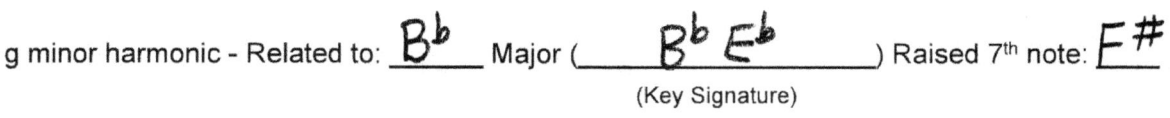

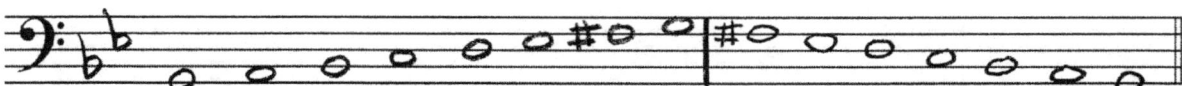

HARMONIC MINOR SCALES - TONES (WHOLE STEPS) and SEMITONES (HALF STEPS)

Harmonic Minor Scale Pattern:
$\hat{1}$ tone $\hat{2}$ semitone $\hat{3}$ tone $\hat{4}$ tone $\hat{5}$ semitone $\hat{6}$ tone + semitone $\hat{7}$ semitone $\hat{8}(\hat{1})$

In a **HARMONIC MINOR** scale, semitones are between degrees (notes) $\hat{2}$-$\hat{3}$, $\hat{5}$-$\hat{6}$ and $\hat{7}$-$\hat{8}(\hat{1})$.

♪ **Note:** When using accidentals, a harmonic minor scale written **WITH** a center bar line will repeat the accidentals in the descending scale.

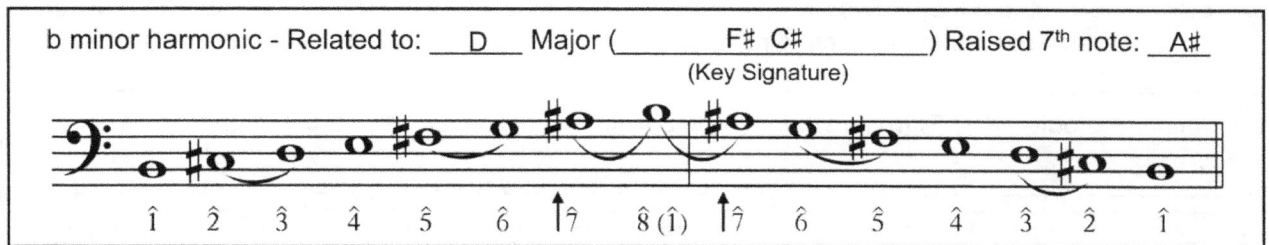

♪ **Note:** When using accidentals, a harmonic minor scale written **WITHOUT** a center bar line will only use accidentals in the ascending scale.

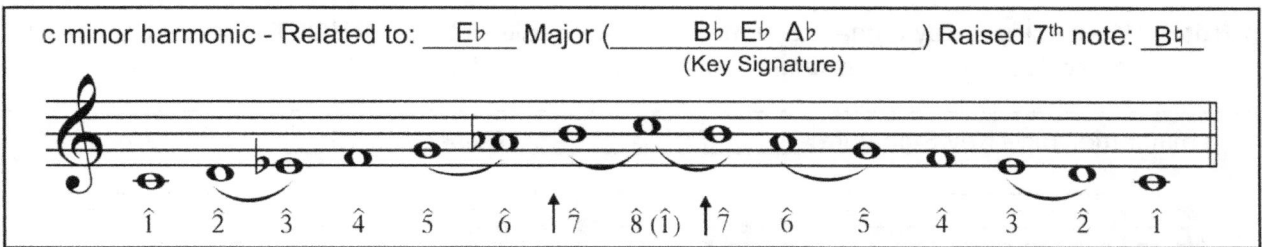

♪ **Note:** "Semitone Slurs" are written under the notes and do not touch the noteheads.

1. a) Name the relative Major key, the Key Signature and the raised 7th note of the harmonic minor.
   b) Write the harmonic minor scale, ascending and descending. Use accidentals. Use whole notes.
   c) Mark the semitones (half steps) with a slur.

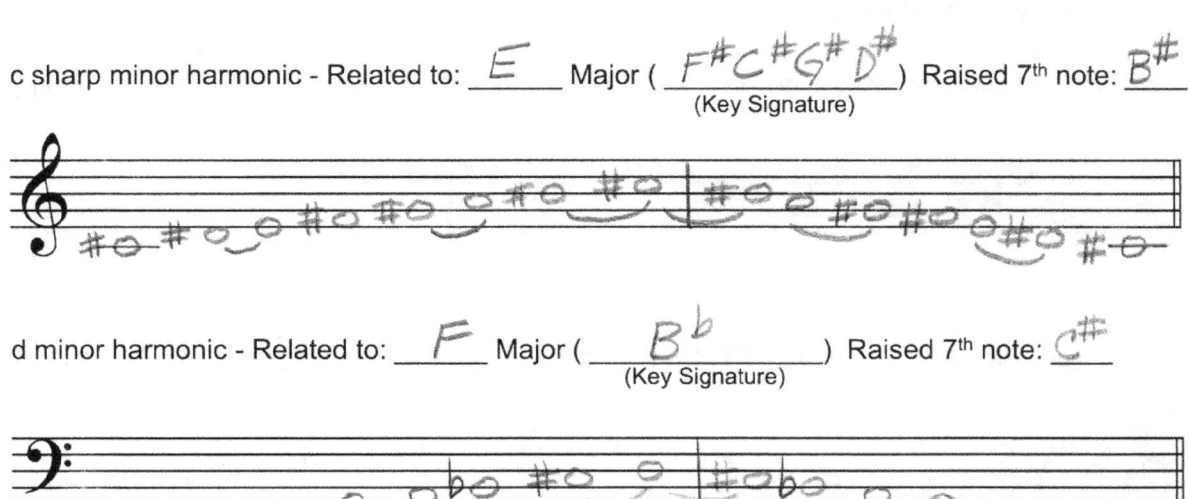

77

MELODIC MINOR SCALE

A **MELODIC MINOR** scale has the **SAME** Key Signature as its relative Major. In the melodic minor scale, the **6ᵗʰ** and **7ᵗʰ** notes are **RAISED** one chromatic semitone **ASCENDING** and **LOWERED** one chromatic semitone **DESCENDING**.

When using a Key Signature, the raised and lowered 6ᵗʰ and 7ᵗʰ notes are written with accidentals.

♪ **Note:** When using a Key Signature, a melodic minor scale written **WITH** a center bar line will only use accidentals in the ascending scale.

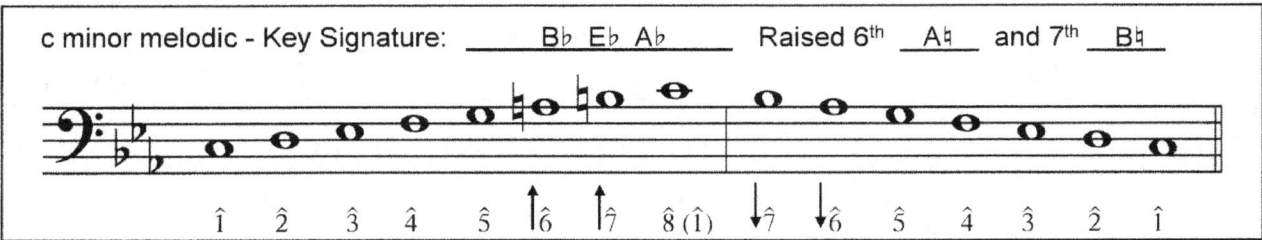

♪ **Note:** When using a Key Signature, a melodic minor scale written **WITHOUT** a center bar line will use accidentals in the ascending and descending scales.

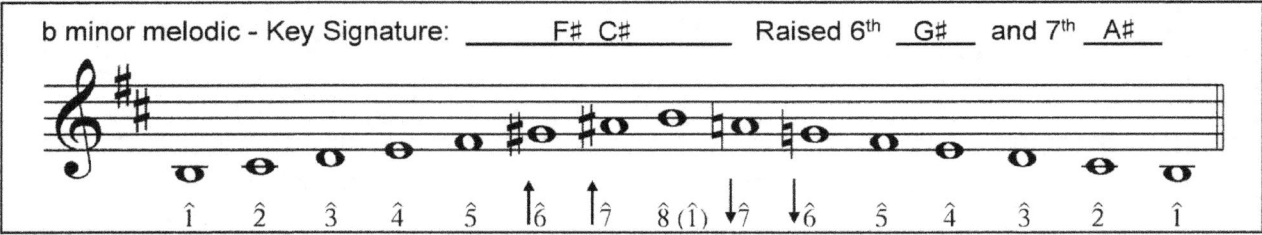

1. a) Name the Key Signature, the raised 6ᵗʰ note and the raised 7ᵗʰ note of the melodic minor.
   b) Write the melodic minor scale, ascending and descending. Use a Key Signature and any necessary accidentals. Use whole notes.

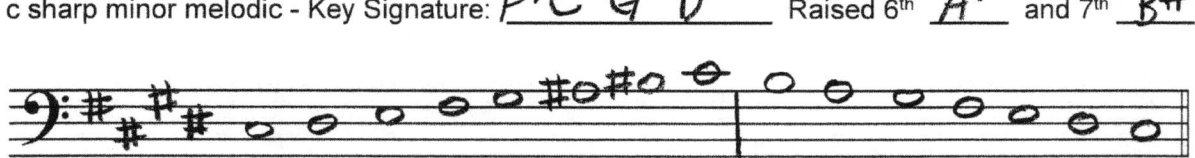

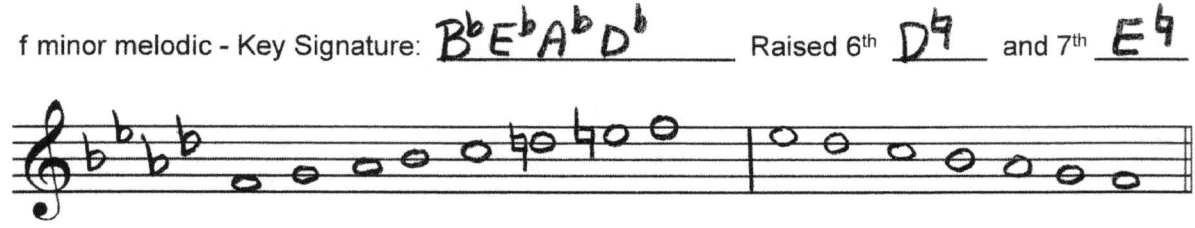

MELODIC MINOR SCALES - TONES (WHOLE STEPS) and SEMITONES (HALF STEPS)

Melodic Minor Scale Pattern:
    Ascending: 1̂ tone 2̂ semitone 3̂ tone 4̂ tone 5̂ tone 6̂ tone 7̂ semitone 8̂ (1̂)
    Descending: (8̂) tone 7̂ tone 6̂ semitone 5̂ tone 4̂ tone 3̂ semitone 2̂ tone 1̂

In a **MELODIC MINOR s**cale, semitones are between degrees (notes) 2̂ - 3̂ and 7̂ - 8̂ (1̂) **ASCENDING** and between degrees (notes) 2̂ - 3̂ and 5̂ - 6̂ **DESCENDING**.

♪ **Note:** When using accidentals, a melodic minor scale written **WITH** a center bar line will use accidentals in the ascending and descending scales.

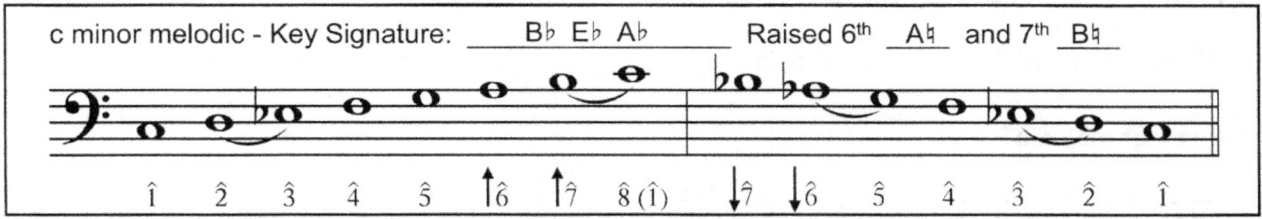

♪ **Note:** When using accidentals, a melodic minor scale written **WITHOUT** a center bar line will use accidentals in the ascending and descending scales.

1. a) Name the Key Signature, the raised 6th note and the raised 7th note of the melodic minor.
   b) Write the melodic minor scale, ascending and descending. Use accidentals. Use whole notes.
   c) Mark the semitones (half steps) with a slur.

d minor melodic - Key Signature: __B♭__   Raised 6th __B♮__ and 7th __C♯__

a minor melodic - Key Signature: __—__   Raised 6th __F♯__ and 7th __G♯__

WRITING NATURAL, HARMONIC and MELODIC MINOR SCALES

NATURAL MINOR SCALE: Nothing is added.
♪ **Note:** Like "N" in "Natural.

HARMONIC MINOR SCALE: Raise the 7th note ONE chromatic semitone ascending and descending.
♪ **Note:** Find the 7 in the H.

MELODIC MINOR SCALE: Raise the 6th and 7th notes ONE chromatic semitone ascending and lower the 6th and 7th notes ONE chromatic semitone descending.
♪ **Note:** Find the 6 and 7 in the M.

1. Write the following scales, ascending and descending. Use accidentals. Use whole notes.

a) c minor melodic

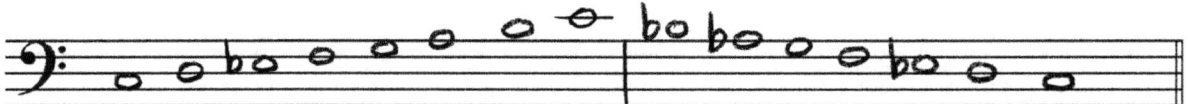

b) f minor harmonic

c) e minor natural

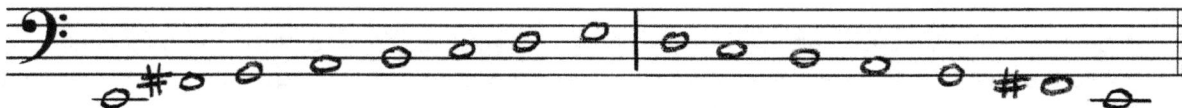

d) a minor melodic

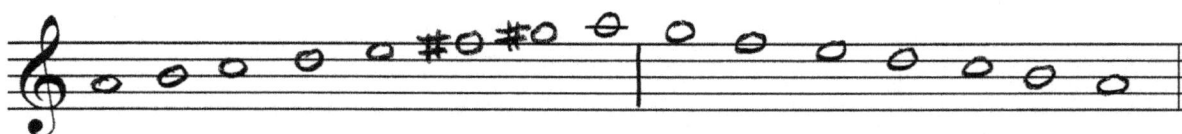

e) f sharp minor harmonic

Lesson 6   Review Test

Total Score: ____ / 100

1. a) Write the following notes **ABOVE** the **Treble Clef**. Use ledger lines. Use whole notes.

___/10

Eb   G   D#   B   Ab

b) Name the following notes **BELOW** the **Bass Clef**.

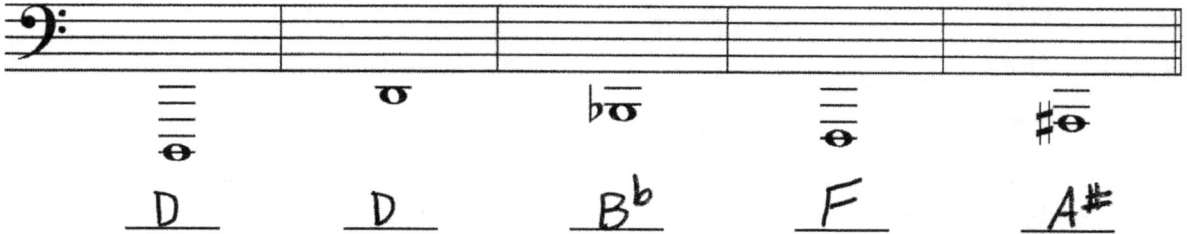

D   D   Bb   F   A#

2. Write the following **HARMONIC** intervals **ABOVE** each of the given notes. Use whole notes.

___/10

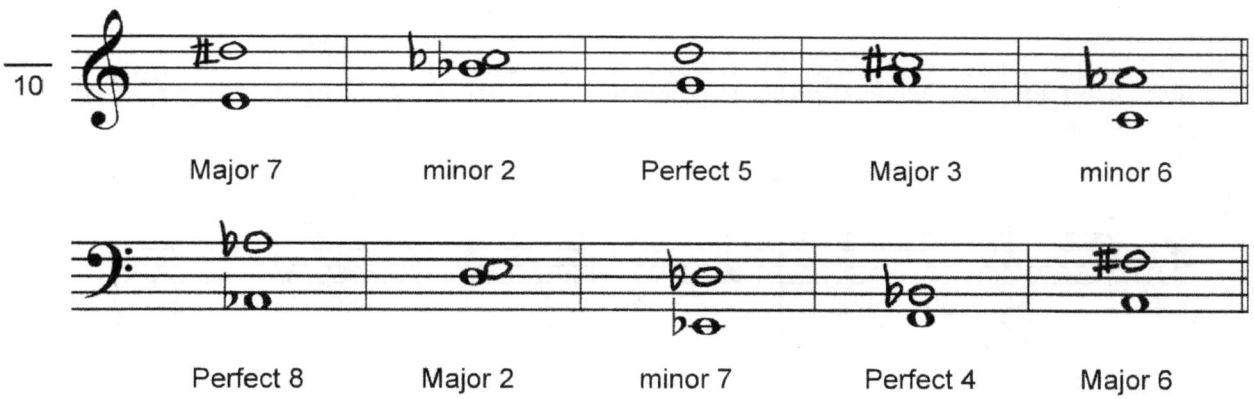

Major 7   minor 2   Perfect 5   Major 3   minor 6

Perfect 8   Major 2   minor 7   Perfect 4   Major 6

3. Write the following notes in the Bass Clef. Use the the correct **KEY SIGNATURE**. Use half notes.

___/10

a) the TONIC note of e minor
b) the TONIC note of c sharp minor
c) the TONIC note of b minor
d) the TONIC note of f minor
e) the TONIC note of d minor

a)   b)   c)   d)   e)

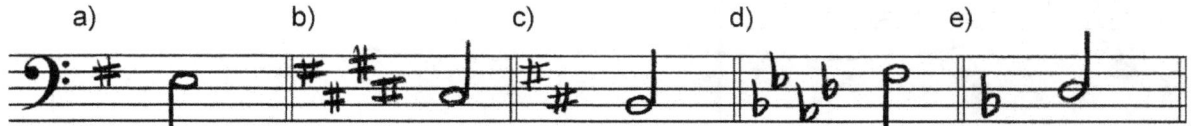

4. Match each musical term or sign with the English definition. (Not all definitions will be used.)

Term		Definition
natural minor	k	a) sweet, gentle
prestissimo	g	b) raise the 7th note ascending and descending
harmonic minor	b	c) right hand
mano sinistra, M.S.	f	d) very slow
melodic minor	j	e) first note of a Major or minor key
dal segno, D.S.	h	f) left hand
largo	d	g) as fast as possible
dolce	a	h) from the sign
Tonic note	e	i) 3 semitones and 3 letter names
distance between Major and relative minor keys	i	j) raise the 6th and 7th notes ascending and lower the 6th and 7th notes descending
		k) same Key Signature as its relative Major, nothing added

5. Add **ONE REST** below each bracket to complete the measure. Cross off the count as each beat is completed.

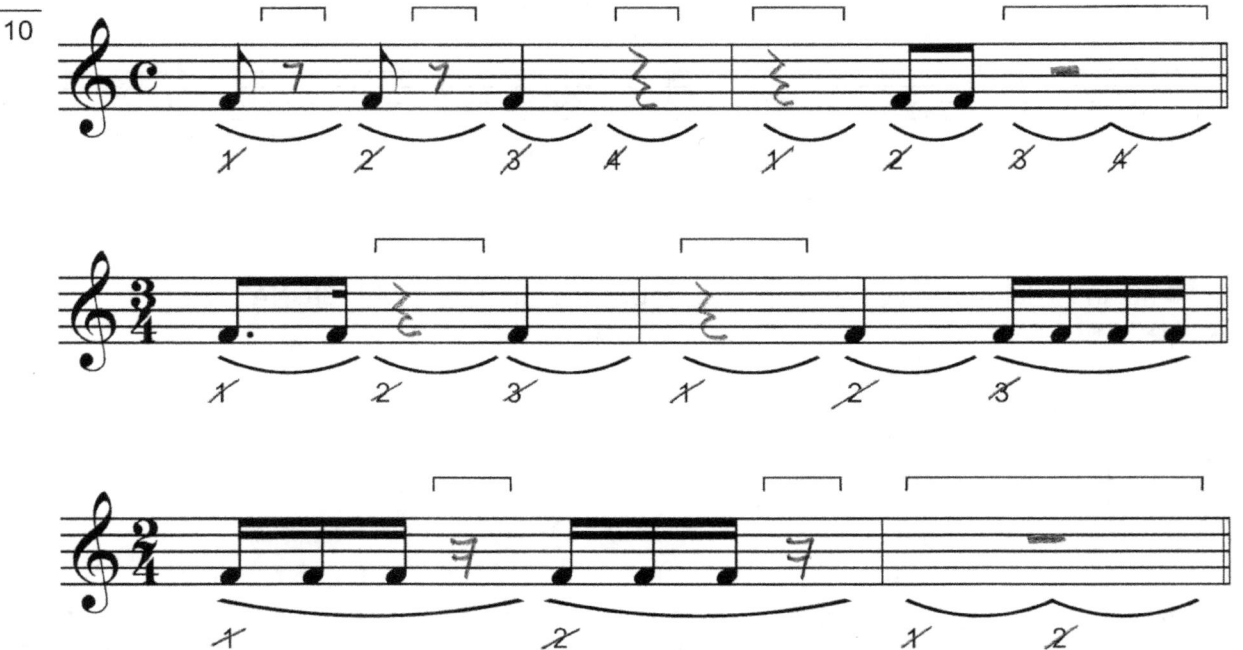

6. Name each of the following as: **d.s.** (diatonic semitone), **c.s.** (chromatic semitone), **w.t.** (whole tone) or **e.e.** (enharmonic equivalent).

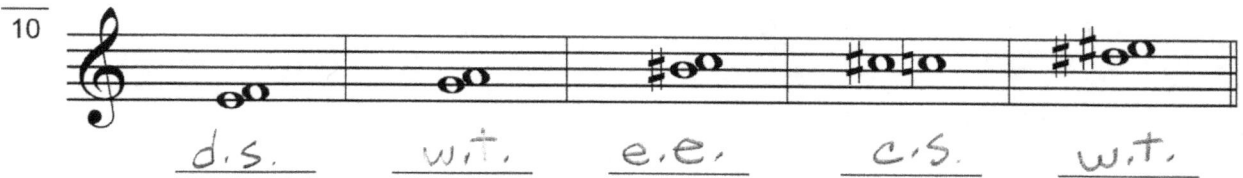

7. Write the **ENHARMONIC EQUIVALENT** for each of the following notes. Use whole notes. Name **BOTH** notes.

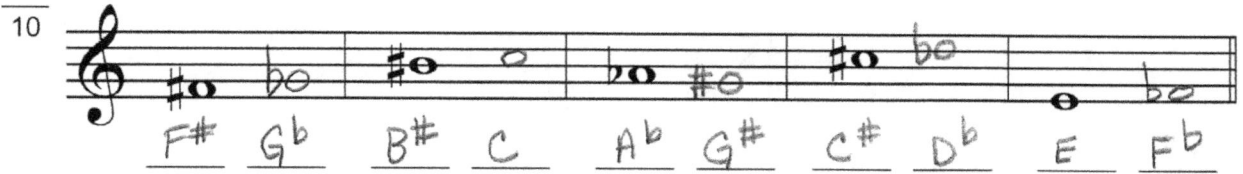

8. a) Name the key of the following melody. Rewrite it at the **SAME PITCH** in the **Treble Clef**.

Key: E Major

b) Name the key of the following melody. Rewrite it at the **SAME PITCH** in the **Bass Clef**.

Key: B♭ Major

9. Complete the **CIRCLE OF FIFTHS**:
   a) Write the order of flats and sharps.
   b) Write the Major keys on the OUTSIDE of the circle.
   c) Write the relative minor keys on the INSIDE of the circle.

10

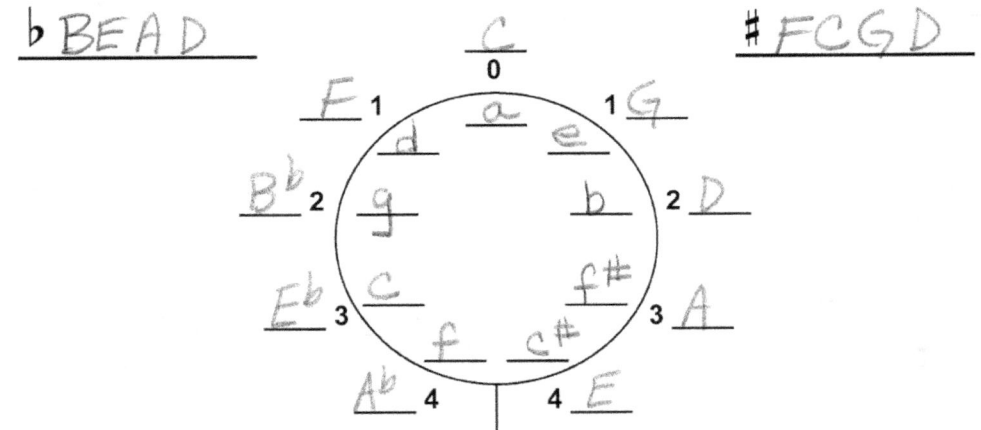

Write the following scales, ascending and descending, using the correct **KEY SIGNATURE** and any necessary accidentals for each. Use whole notes.

   a) E flat Major in the Treble Clef
   b) f sharp minor harmonic in the Bass Clef
   c) c minor melodic in the Bass Clef
   d) g minor natural in the Bass Clef
   e) E Major in the Treble Clef

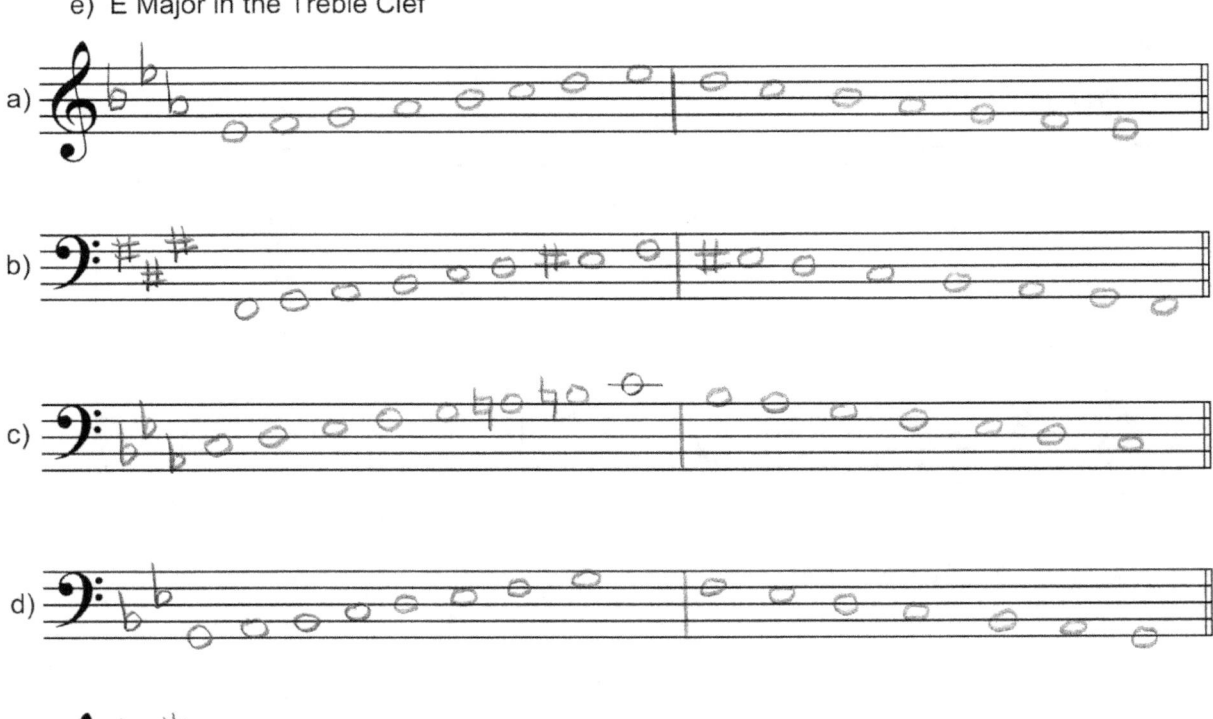

10. Analyze the following piece of music by answering the questions below.

a) How many measures are in this piece? __eight__

b) Name the composer of this piece. __Franz Joseph Haydn__

c) Explain the sign at the letter **A**. __mezzo forte - moderately loud__

d) Name the interval at the letter **B**. __Major 2__

e) Name the note at the letter **C**. __A#__

f) Name the interval at the letter **D**. __Perfect 5__

g) Name the highest note in this piece. __A__

h) Locate and circle a diatonic semitone in this piece. Label it as d.s.

i) Locate and circle a whole tone in this piece. Label it as w.t.

j) Explain the meaning of **Moderato**. __at a moderate tempo__

Lesson 7 Triads - Major and Minor: Tonic, Subdominant and Dominant

SOLID ROOT POSITION TRIADS

A **TRIAD** is a three note chord: the root (the lowest note), a third above the root and a fifth above the root.
A **SOLID** (blocked) triad is written one note above the other (three notes played together).

F Major triad

♪ Note: A **ROOT** position triad is ALL lines or ALL spaces. The lowest note names the root.

1. Copy the following solid root position triads. Name the root.

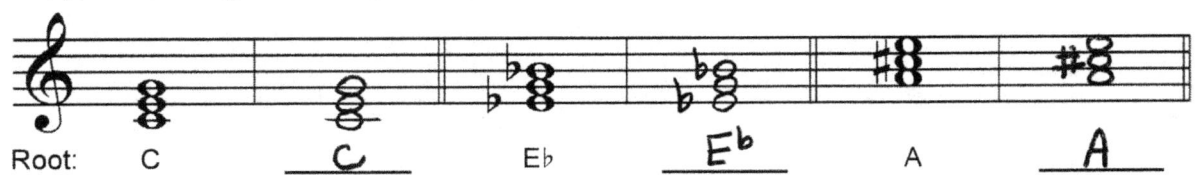

Root: C   _C_   E♭   _E♭_   A   _A_

The **Major** triad is written using: Major 3 + Perfect 5 = Major triad
The **minor** triad is written using: minor 3 + Perfect 5 = minor triad

C - E   C - G   C E G   C - E♭   C - G   C E♭ G

2. Following the example, write the intervals above the given notes. Write the Major triads.

Maj 3 + Per 5 = D Major triad   Maj 3 + Per 5 = G Major triad   Maj 3 + Per 5 = A Major triad

3. Following the example, write the intervals above the given notes. Write the minor triads.

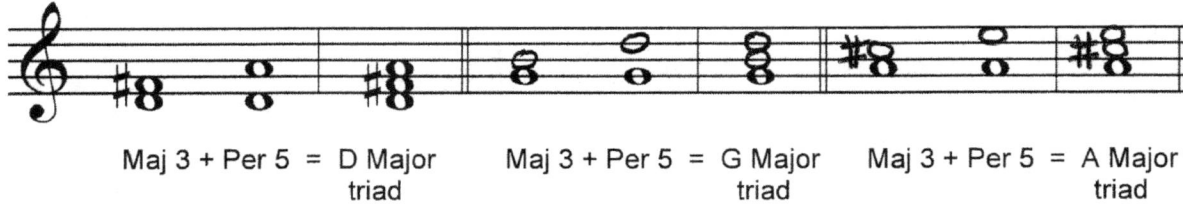

min 3 + Per 5 = d minor triad   min 3 + Per 5 = g minor triad   min 3 + Per 5 = a minor triad

4. Identify the type/quality of the following triads as Major or minor.

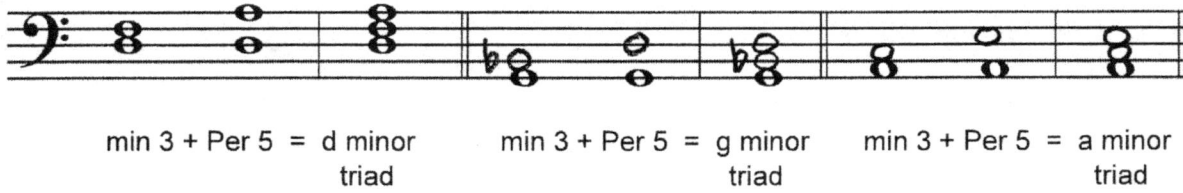

Major   _minor_   _Major_   _minor_   _Major_   _minor_

TONIC TRIADS and SUBDOMINANT TRIADS

TRIADS are built on any degree of a scale. Roman Numerals are used to indicate the scale degree of the root (lowest note). Use UPPER case for Major triads and lower case for minor triads.

Tonic triad - first degree of the scale   I Major   i minor
Subdominant triad - fourth degree of the scale   IV Major   iv minor
Dominant triad - fifth degree of the scale   V Major   V Major

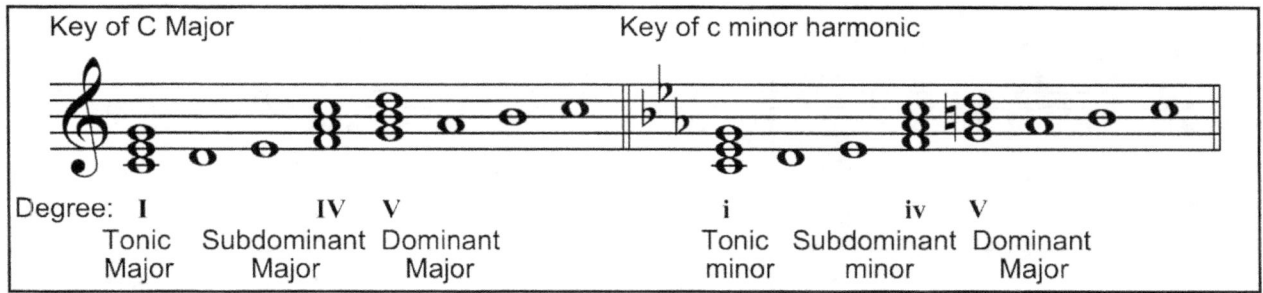

A **TONIC** triad is built on the first degree of the scale.
A Tonic triad uses the $\hat{1}$ (Tonic), $\hat{3}$ (Mediant) and $\hat{5}$ (Dominant) degrees of the scale.

1. a) Write the following Tonic triads in root position. Use a Key Signature. Use whole notes.
   b) Name the Tonic note. Label the Tonic triad as **I** (Major) or **i** (minor).

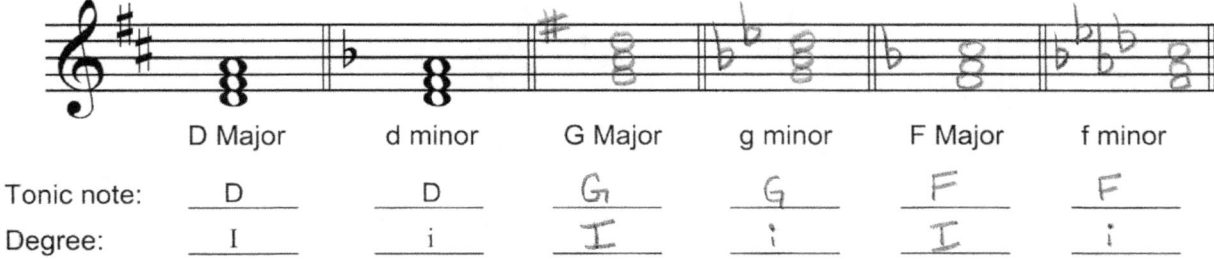

	D Major	d minor	G Major	g minor	F Major	f minor
Tonic note:	D	D	G	G	F	F
Degree:	I	i	I	i	I	i

A **SUBDOMINANT** triad is built on the fourth degree of the scale. Count **UP** 4 notes from the Tonic.
A Subdominant triad uses the $\hat{4}$ (Subdominant), $\hat{6}$ (Submediant) and $\hat{1}$ (Tonic) degrees of the scale.

2. a) Write the following Subdominant triads in root position. Use a Key Signature. Use whole notes.
   b) Name the Subdominant note. Label the Subdominant triad as **IV** (Major) or **iv** (minor).

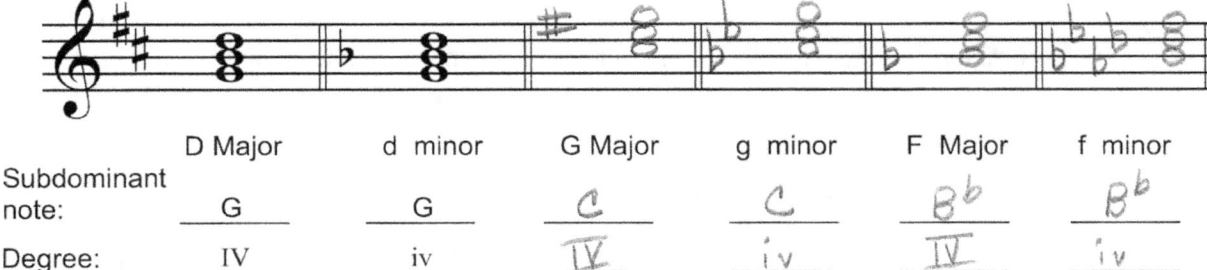

	D Major	d minor	G Major	g minor	F Major	f minor
Subdominant note:	G	G	C	C	B♭	B♭
Degree:	IV	iv	IV	iv	IV	iv

DOMINANT TRIADS

A **DOMINANT** triad is built on the fifth degree of the scale. Count **UP** 5 notes from the Tonic.
A Dominant triad uses the $\hat{5}$ (Dominant), $\hat{7}$ (Leading note) and $\hat{2}$ (Supertonic) degrees of the scale.

1. a) Write the following Dominant triads in root position. Use a Key Signature. Use whole notes.
   Use the musical alphabet to find the fifth note above each Tonic.
   A B C D E F G A B C D E F G
   b) Name the Dominant note. Label the Dominant triad as **V** (Major).

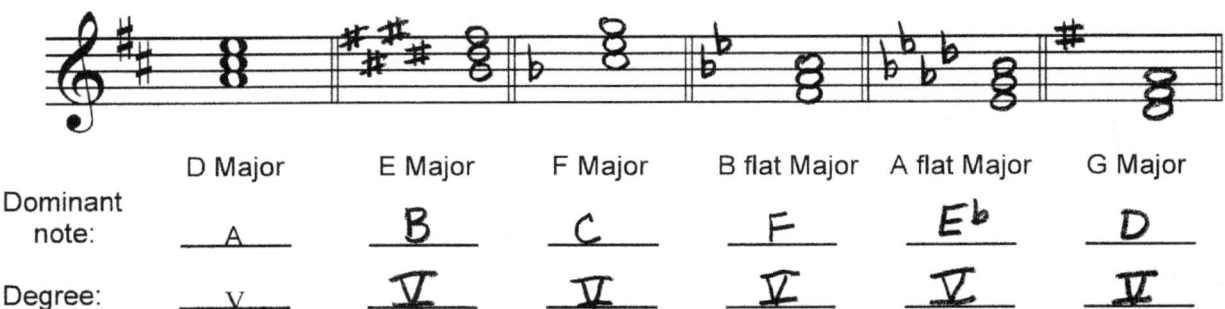

	D Major	E Major	F Major	B flat Major	A flat Major	G Major
Dominant note:	A	B	C	F	E♭	D
Degree:	V	V	V	V	V	V

♪ **Note**: A Dominant triad of a minor key uses the raised 7th note of the harmonic minor scale.
A Dominant triad is **ALWAYS** Major.

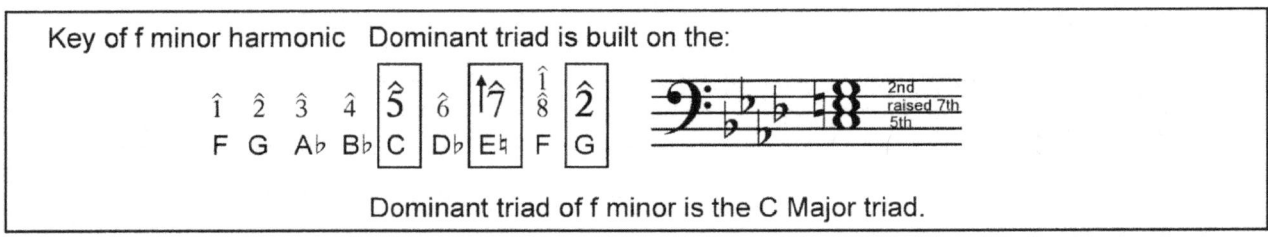

Key of f minor harmonic Dominant triad is built on the:

$\hat{1}$ $\hat{2}$ $\hat{3}$ $\hat{4}$ | $\hat{5}$ | $\hat{6}$ | ↑$\hat{7}$ | $\hat{8}$ $\hat{2}$
F G A♭ B♭ | C | D♭ | E♮ | F G

Dominant triad of f minor is the C Major triad.

In Music, when a Key Signature changes to C Major or a minor, natural signs are used to cancel the outgoing Key Signature in the first measure. In Theory Exercises where a Key Signature is changed with each measure, cancelling the outgoing Key Signature is optional (and is not a requirement).

2. a) Write the following solid Dominant triads in root position. Use a Key Signature and any necessary accidentals. Use whole notes.
   b) Name the Dominant note. Label the Dominant triad as **V** (Major). Name the raised 7th note.

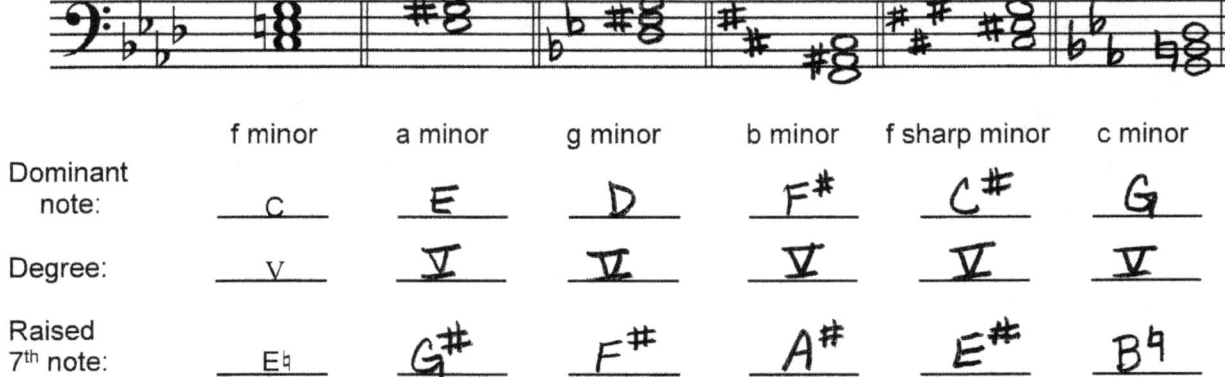

	f minor	a minor	g minor	b minor	f sharp minor	c minor
Dominant note:	C	E	D	F♯	C♯	G
Degree:	V	V	V	V	V	V
Raised 7th note:	E♮	G♯	F♯	A♯	E♯	B♮

WRITING TRIADS USING ACCIDENTALS

When the triad contains **TWO** accidentals, the accidental is written closest to the higher note and further away from the lower note.

When the triad contains **THREE** accidentals, the highest and lowest accidentals are written the same as above. The middle accidental is written furthest away from the middle note.

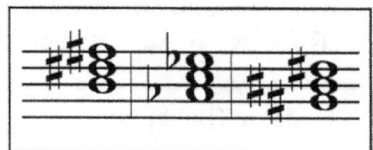

1. Copy the following Dominant triads. Name the ROOT (lowest note).

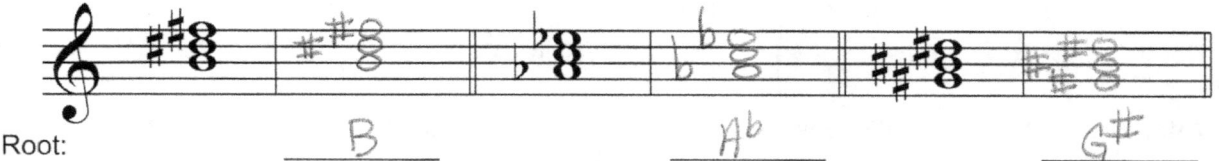

Root: _____ B _____ _____ Ab _____ _____ G# _____

Each Dominant triad belongs to a Major key and a minor key. To identify the key of the Dominant triad, count **DOWN** 5 notes from the Dominant (a Perfect fifth) to find the Tonic note. This names BOTH the Tonic Major key and the Tonic minor key.

The Tonic Major key and the Tonic minor key have the **SAME Tonic note** and the **SAME Dominant triad**.

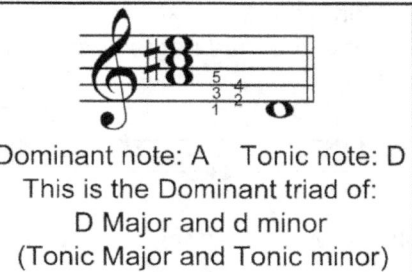

Dominant note: A   Tonic note: D
This is the Dominant triad of:
D Major and d minor
(Tonic Major and Tonic minor)

♫ **Note:** When using **accidentals**, the Dominant triad belongs to **BOTH** the Tonic Major key and the Tonic minor key.

2. Name both the Tonic Major key and Tonic minor key for each of the following Dominant triads.

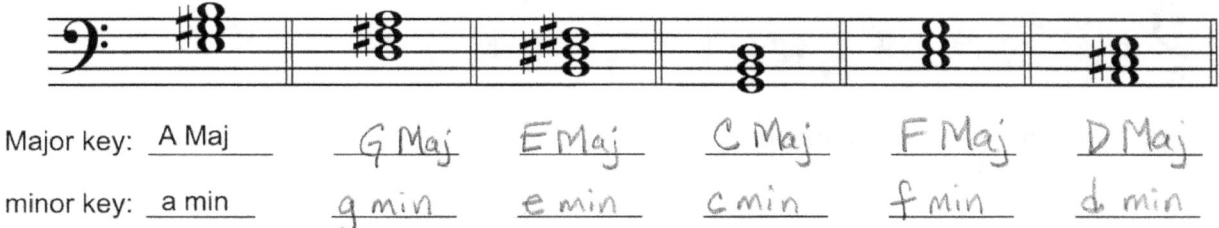

Major key: A Maj   G Maj   E Maj   C Maj   F Maj   D Maj
minor key: a min   g min   e min   c min   f min   d min

♫ **Note:** When using a **Key Signature**, the Dominant triad belongs to only **ONE** key. If the Dominant triad contains an accidental (the raised 7th note of the harmonic minor scale), it belongs to the minor key.

3. Name the correct key (Major or minor) for each of the following Dominant triads.

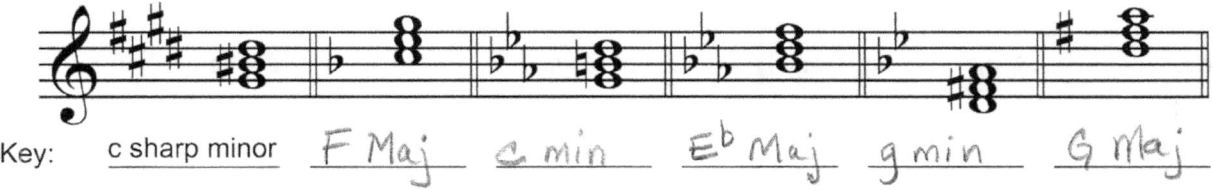

Key: c sharp minor   F Maj   c min   Eb Maj   g min   G Maj

BROKEN TRIADS

A **SOLID (BLOCKED) TRIAD** is written one note above the other (together).
A **BROKEN TRIAD** is written one note after the other. The notes are played one at a time (separately).

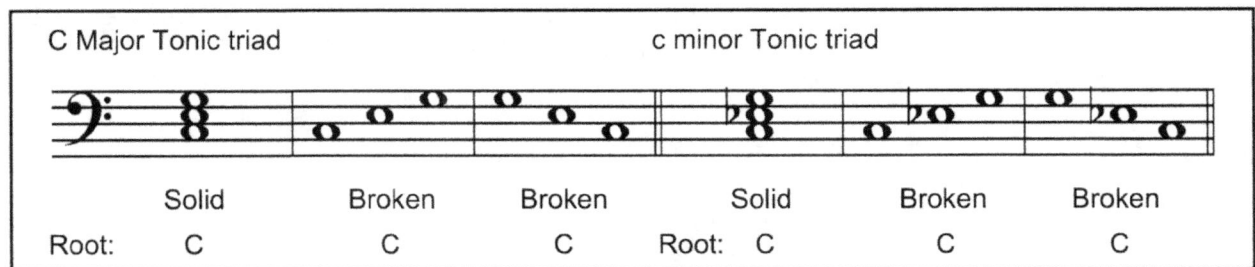

♪ **Note:** Broken triads in ROOT position may be written in the SKIPPING UP pattern or the SKIPPING DOWN pattern. The lowest note is ALWAYS the Root of the triad.

1. Name the Major key for each of the following broken triads. Name the Root.
   Label the triad degree as: I (Tonic Major), IV (Subdominant Major) or V (Dominant Major).

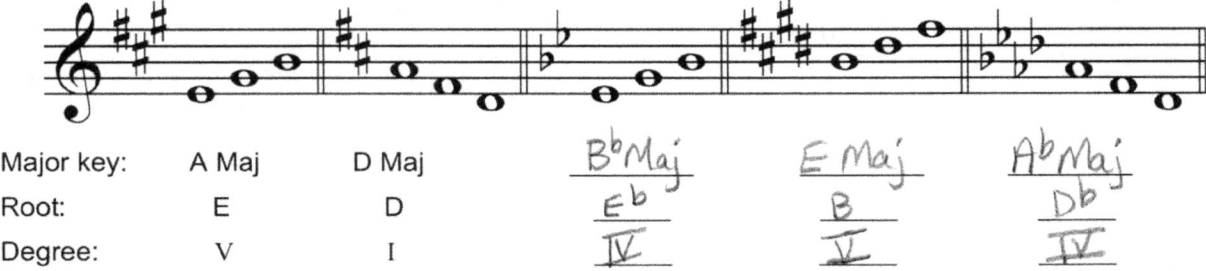

Major key:	A Maj	D Maj	B♭ Maj	E Maj	A♭ Maj
Root:	E	D	E♭	B	D♭
Degree:	V	I	IV	V	IV

2. Name the minor key for each of the following broken triads. Name the Root.
   Label the triad degree as: i (Tonic minor), iv (Subdominant minor) or V (Dominant Major).

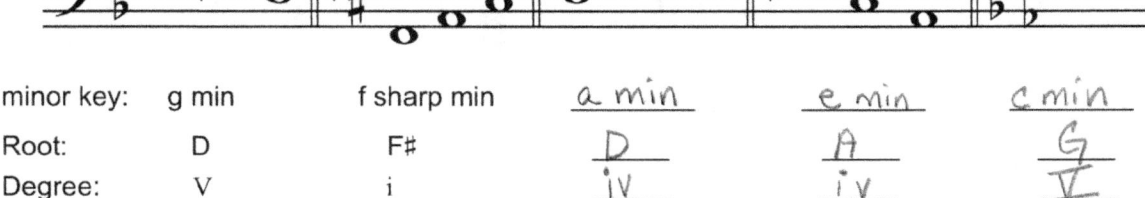

minor key:	g min	f sharp min	a min	e min	c min
Root:	D	F#	D	A	G
Degree:	V	i	iv	iv	V

3. Name the Root. Label the triad degree as: I (Tonic Major), i (Tonic minor),
   IV (Subdominant Major), iv (Subdominant minor) or V (Dominant Major).

Key:	A Major	g minor	E flat Major	f minor	c sharp minor
Root:	A	C	B♭	F	G#
Degree:	I	iv	V	i	V

Lesson 7 — Review Test

Total Score: ____ / 100

1. Name the following notes in the **Bass Clef**.

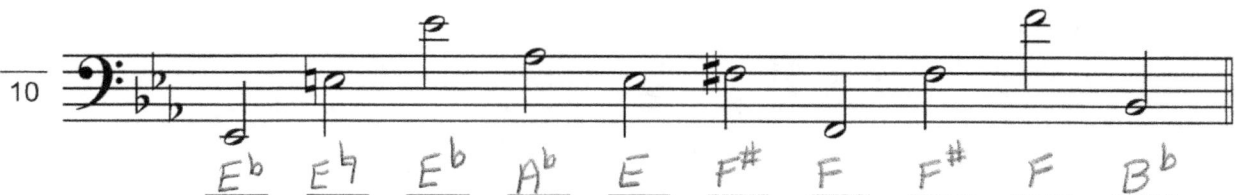

2. a) Name the following **MELODIC** intervals.

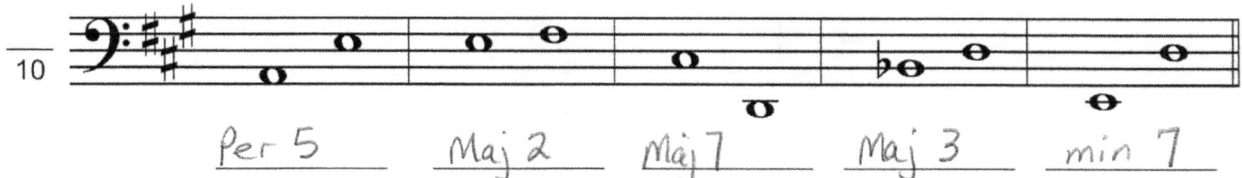

b) Name the following **HARMONIC** intervals.

3. Write the following **SOLID** triads in **ROOT** position in the Bass Clef using **ACCIDENTALS**. Use whole notes.

a) the DOMINANT (V) triad of f sharp minor harmonic
b) the TONIC (I) triad of B flat Major
c) the SUBDOMINANT (iv) triad of a minor harmonic
d) the DOMINANT (V) triad of E Major
e) the SUBDOMINANT (iv) triad of c minor harmonic

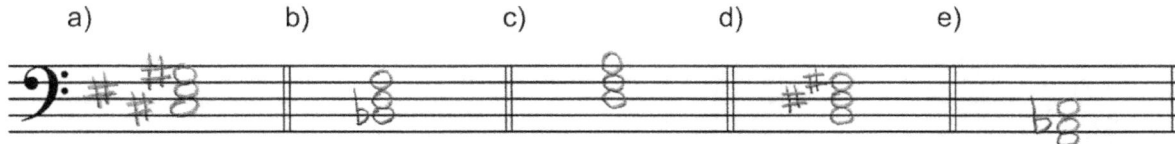

4. a) Name the **MAJOR** key for each of the following Key Signatures.
b) Identify the technical degree name of the ROOT for the following broken triads as:

T (Tonic), SD (Subdominant) or D (Dominant).

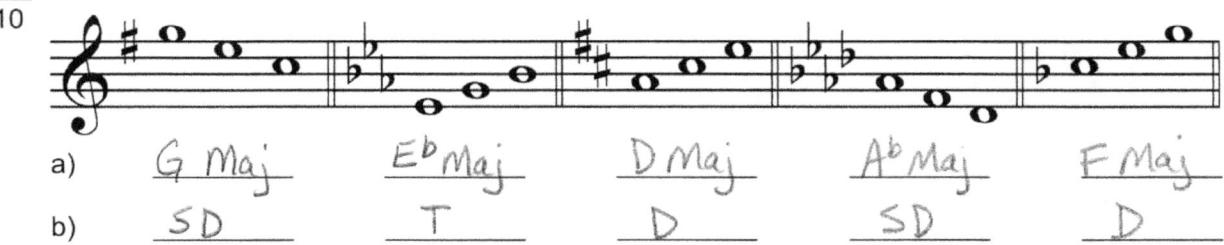

5. Complete the **CIRCLE OF FIFTHS**:
   a) Write the order of flats and sharps.
   b) Write the Major keys on the OUTSIDE of the circle.
   c) Write the relative minor keys on the INSIDE of the circle.

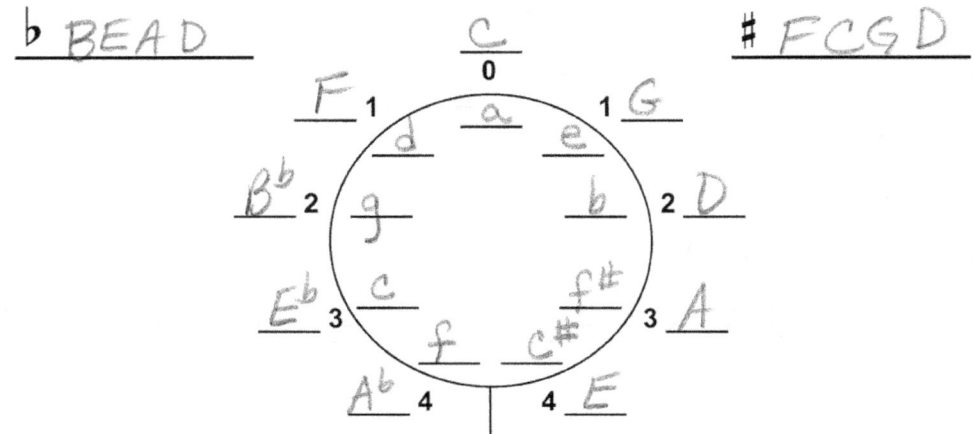

Write the following scales, ascending and descending, using the correct **KEY SIGNATURE** and any necessary accidentals for each. Use whole notes.

   a) E flat Major in the Treble Clef
   b) c sharp minor harmonic in the Bass Clef
   c) d minor melodic in the Treble Clef
   d) D Major in the Bass Clef
   e) a minor natural in the Treble Clef

6. Match each musical term with the English definition. (Not all definitions will be used.)

Term		Definition
Tonic	f	a) fourth degree of a scale
a tempo	h	b) Major 3 + Perfect 5 =
Subdominant	a	c) not as slow as *largo*; fairly slow and broad
con pedale, con ped.	j	d) marked or stressed
Dominant	i	e) minor 3 + Perfect 5 =
larghetto	c	f) first degree of a scale
marcato, marc.	d	g) graceful
solid triad	k	h) return to the original tempo
Major triad	b	i) fifth degree of a scale
minor triad	e	j) with pedal
		k) three note chord: root, 3rd and 5th written one note above the other

7. Name the key of the following melody. Rewrite it at the **SAME PITCH** in the **Bass Clef**.

Key: d minor

8. Add the correct **TIME SIGNATURE** below each bracket to complete the following rhythms.

9. a) Name the **MINOR** key for each of the following Key Signatures.
    b) Identify the technical degree name of the given note as:
       T (Tonic),   **SD** (Subdominant)   or   **D** (Dominant).

a) f#min   d min   b min   f min   a min
b) D   T   SD   D   SD

10. Analyze the following piece of music by answering the questions below.

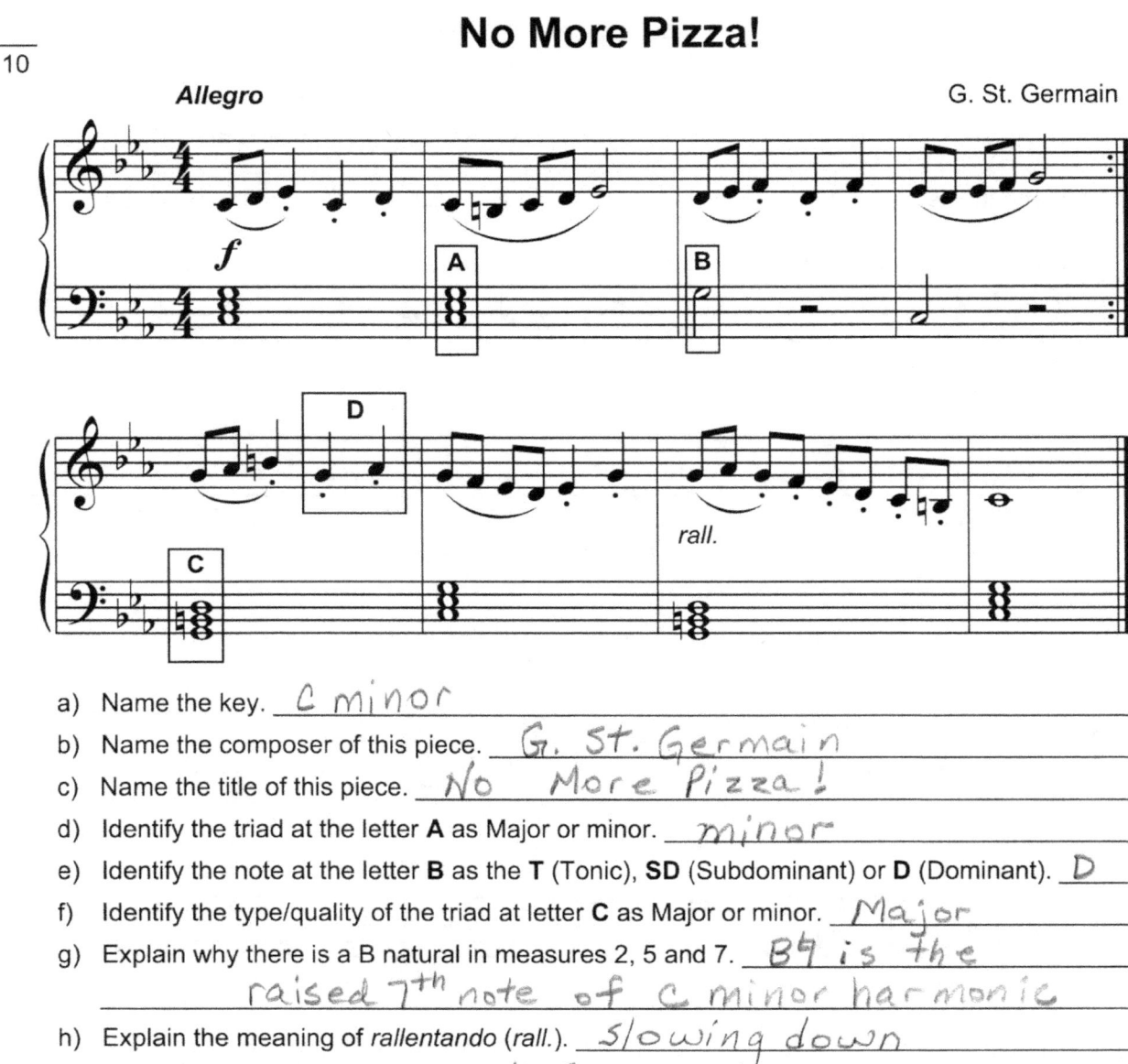

a) Name the key. C minor
b) Name the composer of this piece. G. St. Germain
c) Name the title of this piece. No More Pizza!
d) Identify the triad at the letter **A** as Major or minor. minor
e) Identify the note at the letter **B** as the **T** (Tonic), **SD** (Subdominant) or **D** (Dominant). D
f) Identify the type/quality of the triad at letter **C** as Major or minor. Major
g) Explain why there is a B natural in measures 2, 5 and 7. B♮ is the raised 7th note of C minor harmonic
h) Explain the meaning of *rallentando* (rall.). Slowing down
i) Name the interval at letter **D**. min 2
j) When observing the repeat sign, how many measures of music are played? 12

Lesson 8   Simple Time - Duple, Triple and Quadruple

TIME SIGNATURES

A **TIME SIGNATURE** is written at the beginning of the music and is placed after the Key Signature. TWO numbers are used for a TIME SIGNATURE.

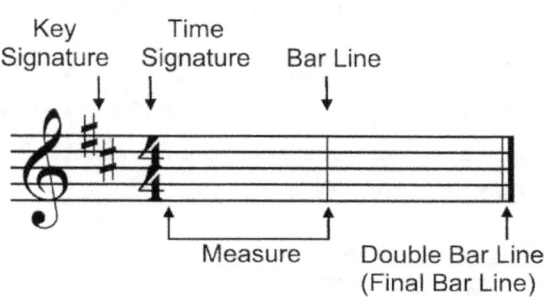

4	The **TOP NUMBER** indicates how many beats in a measure. (Example: 4 - **FOUR BEATS** per measure)
4	The **BOTTOM NUMBER** indicates what kind of note equals one beat. (Example: 4 - a **QUARTER** note equals **ONE BEAT**)

In **SIMPLE TIME** the **TOP NUMBER** is: **2, 3** or **4**.

    2 "DUPLE"   **TWO** beats per measure

    3 "TRIPLE"   **THREE** beats per measure

    4 "QUADRUPLE"   **FOUR** beats per measure

The **BOTTOM** number indicates what kind of note equals **ONE** beat. This is called the **BASIC BEAT**.

    ♩   **2**   HALF NOTE   =   **ONE** Basic Beat

    ♩   **4**   QUARTER NOTE   =   **ONE** Basic Beat

    ♪   **8**   EIGHTH NOTE   =   **ONE** Basic Beat

♪ **Note:**   **C** is the symbol for **COMMON TIME**: $\frac{4}{4}$ Time

             ¢ is the symbol for **CUT TIME** or **ALLA BREVE**: $\frac{2}{2}$ Time

1. Top Number: Write the number of beats (2, 3 or 4) per measure for each Time Signature.
   Bottom Number: Draw the kind of note that equals one beat (half, quarter or eighth note).

   2/4   = _2_ beats per measure   **3/8**   = _3_ beats per measure
          = _♩_ note equals one beat   = _♪_ note equals one beat

   3/2   = _3_ beats per measure   **C**   = _2_ beats per measure
          = _♩_ note equals one beat   = _♩_ note equals one beat

   4/4   = _4_ beats per measure   **4/2**   = _4_ beats per measure
          = _♩_ note equals one beat   = _♩_ note equals one beat

SIMPLE "DUPLE" TIME - TWO BASIC BEATS per MEASURE

A **GROUP** is a single note or rest, or a combination of notes or rests, that equal **ONE** BASIC BEAT.

1. Following the examples, scoop each beat. Write the Basic Beat below each scoop.
   Add the correct Time Signature below each bracket.

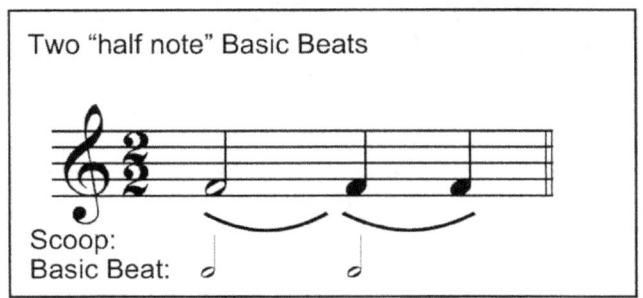 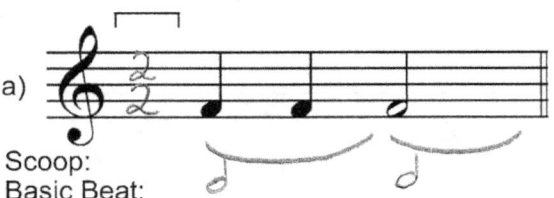

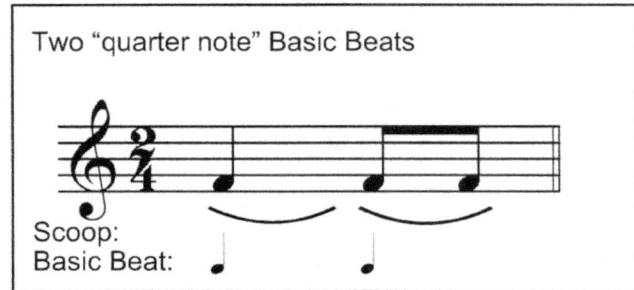 

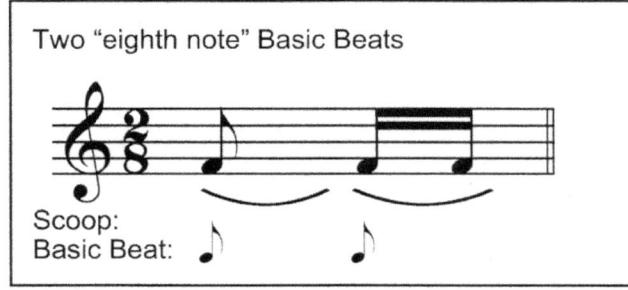 

2. Scoop each beat. Write the Basic Beat below each scoop. Add bar lines.

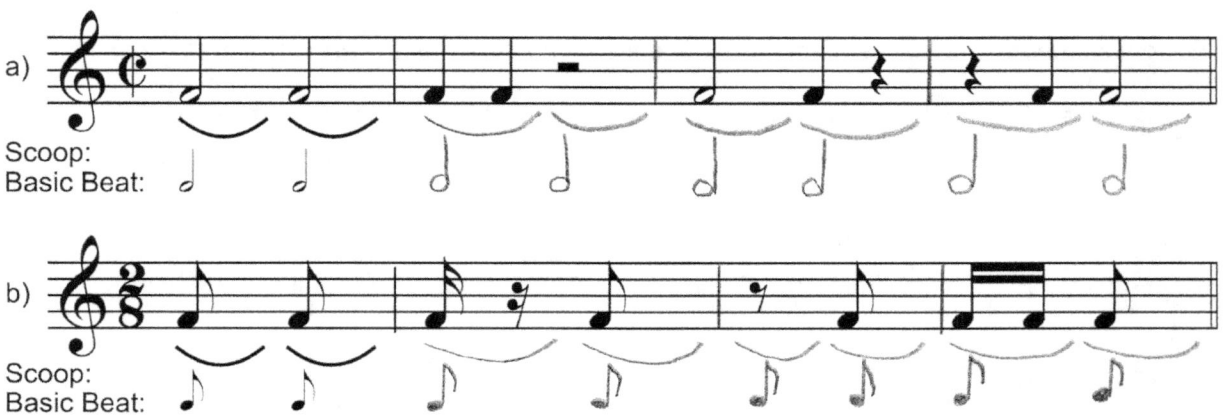

PULSE and ADDING RESTS in "DUPLE" Time

In "**DUPLE**" Time, the **TOP** number is **2**: two beats (pulses) per measure. The **PULSE** is where the rhythmic emphasis falls in a measure. **Pulse:**   S = Strong   w = weak

        Duple Pulse: 1 - Strong   2 - weak

♪ **Note:** Use UPPER CASE **S** for Strong and lower case **w** for weak. When adding rests, complete ONE Basic Beat at a time.

1. Write the Basic Beat and pulse below each measure. Add rests below each bracket to complete the measure. Cross off the Basic Beat as each beat is completed.

♪ **Note:** Time Signature: The TOP number is the number of Basic Beats (equal groups) per measure. The BOTTOM number is what kind of note equals one beat (group). Look for equal groups.

2. Write the Basic Beat below each scoop. Add the correct Time Signature below each bracket.

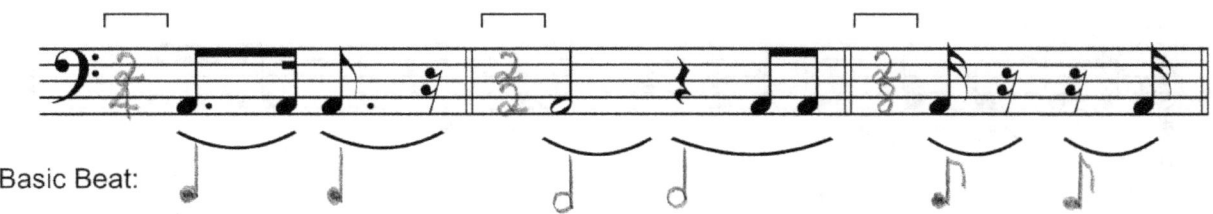

SIMPLE "TRIPLE" TIME - THREE BASIC BEATS per MEASURE

1. Following the examples, scoop each beat. Write the Basic Beat below each scoop.
   Add the correct Time Signature below each bracket.

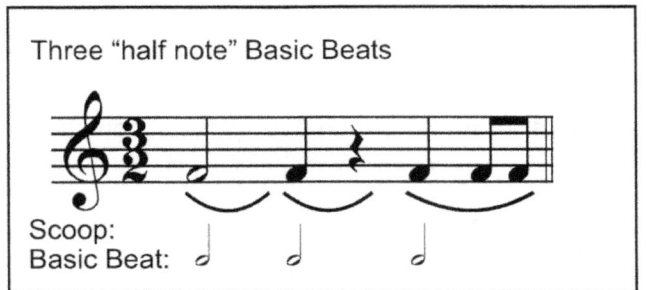

♫ **Note:** In 3/2 time, a **whole rest** receives 3 beats of silence and is used for a whole measure.

In 3/2 time, a **whole rest** receives 2 beats of silence for beats 1 and 2 (Strong - weak) when a half note value is on beat 3.

2. Scoop each beat. Write the Basic Beat below each scoop. Add bar lines.

PULSE and ADDING RESTS in "TRIPLE" TIME

In "**TRIPLE**" Time, the **TOP** number is **3**: three beats (pulses) per measure. The **PULSE** is where the rhythmic emphasis falls in a measure. **Pulse: S = Strong   w = weak**

Triple Pulse: 1 - Strong   2 - weak   3 - weak

♫ **Note:** When adding **MORE THAN ONE REST** to complete ONE Basic Beat, start with the given note and add the equal rest value to complete the beat. Complete EACH beat ONE beat at a time.

1. Write the Basic Beat and pulse below each measure. Add rests below each bracket to complete the measure. Cross off the Basic Beat as each beat is completed.

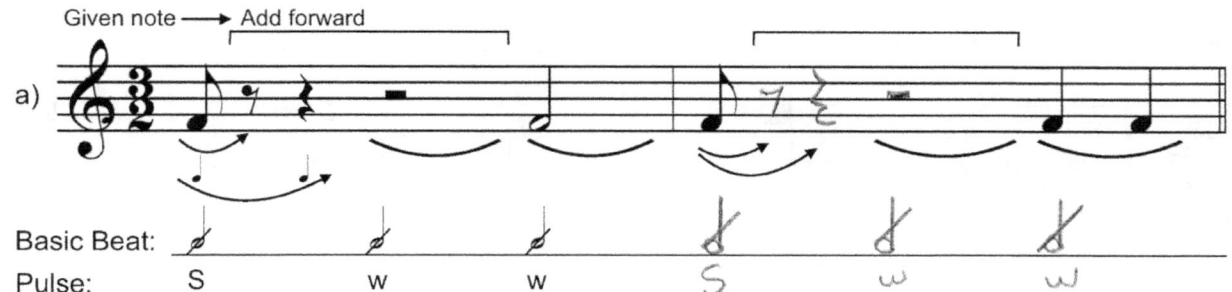

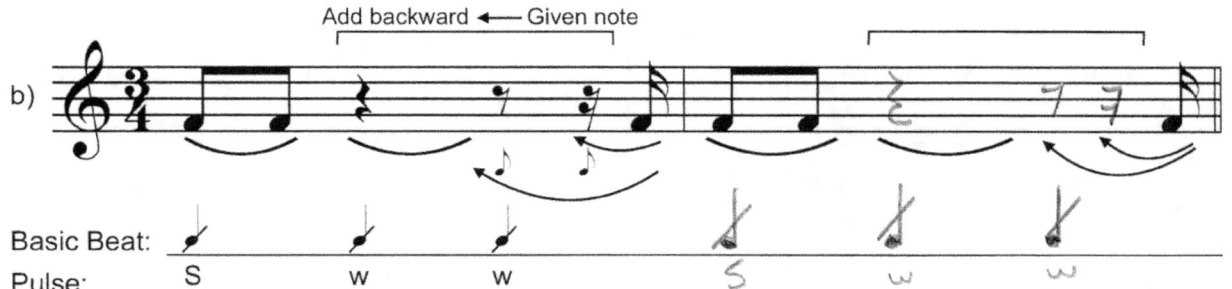

♫ **Note:** When eighth notes or sixteenth notes are **BEAMED together**, they belong to the **SAME** group. When they are **NOT beamed together**, they belong to **DIFFERENT** groups.

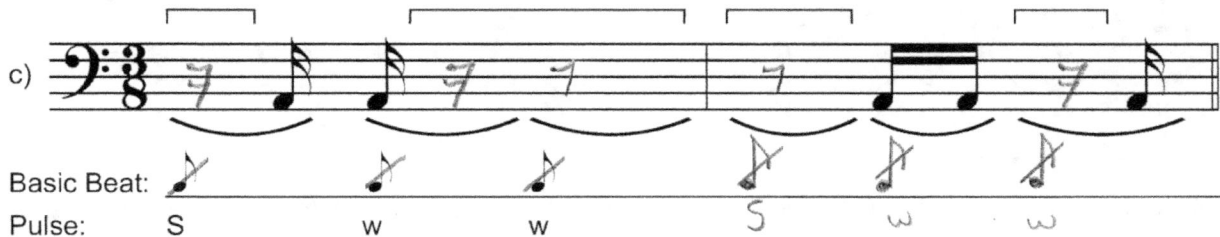

2. Write the Basic Beat below each scoop. Add the correct Time Signature below each bracket.

SIMPLE "QUADRUPLE" TIME - FOUR BASIC BEATS per MEASURE

1. Following the examples, scoop each beat. Write the Basic Beat below each scoop. Add the correct Time Signature below each bracket.

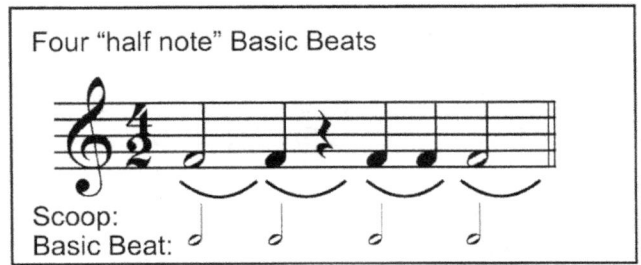
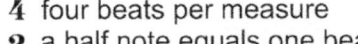
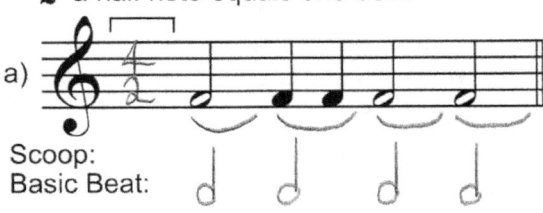

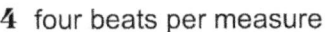

♪ **Note:** 𝄴 is the symbol for $\frac{4}{4}$ time, also called Common Time.

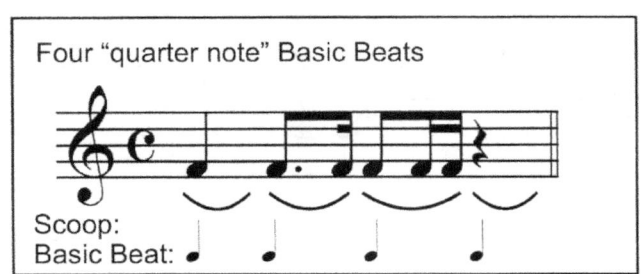
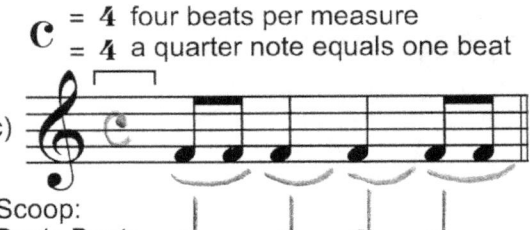

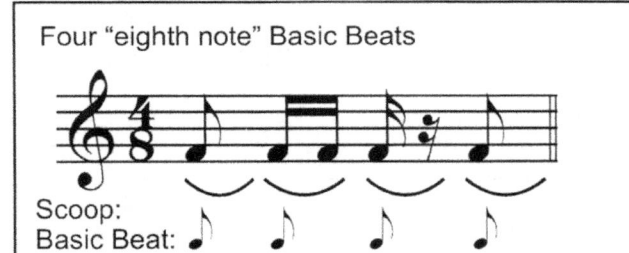
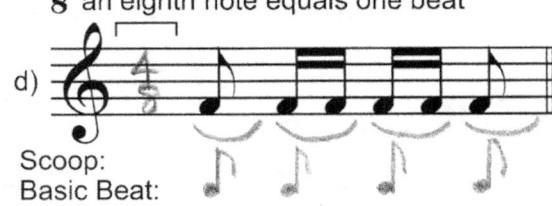

♪ **Note:** In $\frac{4}{2}$ time, the **BREVE** (double whole note: 𝄁o𝄁) or **BREVE REST** (double whole rest: ▬) is equal to 4 beats (4 half notes). The **WHOLE** rest is equal to 2 beats (2 half notes).

2. Scoop each beat. Write the Basic Beat below each scoop. Add bar lines.

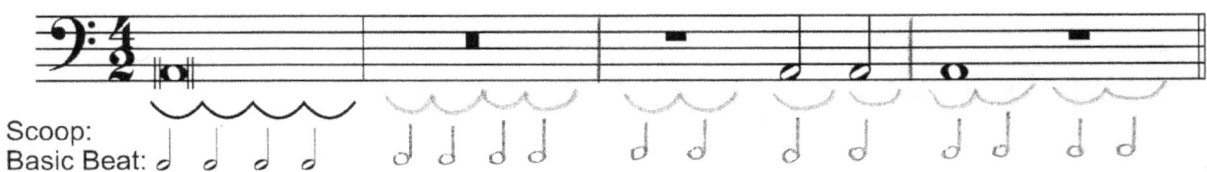

PULSE and ADDING RESTS in "QUADRUPLE" TIME

In "**QUADRUPLE**" Time, the **TOP** number is 4: four beats (pulses) per measure. The **PULSE** is where the rhythmic emphasis falls in a measure. **Pulse: S = Strong   w = weak   M = Medium**

Quadruple Pulse: 1 - Strong   2 - weak   3 - Medium   4 - weak

REST RULES:
A Strong joins a weak into one rest (**S + w**). A Medium joins a weak into one rest (**M + w**).
A weak can not be joined to a Medium or a weak. It must use 2 separate rests (**w ~ M** and **w ~ w**).

The **plus (+)** sign indicates to **join** the Strong + weak (**S + w**) and the Medium + weak (**M + w**) pulses.

The **tilde (~)** sign (pronounced TILL-day), indicates to **NOT** join the weak ~ Medium (**w ~ M**) pulses or the weak ~ weak (**w ~ w**) pulses.

♪ **Note:** A whole rest fills a whole measure with silence and combines all pulses into ONE rest.
A Strong pulse is then combined with ALL the pulses into ONE whole rest.

1. a) Add rests below each bracket to complete the measure. The "+" sign indicates to join pulses and the "~" sign indicates to separate (not join) pulses.
   b) Cross off the Basic Beat as each beat is completed.

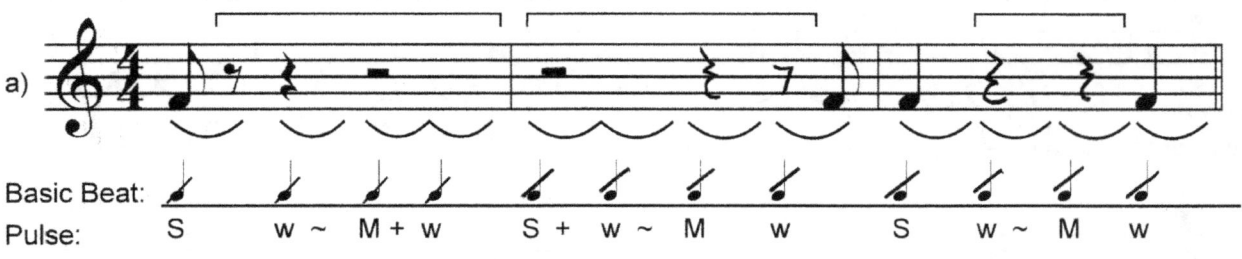

2. Write the Basic Beat below each scoop. Add the correct Time Signature below each bracket.

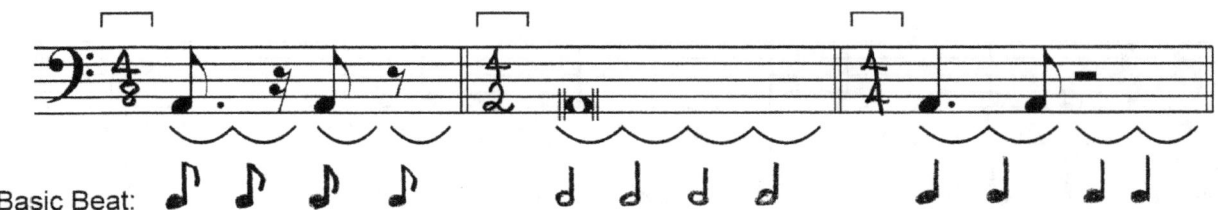

WHOLE RESTS and BAR LINES

A **WHOLE REST** fills an entire measure of silence in **ANY** time signature. The **TOP NUMBER** indicates the number of beats given to the **WHOLE** rest.

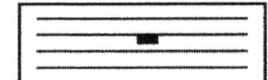

♫ **Note:** The exception to the rule is $\frac{4}{2}$ time in which a BREVE REST (▮) fills the whole measure.

1. Write the number of beats given to the rest in each measure.

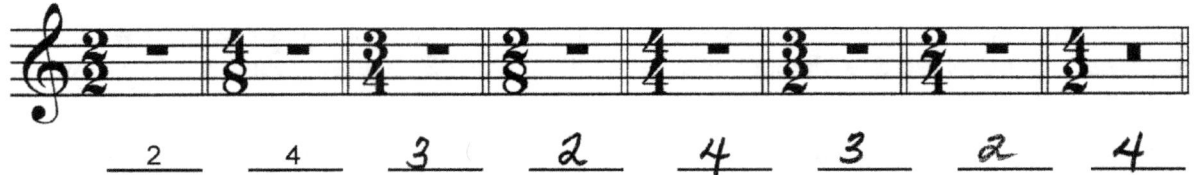

2 4 3 2 4 3 2 4

2. Scoop each beat. Write the Basic Beat below each scoop. Add bar lines.

a)
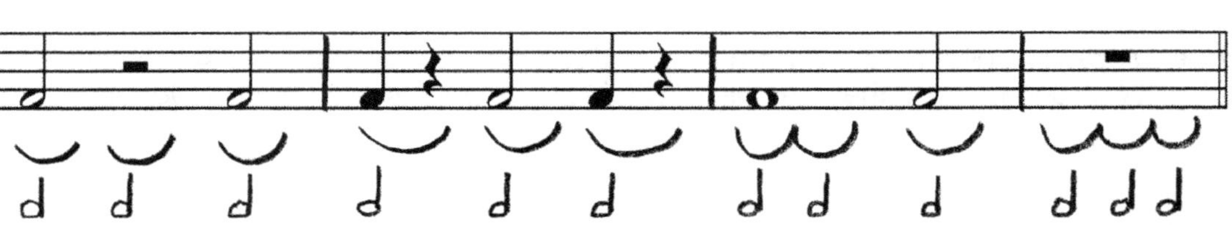
Scoop:
Basic Beat:

b)
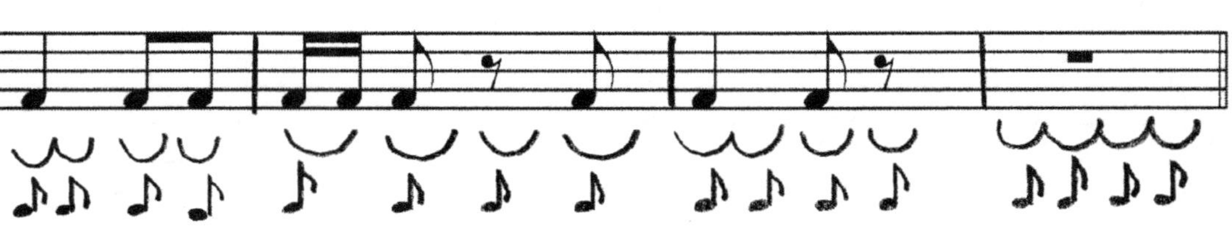
Scoop:
Basic Beat:

c)
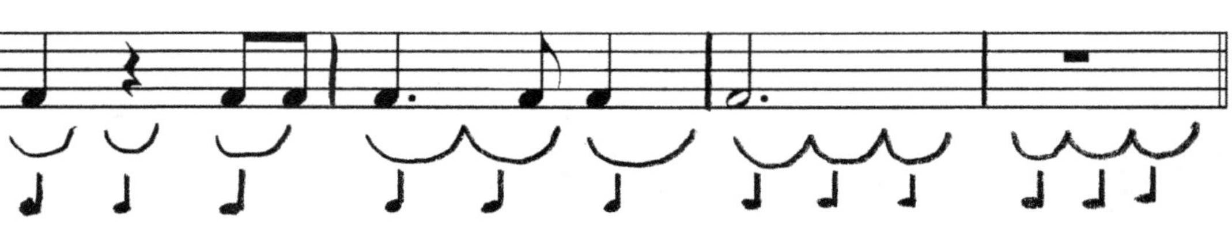
Scoop:
Basic Beat:

d)
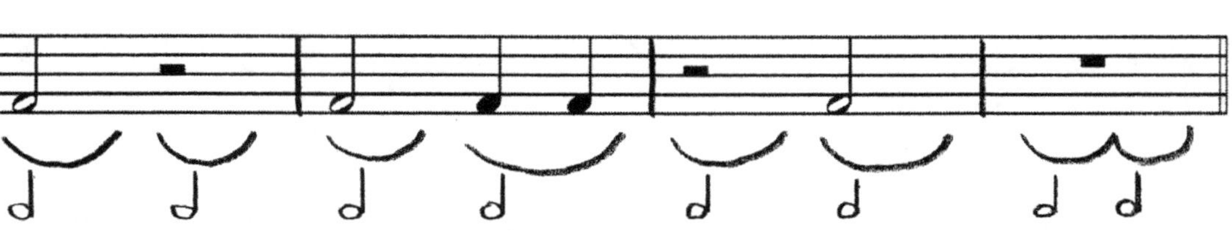
Scoop:
Basic Beat:

e)
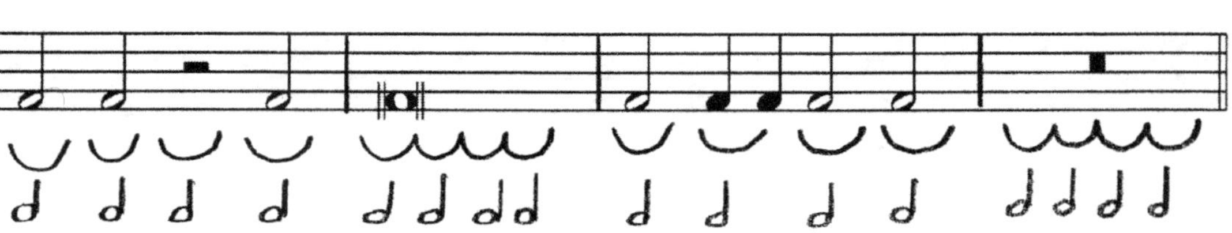
Scoop:
Basic Beat:

COMBINING TWO BASIC BEATS using RESTS

When **COMBINING TWO BASIC BEATS** using rests:

A Strong pulse (beat) joins a weak pulse (beat) into one rest (**S + w**).
A Medium pulse (beat) joins a weak pulse (beat) into one rest (**M + w**).
A weak can NOT be joined to a Medium or a weak. It must use 2 separate rests (**w ~ M** and **w ~ w**).

♩ **Note:** A **WEAK** beat can **NOT** hold on to another beat.
　　　　A weak beat (pulse) always stands alone.　w ~ M　or　w ~ w

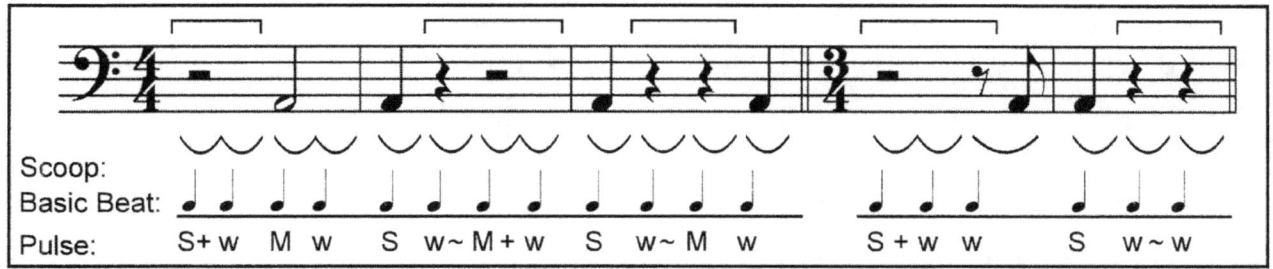

1. a) Scoop each beat. Add the "+" sign when joining pulses (S + w or M + w) and the "~" sign when not joining the pulses (w ~ M or w ~ w).
   b) Add rests below each bracket to complete the measure.
   c) Cross off the Basic Beat as each beat is completed.

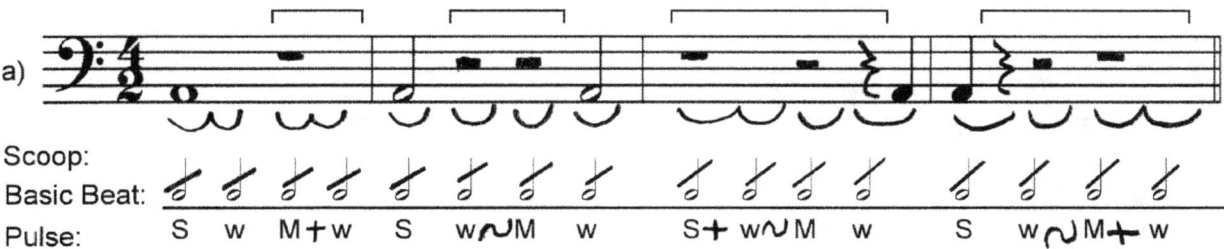

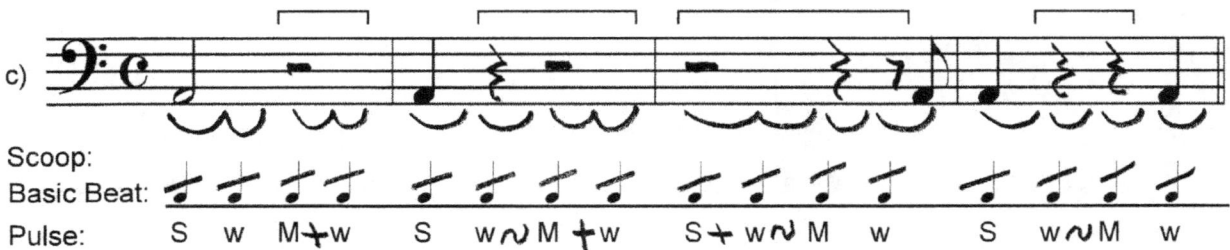

TRIPLET and the ANACRUSIS

A **TRIPLET** is indicated by the number "**3**" written above or below a group of three notes. A triplet is a group of three notes played in the time of two notes of the same note value.

1. Copy the chart below.

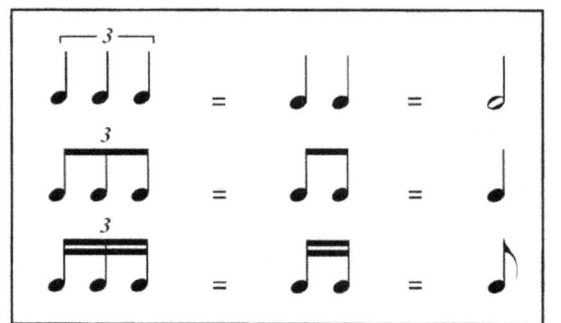
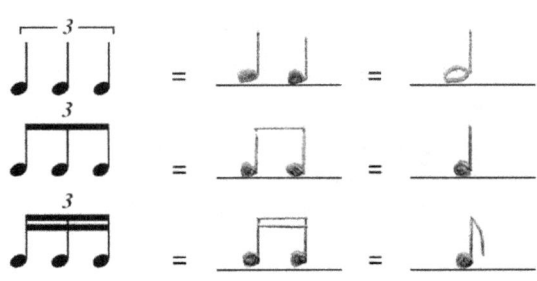

An **ANACRUSIS, PICK-UP** or **UPBEAT** is a note or group of notes in the FIRST incomplete measure at the beginning of the music. The LAST (final) measure at the end of the music will also be an incomplete measure. Together they equal one COMPLETE measure.

♪ **Note:** When numbering the measures, the first COMPLETE measure (not the anacrusis) is counted as measure number one. [1]

2. Add bar lines to complete the following rhythms. Write the counts under each measure.

104

ADDING TIME SIGNATURES and INCOMPLETE MEASURES

When **ADDING** a **TIME SIGNATURE**, the first measure may be an **INCOMPLETE MEASURE** (anacrusis or upbeat). Begin at the SECOND MEASURE to find the total number of beats.

♪ **Note:** If the first measure is an anacrusis, the beats in the first and last measures combined will equal one complete measure. The **LAST** measure will begin with the **Strong** pulse.

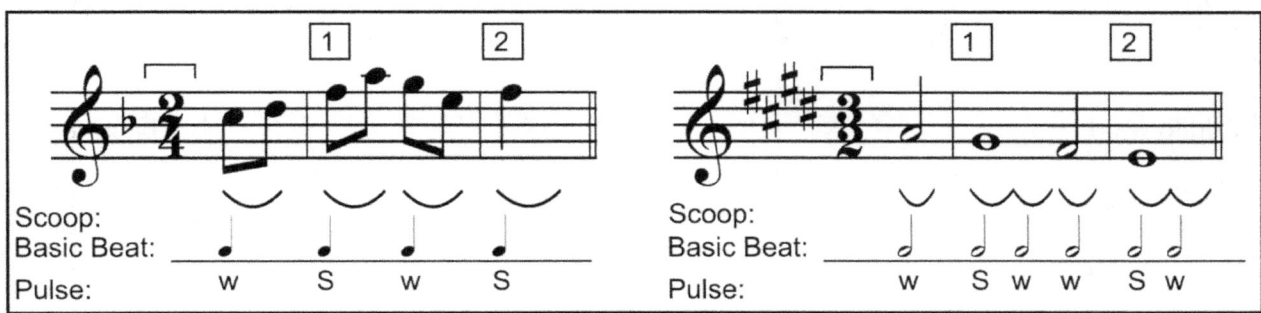

1. a) Beginning at the first complete measure, scoop each beat. Write the Basic Beat and pulse below each scoop.
   b) Add the correct Time Signature below each bracket.
   c) Write the measure numbers in the square box at the beginning of each measure.

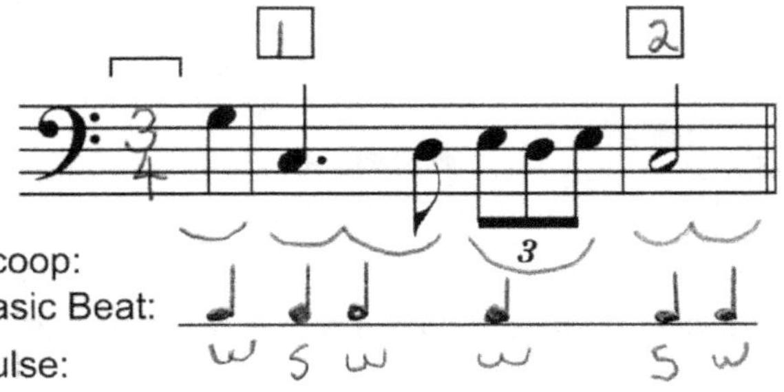

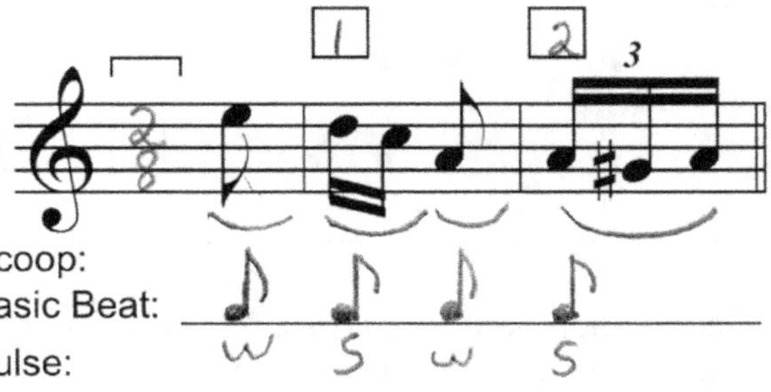

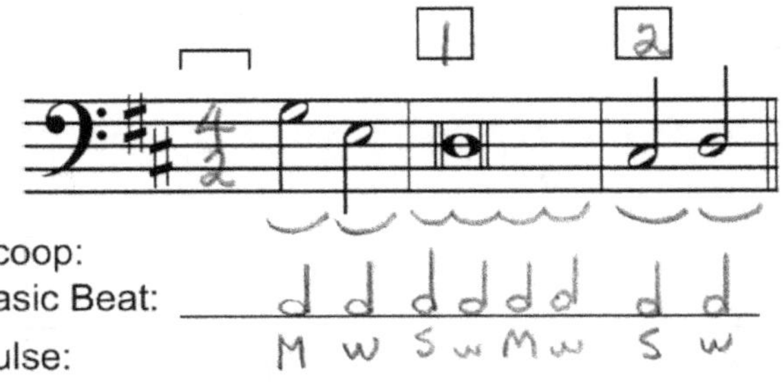

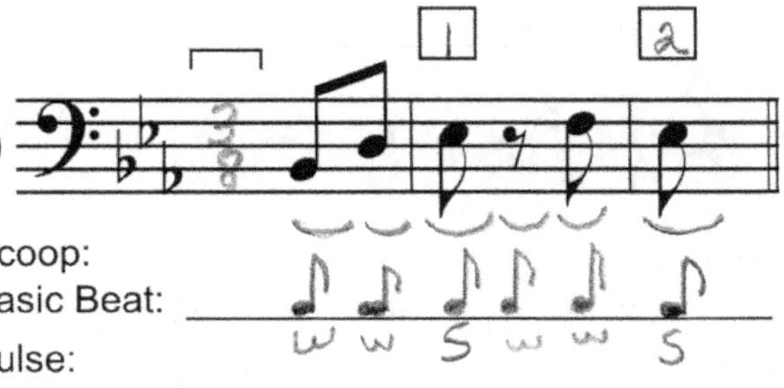

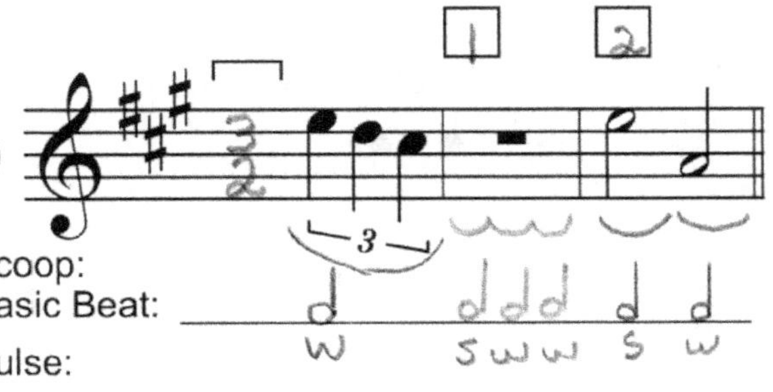

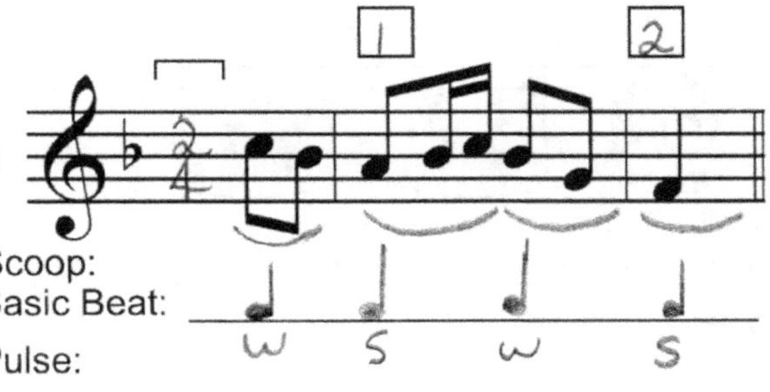

COMPLETING A BASIC BEAT with MORE THAN ONE REST

When adding **MORE THAN ONE REST** to complete **ONE BASIC BEAT**, start with the **GIVEN NOTE** and add the equal rest value to complete the beat.

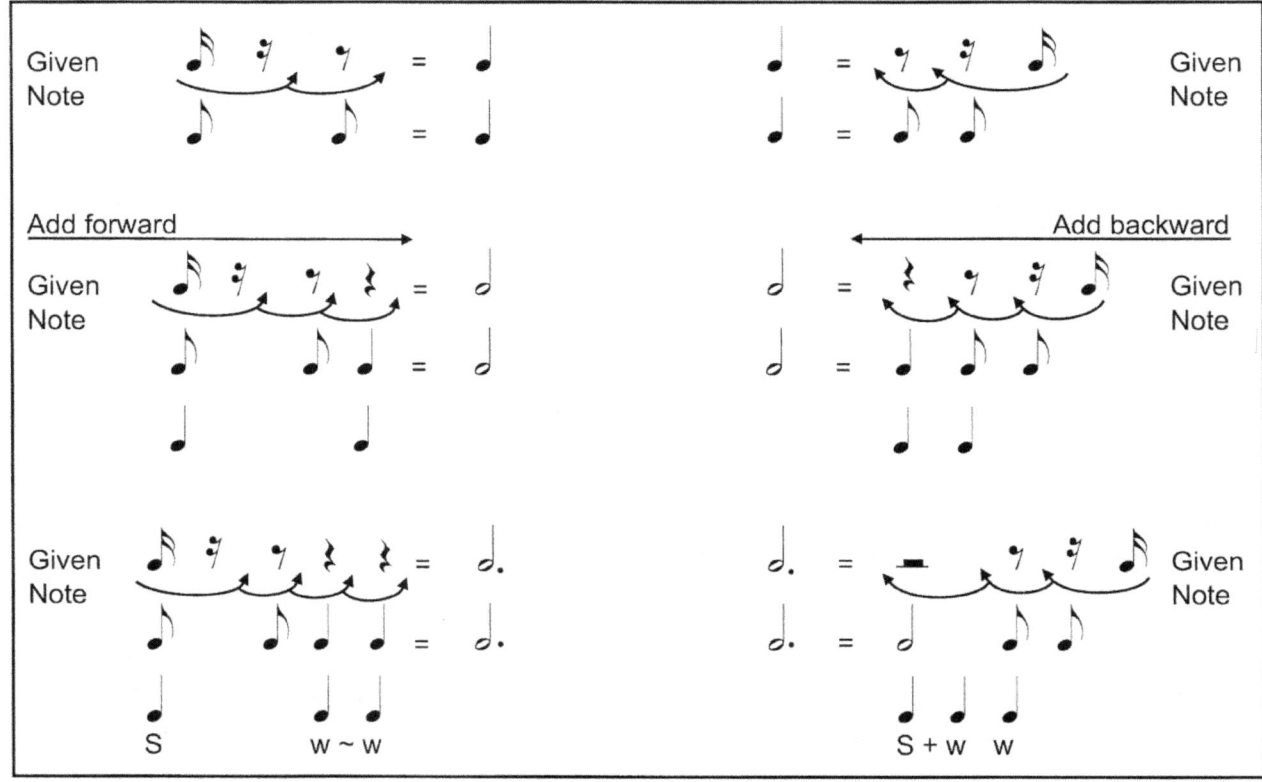

1. Scoop each beat. Add rests below each bracket. Start with the given note and move forwards or backwards to complete one beat at a time. Cross off the Basic Beat as each is completed.

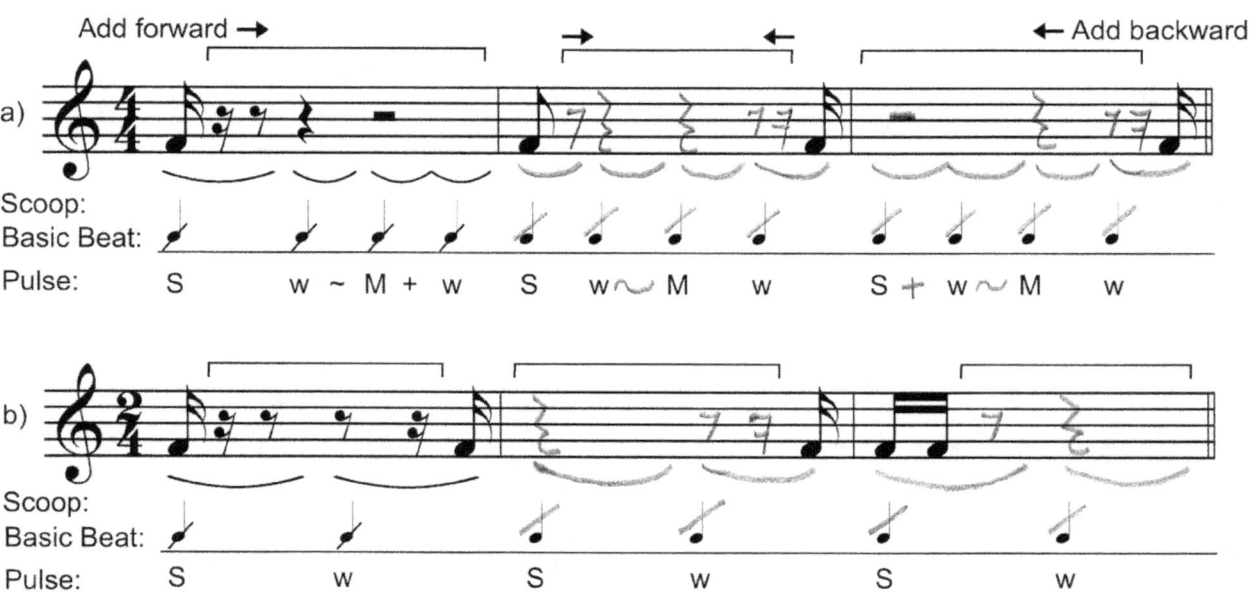

ADDING RESTS

Before **ADDING RESTS**, determine if the Basic Beat is an eighth note, quarter note or half note.

♪ **Note:** The bottom number of the Time Signature determines the value of the Basic Beat.

1. Write the Basic Beat and the pulse below each measure. Add rests below each bracket to complete the measure. Cross off the Basic Beat as each beat is completed.

ADDING BAR LINES

When **ADDING BAR LINES**, look for equal groups of the Basic Beat. Determine how many Basic Beats are in a measure. The first measure may be an anacrusis (incomplete measure).

♪ **Note:** A whole rest indicates silence for a whole measure in every Time Signature except for $\frac{4}{2}$. In $\frac{4}{2}$, a **BREVE REST** (■) is used to indicate a whole measure of silence.

1. Add bar lines. Write the Basic Beat and the pulse below each measure.

ADDING TIME SIGNATURES

When **ADDING TIME SIGNATURES**, look for equal groups. Determine how many Basic Beats are in a measure.

1. Add the correct Time Signature below each bracket to complete the following rhythms.

   a) 3/4   b) 2/4

   c) 3/8   d) 4/2

   e) 3/2   f) 4/4

   g) 2/8 (?)   h) 2/2

   i) 2/4   j) 4/8

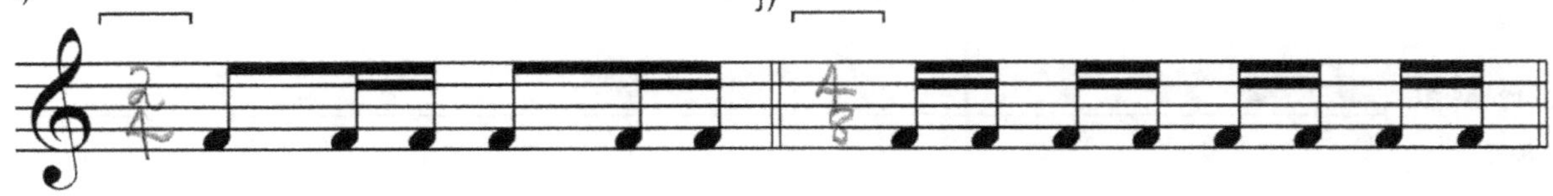

2. Identify if the rests under the brackets are CORRECT or INCORRECT.

   a) correct   b) incorrect   c) incorrect

   d) correct   e) incorrect   f) correct

ADDING RESTS in SIMPLE TIME

1. Write the Basic Beat and the pulse below each measure. Add rests below each bracket to complete the measure. Cross off the Basic Beat as each beat is completed.

Lesson 8 — Review Test

Total Score: ____ / 100

1. a) Write the following notes in the **Treble Clef**. Use single **eighth** notes.

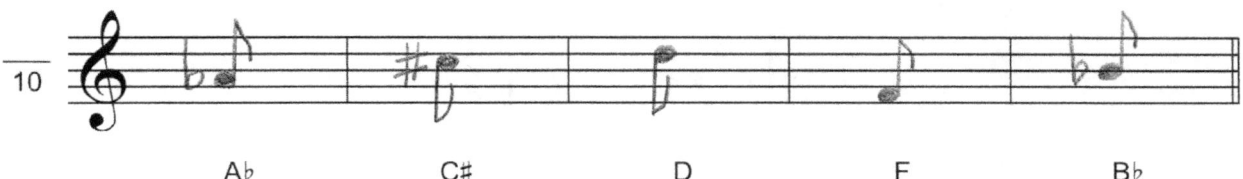

Ab   C#   D   F   Bb

b) Name the note below each bracket.

G#   F   E   E   A

2. a) Write the following **HARMONIC** intervals **ABOVE** the given notes.

Per 4   Maj 7   min 3   Maj 2   min 6

b) Name the following **MELODIC** intervals.

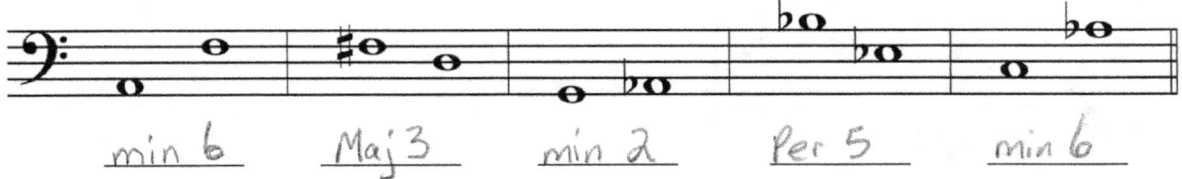

min 6   Maj 3   min 2   Per 5   min 6

3. Write the following **SOLID** triads in **ROOT** position in the Bass Clef using the correct **KEY SIGNATURE** and any necessary accidentals. Use whole notes.

a) the DOMINANT (V) triad of c sharp minor harmonic
b) the TONIC (I) triad of A flat Major
c) the SUBDOMINANT (iv) triad of e minor harmonic
d) the SUBDOMINANT (IV) triad of C Major
e) the DOMINANT (V) triad of g minor harmonic

a)   b)   c)   d)   e)

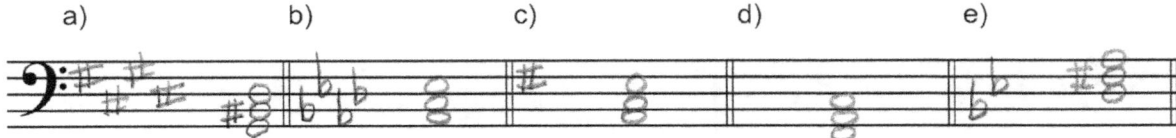

4. Complete the **CIRCLE OF FIFTHS**:
   a) Write the order of flats and sharps.
   b) Write the Major keys on the OUTSIDE of the circle.
   c) Write the relative minor keys on the INSIDE of the circle.

10

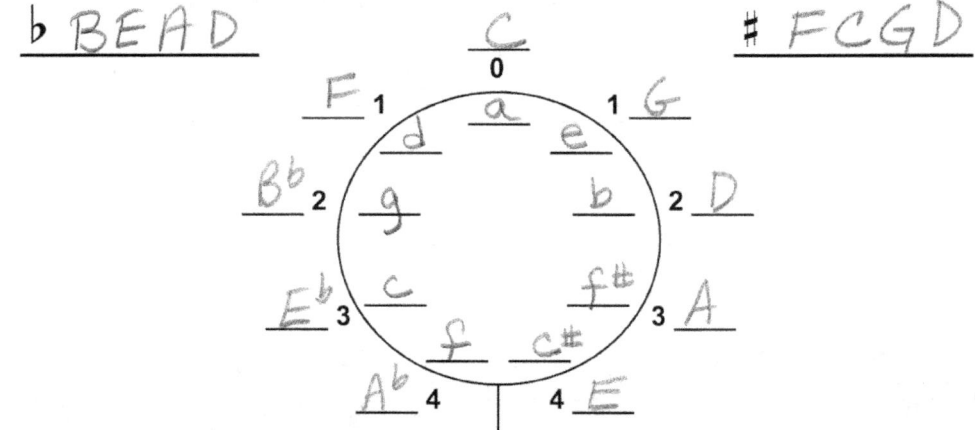

Write the following scales, ascending and descending, using **ACCIDENTALS** instead of a Key Signature for each. Use whole notes.

   a) B flat Major in the Bass Clef
   b) f sharp minor natural in the Treble Clef
   c) F Major in the Bass Clef
   d) b minor melodic in the Treble Clef
   e) c minor harmonic in the Bass Clef

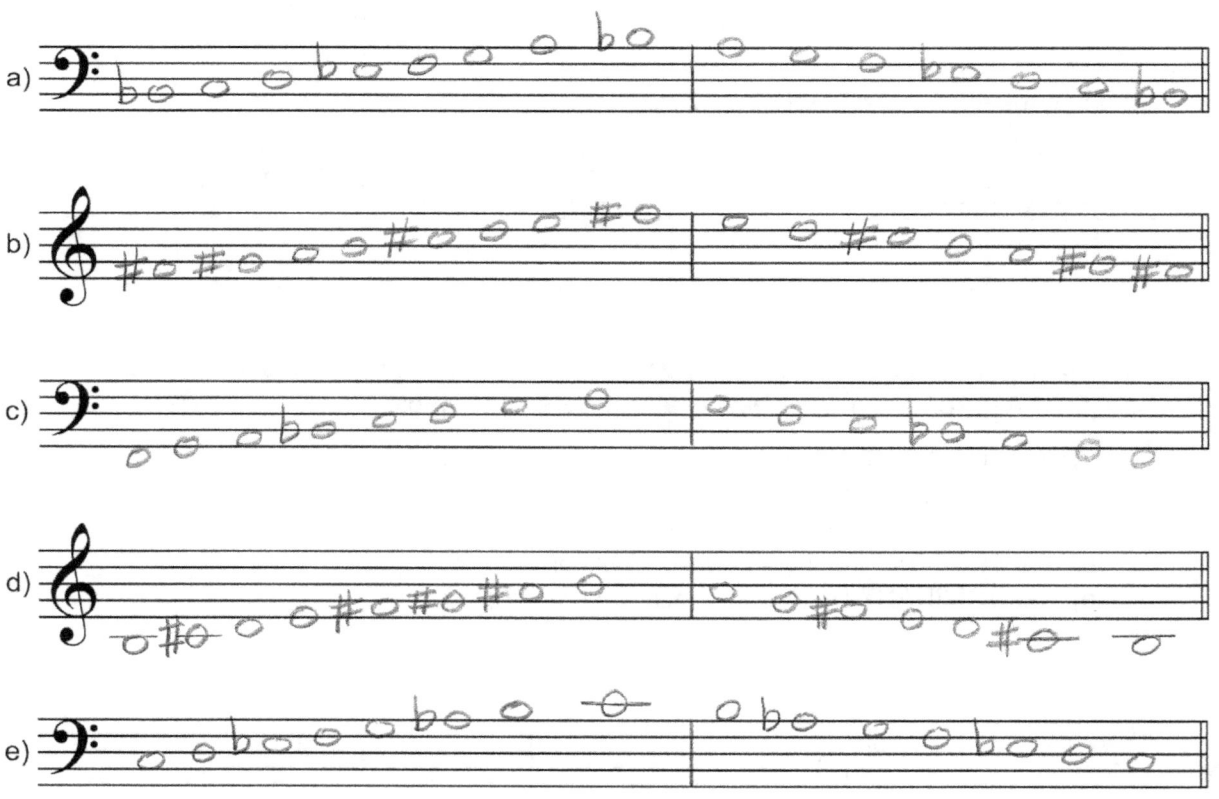

5. Match each musical term or sign with the English definition. (Not all definitions will be used.)

___10___

Terms		Definitions
Simple "Duple" Time	b	a) $\frac{4}{4}$ Time Signature
tenuto	e	b) Groups of 2 beats per measure
allegretto	i	c) Groups of 3 beats per measure
Simple "Triple" Time	c	d) Groups of 4 beats per measure
diminuendo, dim.	h	e) held, sustained
Simple "Quadruple" Time	d	f) the interval of an octave
ottava, 8va	f	g) $\frac{2}{2}$ Time Signature
rallentando	k	h) becoming softer
common time, C	a	i) not as fast as allegro; fairly fast
cut time, ₵	g	j) sharply detached
		k) becoming slower

6. Name the key of the following melody. Rewrite it at the **SAME PITCH** in the **Bass Clef**.

___10___

Key: D Major

7. Name each of the following as: **d.s.** (diatonic semitone), **c.s.** (chromatic semitone),
    w.t. (whole tone)   or   **e.e.** (enharmonic equivalent).

___10___

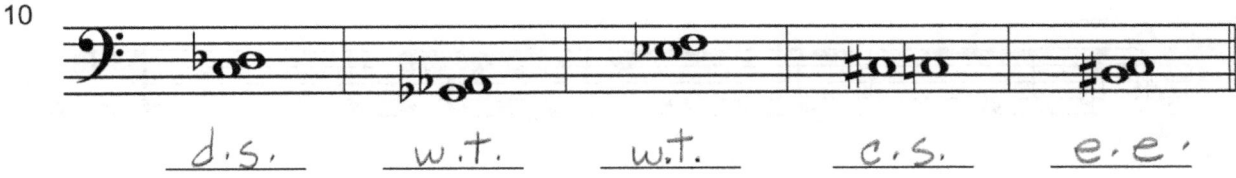

d.s.   w.t.   w.t.   c.s.   e.e.

113

8. a) Name the **MINOR** key for each of the following Key Signatures.
    b) Identify the technical degree name of the ROOT for the following **BROKEN** triads as:
       T (Tonic),   **SD** (Subdominant)   or   **D** (Dominant).

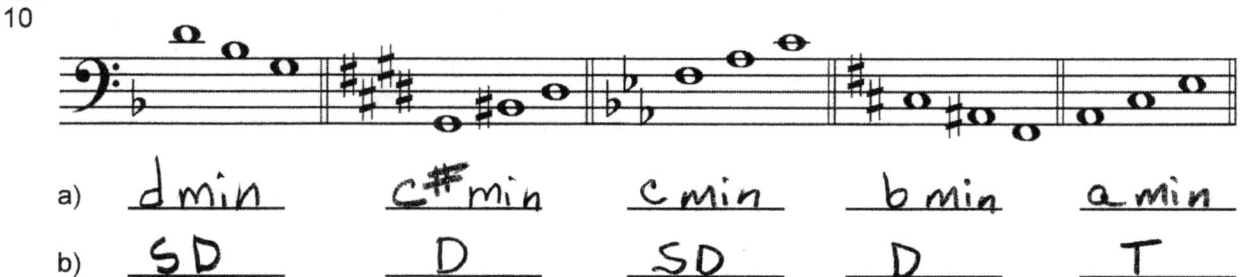

a) d min   c# min   c min   b min   a min
b) SD   D   SD   D   T

9. a) Write the **BASIC BEAT** and the **PULSE** below each measure. Add rests below each bracket to complete the measure. Cross off the Basic Beat as each beat is completed.

b) Add the correct **TIME SIGNATURE** below each bracket to complete the following rhythms.

114

10. Analyze the following piece of music by answering the questions below.

a) Add the correct Time Signature directly on the music.

b) Name the composer of this piece. _Franz Joseph Haydn_

c) Explain the sign at the letter **A**. _slur - play the notes legato (smooth)_

d) Name the interval at the letter **B**. _Perfect 4_

e) Name the interval at the letter **C**. _Maj 3_

f) Identify the type/quality of the triad at the letter **D** as Major or minor. _Major_

g) Name the key of this piece. _D Major_

h) Locate and circle a diatonic semitone in this piece. Label it as d.s.

i) Locate and circle a whole tone in this piece. Label it as w.t.

j) Explain the meaning of **Allegro**. _fast_

Lesson 9   Identifying the Key of a Melody - Major or Minor

When **IDENTIFYING** the **KEY** of a **MELODY** use the following steps:

Step 1: Look at the **KEY SIGNATURE**. The Key Signature identifies the **Major** key or its **relative minor** key for the melody.

Key of D Major

Key Signature: 2 sharps = D Major or b minor

Step 2: Look for **ACCIDENTALS**. A melody in a minor key WILL usually contain the raised 7th note of the harmonic minor scale.

Key of b minor

Accidental: A♯ = Raised 7th note of b minor harmonic

Step 3: Look at the **LAST NOTE**. A melody will often END on the TONIC note of the key.

Key of b minor

Accidentals: G♯ A♯ = Raised 6th and 7th notes of b minor melodic. The last note is B.

♪ **Note:** A melody in a Major key will NOT usually contain the raised 6th or 7th notes of its relative minor key.

1. Name the Major key and its relative minor key for each of the following Key Signatures. Name any accidentals. Name the last note. Name the key of the melody.

Key: __F__ Major or __d__ minor   Accidentals __C♯__   Last note __D__   Key of the Melody __d minor__

Key: __E__ Major or __C♯__ minor   Accidentals __B♯__   Last note __C♯__   Key of the Melody __C♯ minor__

Key: __B♭__ Major or __g__ minor   Accidentals __—__   Last note __B♭__   Key of the Melody __B♭ Major__

FINAL NOTE of a MELODY

The **FINAL NOTE OF A MELODY** is not always the Tonic note. Look at the Key Signature. Determine if the key is Major or minor by looking for accidentals (raised 7th note of the relative harmonic minor key, or the raised 6th and 7th notes of the relative melodic minor key).

♪ **Note:** When naming the melody as a minor key, it is not necessary to identify it as harmonic or melodic. The key is simply called minor.

1. Name the key of each of the following melodies.

a) Key: a minor

b) Key: d minor

c) Key: A Major

d) Key: g minor

e) Key: E Major

f) Key: b minor

Lesson 9   Review Test

Total Score: ____ / 100

1. a) This melody is in the Key of b minor. Name the note under each bracket.
   b) How many times does the **TONIC** note appear in this melody? __7__
   c) How many times does the **DOMINANT** note appear in this melody? __4__

___/10

2. a) Write the following **HARMONIC** intervals **ABOVE** the given notes. Use whole notes.

___/10

   Per 4   Maj 3   min 7   Maj 6   min 2

   b) Name the following **MELODIC** intervals.

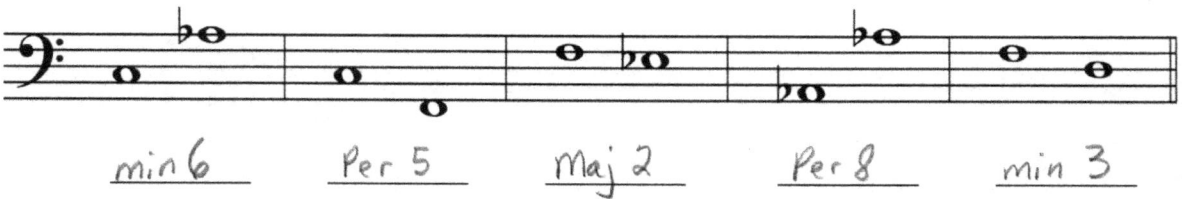

   min 6   Per 5   Maj 2   Per 8   min 3

3. Write the following **SOLID** triads in **ROOT** position in the Bass Clef using **ACCIDENTALS** instead of a Key Signature. Use whole notes.

___/10

   a) the DOMINANT (V) triad of a minor harmonic
   b) the TONIC (I) triad of E Major
   c) the SUBDOMINANT (iv) triad of d minor harmonic
   d) the DOMINANT (V) triad of f sharp minor harmonic
   e) the SUBDOMINANT (IV) triad of A flat Major

4. Complete the **CIRCLE OF FIFTHS**:
   a) Write the order of flats and sharps.
   b) Write the Major keys on the OUTSIDE of the circle.
   c) Write the relative minor keys on the INSIDE of the circle.

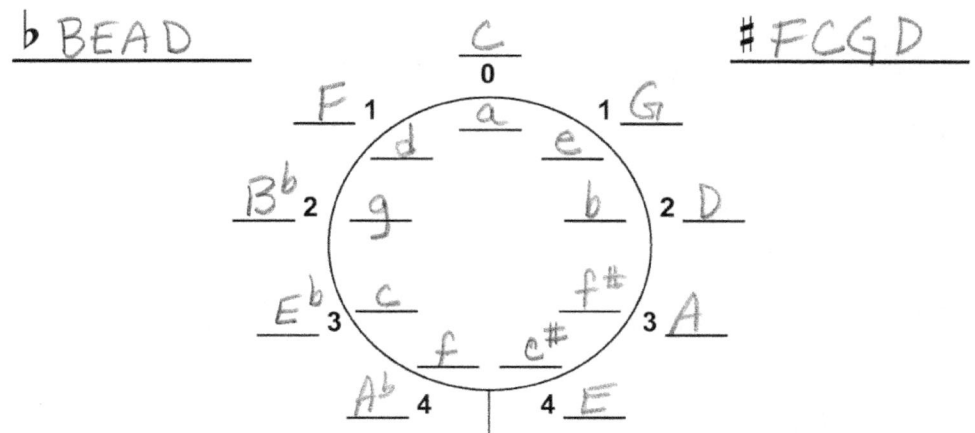

Write the following scales, ascending and descending, using the correct **KEY SIGNATURE** and any necessary accidentals for each. Use whole notes.

   a) a minor harmonic in the Treble Clef
   b) c minor melodic in the Bass Clef
   c) G Major in the Treble Clef
   d) e minor melodic in the Bass Clef
   e) f minor natural in the Treble Clef

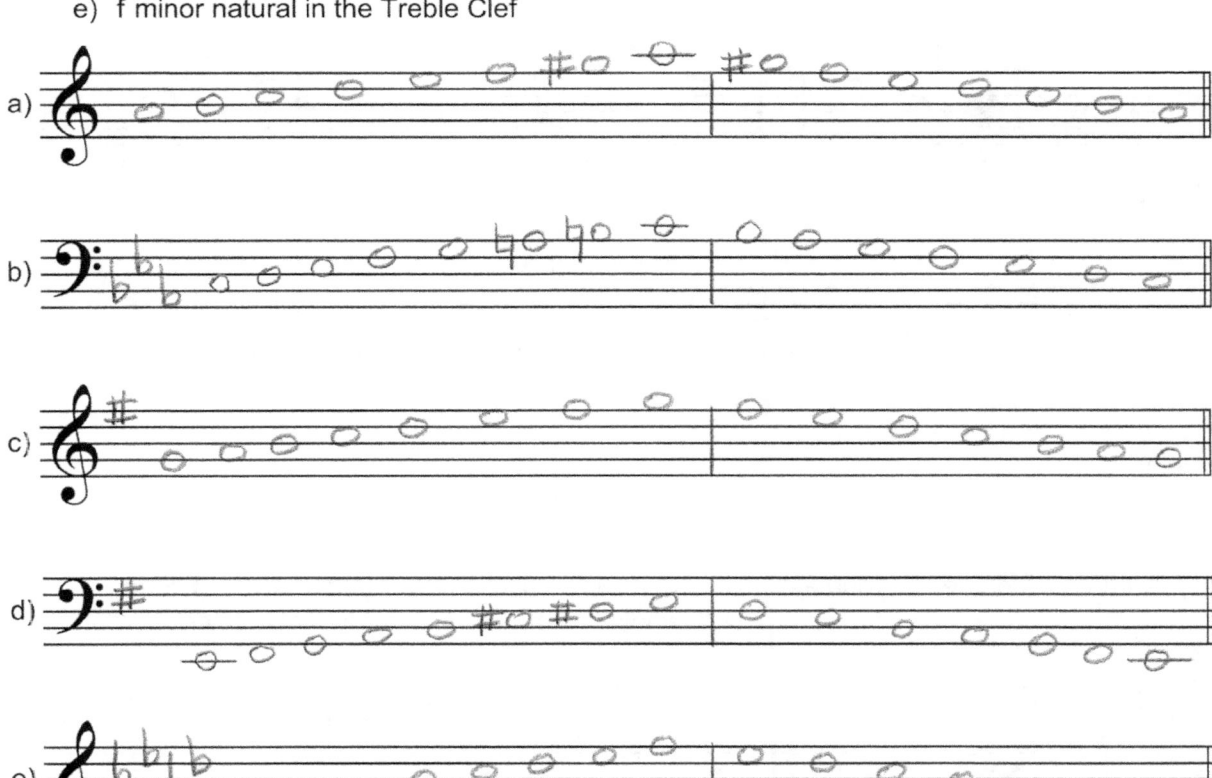

5. Match each musical term or sign with the English definition. (Not all definitions will be used.)

Term   **Definition**

> — c

allegro — h   a) as fast as possible

largo — f   b) speed at which music is performed

prestissimo — a   c) becoming softer

tempo — b   d) pause, hold longer than written value

cantabile — k   e) from the beginning

fermata, 𝄐 — d   f) very slow and broad; a slow and solemn tempo

da capo, D.C. — e   g) play the note sharply detached

maestoso — j   h) fast

staccato — g   i) moderately slow; at a walking pace

     j) majestic

     k) in a singing style

6. Name the key of the following melody. Rewrite it at the **SAME PITCH** in the **Treble Clef**.

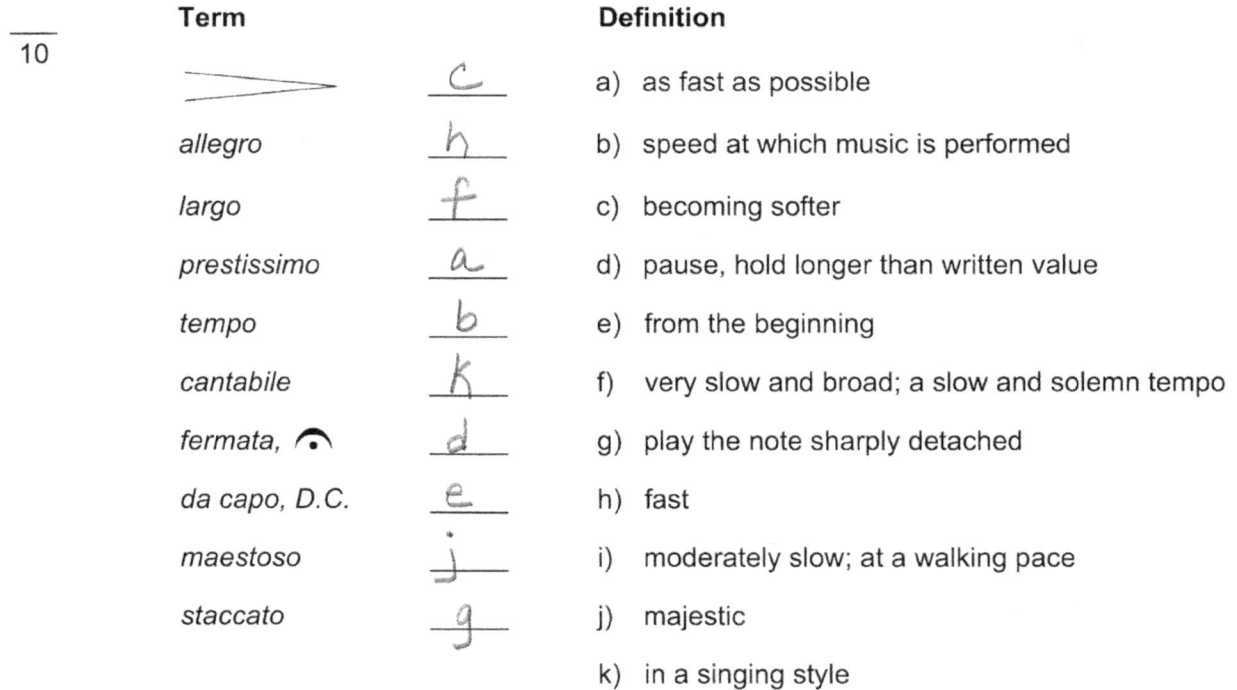

Key: C# minor

7. Name each of the following as: **d.s.** (diatonic semitone), **c.s.** (chromatic semitone), **w.t.** (whole tone) or **e.e.** (enharmonic equivalent).

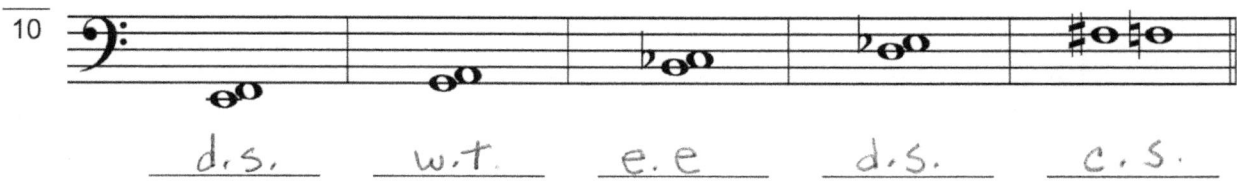

d.s.   w.t.   e.e   d.s.   c.s.

8. Name the **MINOR** key for each of the following Key Signatures. Write the SOLID **Dominant triad** in root position for each. Use whole notes.

f min   e min   a min   g min   f# min

9. a) Write the **BASIC BEAT** and the **PULSE** below each measure. Add rests below each bracket to complete the measure. Cross off the Basic Beat as each beat is completed.

b) Add the correct **TIME SIGNATURE** below each bracket to complete the following rhythms. Name the key.

Key: G Major   Key: c# minor

Key: Ab Major   Key: g minor

Key: d minor   Key: A Major

10. Analyze the following piece of music by answering the questions below.

a) Add the correct Time Signature directly on the music.

b) Name the key of this piece. __g minor__

c) Explain the sign at the letter A. __staccato - play the note sharply detached__

d) Explain the sign at the letter B. __tie - hold for the combined value of the notes__

e) Name the interval at the letter C. __Perfect 4__

f) Explain the F sharp at the letter D. __F# is the raised 7th note of g minor harmonic__

g) Explain the sign at the letter E. __repeat the music from the beginning__

h) Locate and circle a diatonic semitone in this piece. Label it as d.s.

i) Locate and circle a whole tone in this piece. Label it as w.t.

j) Explain the meaning of *Andante*. __moderately slow, at a walking pace__

Lesson 10   Transposition - Up or Down One Octave

TRANSPOSING

TRANSPOSING means playing or writing music at a different pitch from the original by raising or lowering **ALL** the **NOTES** by the **SAME INTERVAL**. A melody may be written one octave higher or one octave lower in the **same** clef or into an **alternate** clef. The Time Signature and Key Signature of the transposed melody will remain the same as the original given melody.

♫ **Note:** A Melody may also be rewritten at the SAME PITCH in an alternate clef.

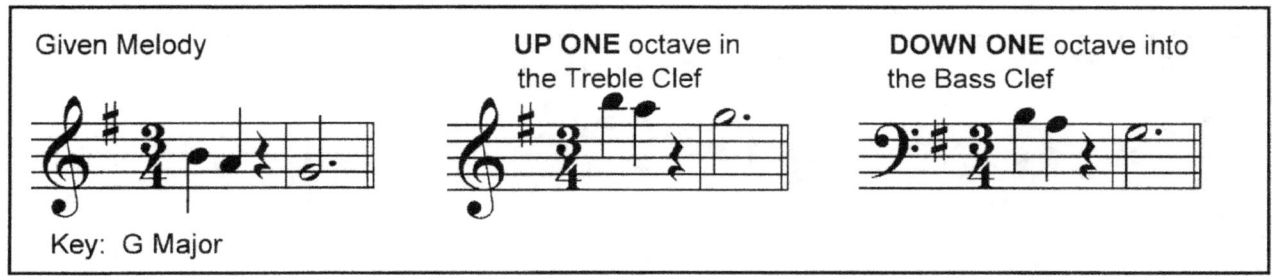

1. Name the key. Transpose the melody down one octave in the Treble Clef.

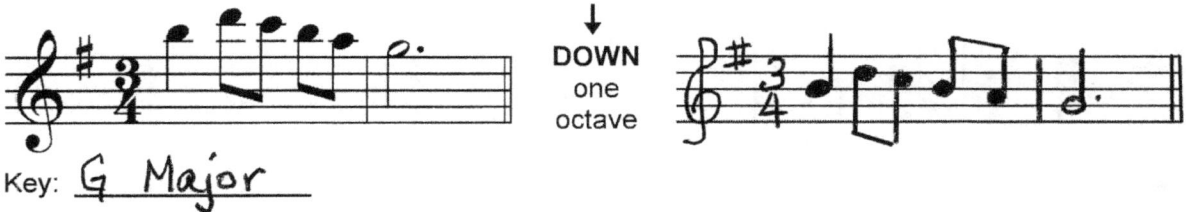

Key: G Major

2. Name the key. Transpose the melody up one octave in the Treble Clef.

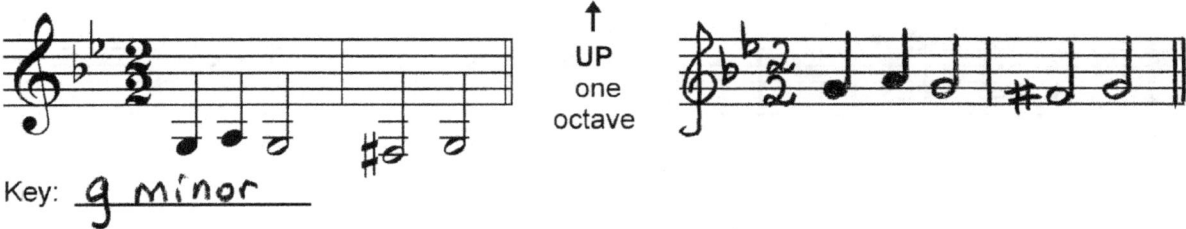

Key: g minor

3. Name the key. Transpose the melody down one octave into the Bass Clef.

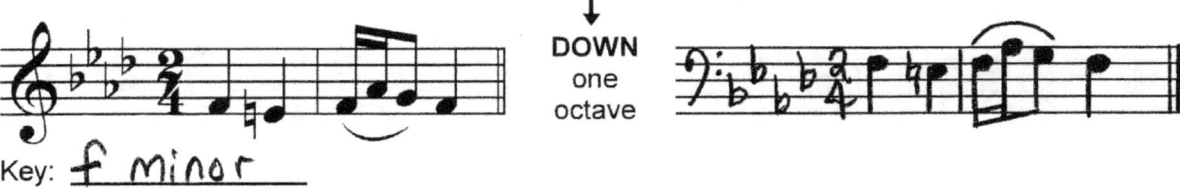

Key: f minor

4. Name the key. Rewrite the melody at the same pitch in the Bass Clef.

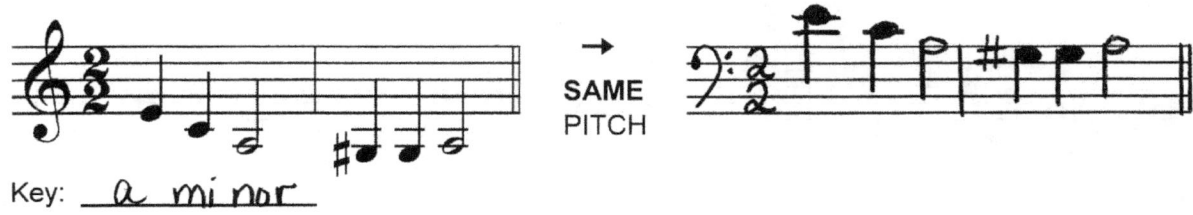

Key: a minor

TIPS for TRANSPOSING

TIPS for TRANSPOSING: Write the Clef sign, Key Signature and Time Signature. Correct the stem direction and add necessary accidentals. Write the dynamics below the Treble Staff and above the Bass Staff. Write all articulation (slurs, fermata, staccatos, etc.) in the correct position. When given, write the tempo, title and composer above the music.

♫ **Note:** When transposing up or down one octave, LINE notes become SPACE notes and SPACE notes become LINE notes. If BOTH the given melody and the transposed melody use LINE notes or SPACE notes, the melody has been transposed TWO octaves instead of ONE.

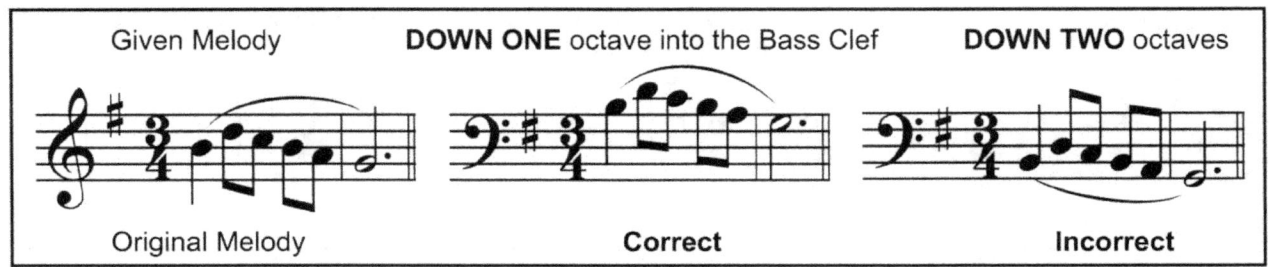

1. Name the key. Transpose the melody up one octave in the Bass Clef.

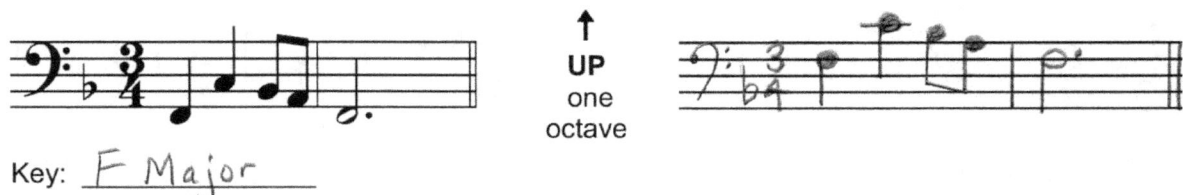

Key: F Major

2. Name the key. Transpose the melody down one octave in the Bass Clef.

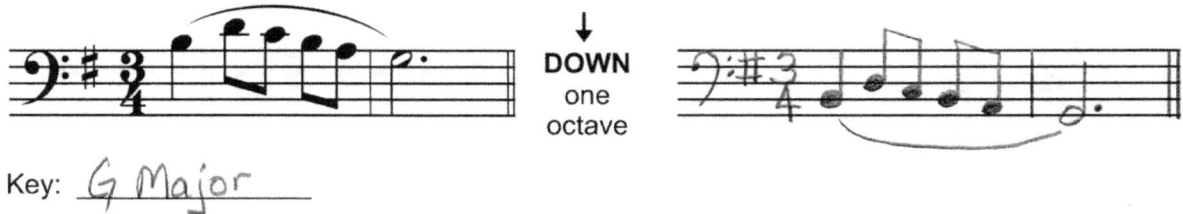

Key: G Major

3. Name the key. Transpose the melody up one octave into the Treble Clef.

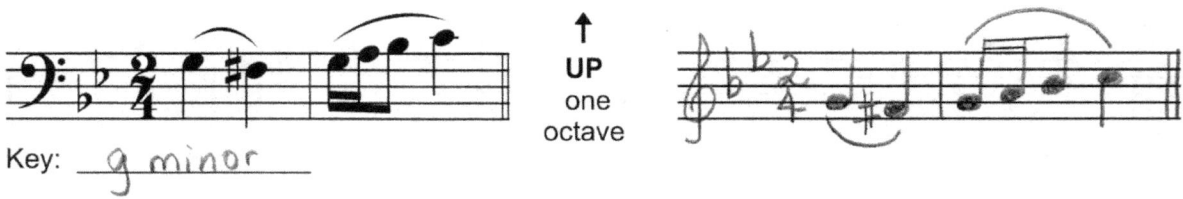

Key: g minor

4. Name the key. Rewrite the melody at the same pitch in the Treble Clef.

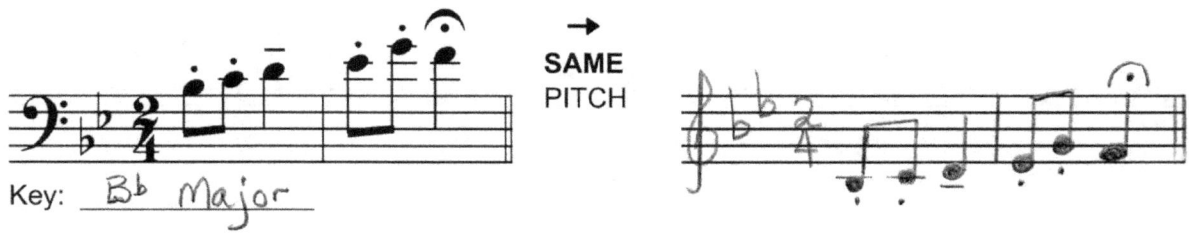

Key: B♭ Major

Lesson 10 Review Test

Total Score: ____ / 100

1. Name the following notes on the **GRAND STAFF**.

___ / 10

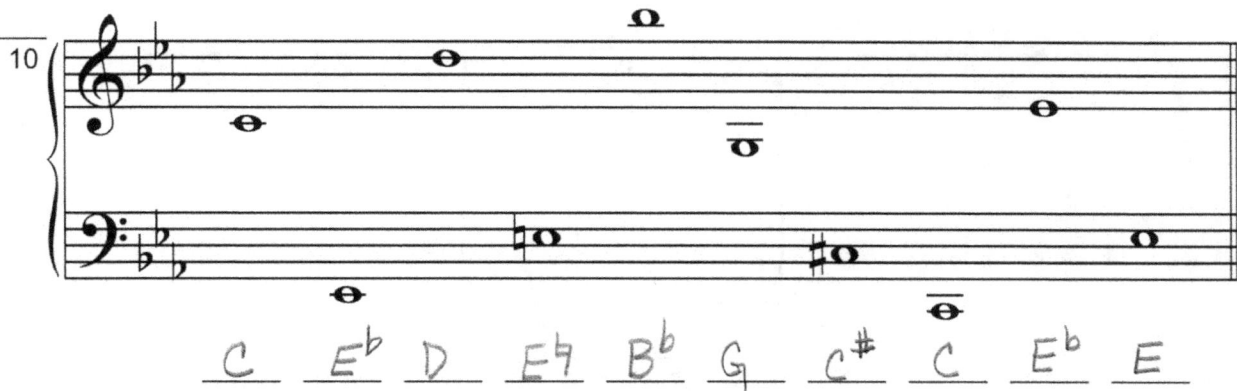

C, E♭, D, E♮, B♭, G, C♯, C, E♭, E

2. a) Write the following **HARMONIC** intervals **ABOVE** the given notes.

___ / 10

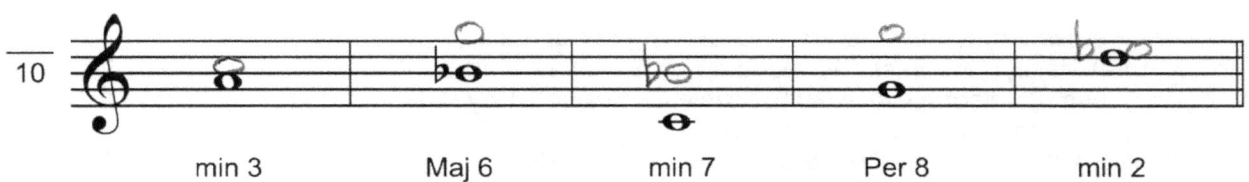

min 3, Maj 6, min 7, Per 8, min 2

b) Name the following **MELODIC** intervals.

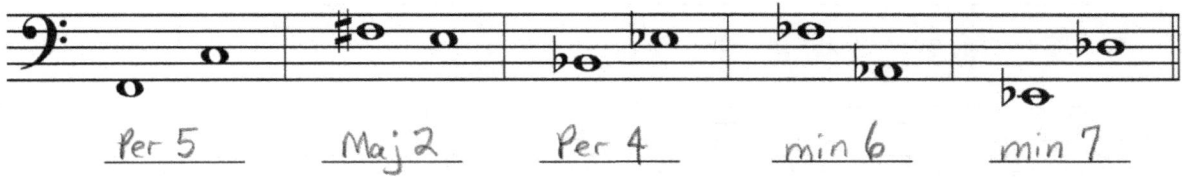

Per 5, Maj 2, Per 4, min 6, min 7

3. For each of the following triads:
  a) Name the ROOT.
  b) Identify the TYPE/QUALITY of the triad as Major or minor.

___ / 10

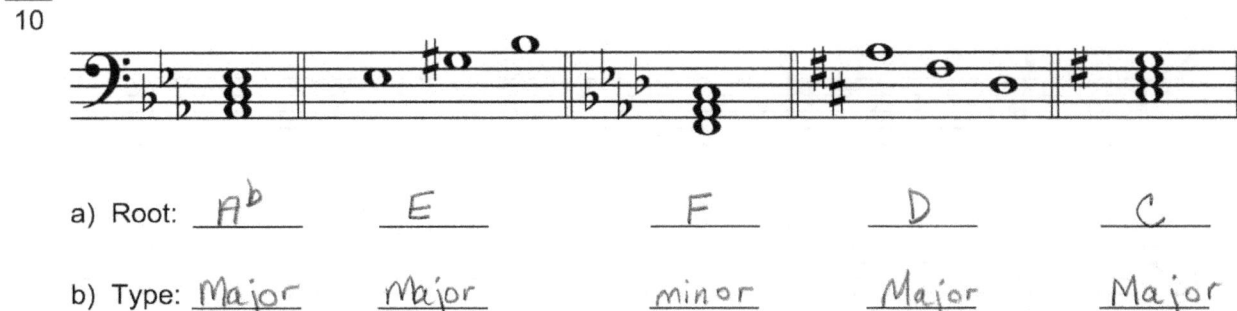

a) Root: A♭, E, F, D, C

b) Type: Major, Major, minor, Major, Major

4. Complete the **CIRCLE OF FIFTHS**:
   a) Write the order of flats and sharps.
   b) Write the Major keys on the OUTSIDE of the circle.
   10 c) Write the relative minor keys on the INSIDE of the circle.

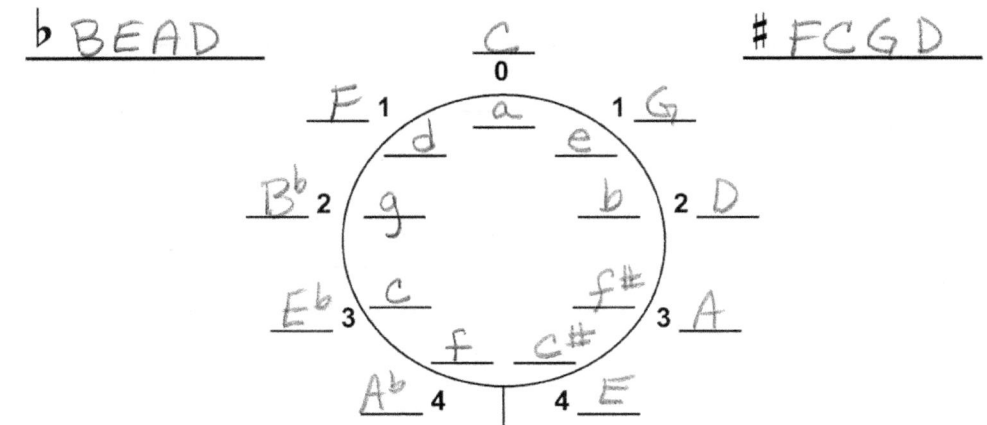

Write the following scales ascending and descending. Use whole notes.

   a) b minor natural in the Treble Clef using accidentals
   b) A Major in the Bass Clef using a Key Signature
   c) f sharp minor melodic in the Treble Clef using a Key Signature
   d) c sharp minor harmonic in the Bass Clef using accidentals
   e) A flat Major in the Treble Clef using accidentals

5. Match each musical sign with the English definition. (Not all definitions will be used.)

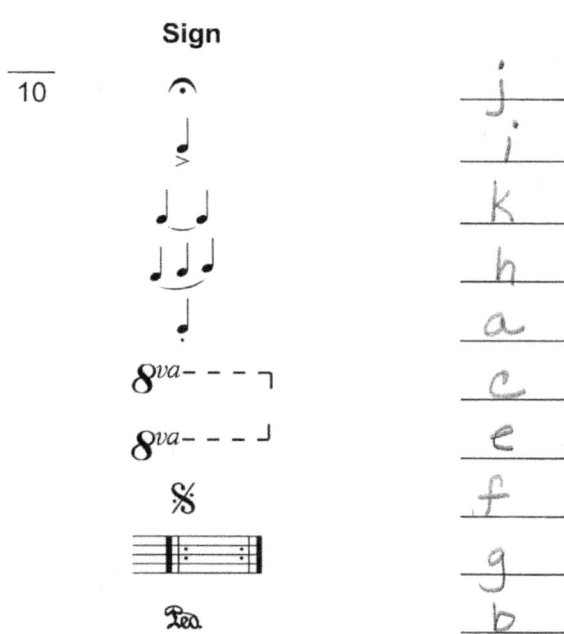

Sign / **Definition**

_j_ a) staccato, detached
_i_ b) pedal marking
_k_ c) play one octave above the written pitch
_h_ d) slowing down gradually
_a_ e) play one octave below the written pitch
_c_ f) dal segno, D.S., from the sign
_e_ g) repeat the music within the double bar lines
_f_ h) slur, play the notes legato
_g_ i) accent, a stressed note
_b_ j) fermata, pause; hold the note or rest longer than its written value
     k) tie, hold for the combined value of the tied notes

6. Name the key of the following melody. Transpose it **UP** one octave into the **Treble Clef**, using the correct Key Signature.

Key: __F Major__

7. Name each of the following as: **d.s.** (diatonic semitone), **c.s.** (chromatic semitone), **w.t.** (whole tone) or **e.e.** (enharmonic equivalent).

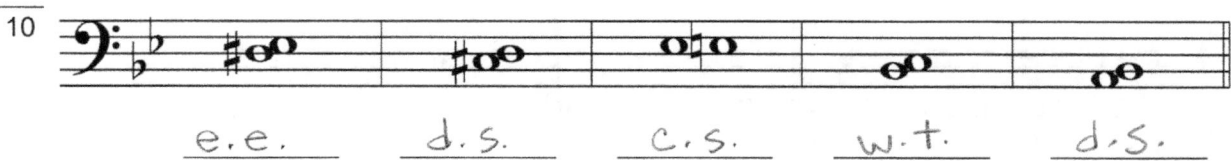

e.e.   d.s.   c.s.   w.t.   d.s.

8. a) Name the **MINOR** key for each of the following Key Signatures.
   b) Identify the technical degree name of the given note as:
      T (Tonic),   **SD** (Subdominant)   or   **D** (Dominant).

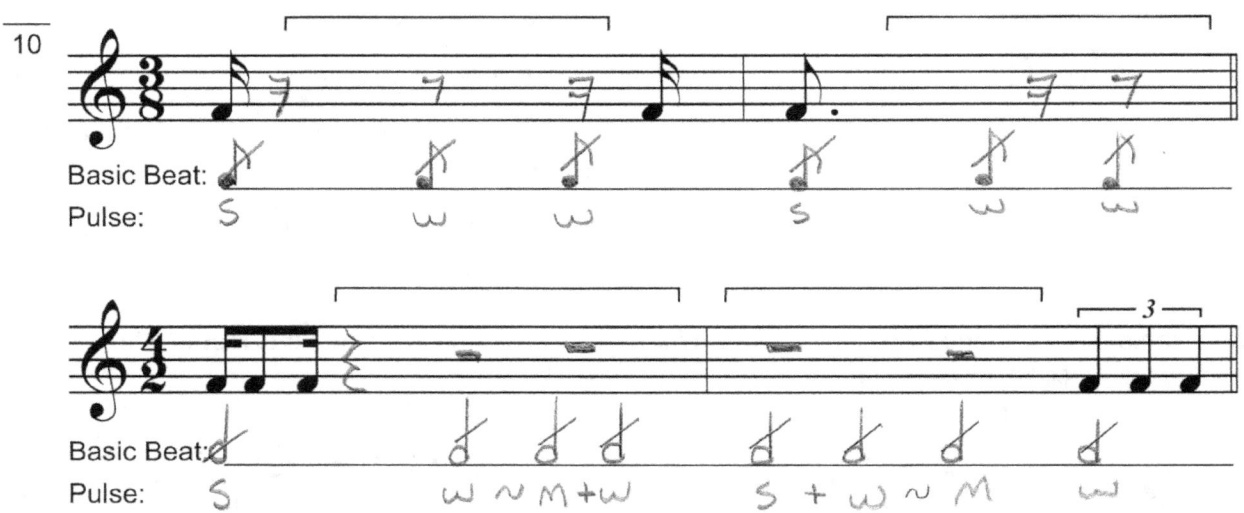

a) g min   e min   a min   c# min   f min
b)   D   SD   T   D   SD

9. a) Write the **BASIC BEAT** and the **PULSE** below each measure. Add rests below each bracket to complete the measure. Cross off the Basic Beat as each beat is completed.

b) Based on the **TIME SIGNATURE**, add **BAR LINES** to complete the following rhythms.

10. Analyze the following piece of music by answering the questions below.

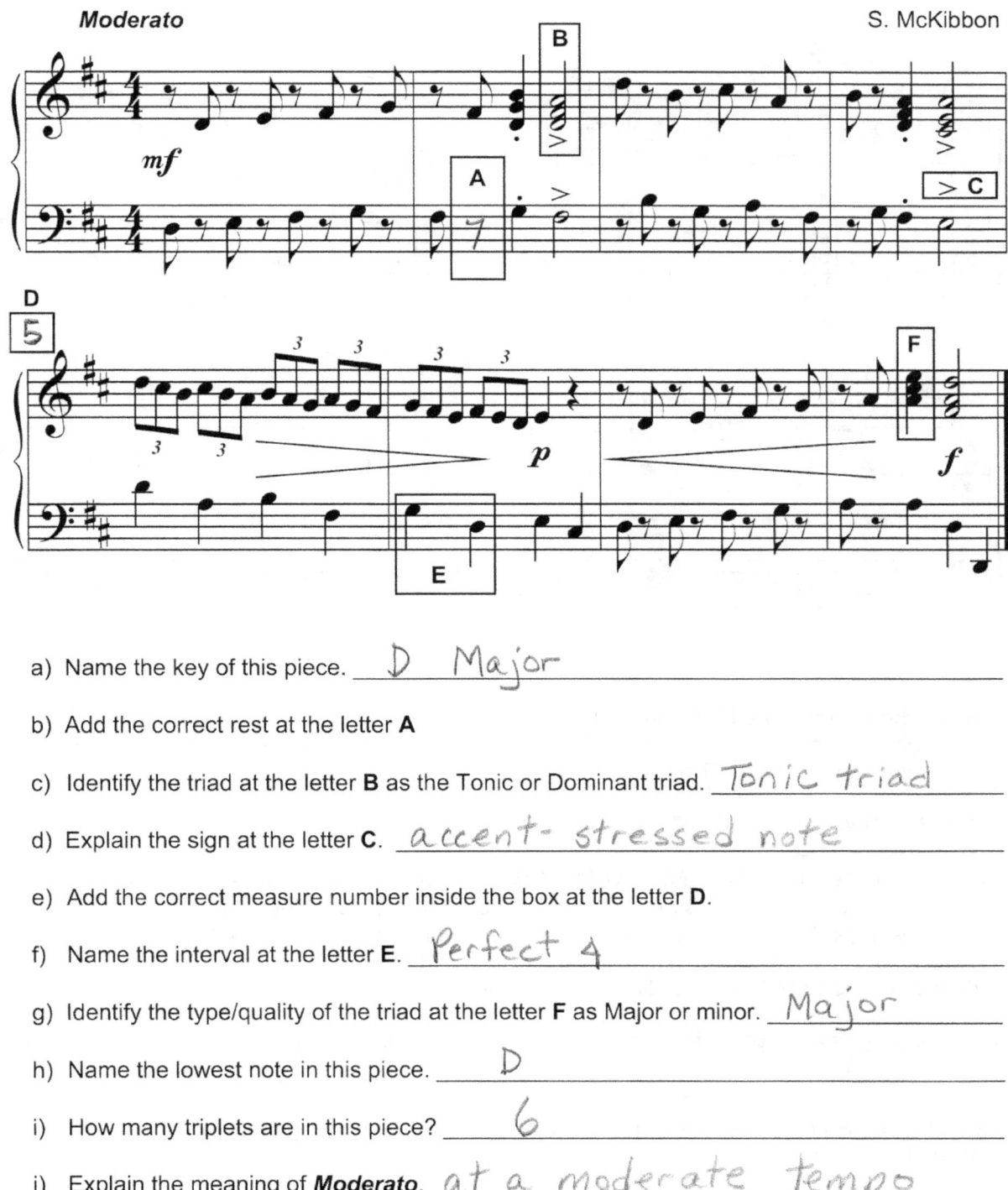

Sniffles and Sneezes...Ah-CHOO!

a) Name the key of this piece. __D Major__

b) Add the correct rest at the letter **A**

c) Identify the triad at the letter **B** as the Tonic or Dominant triad. __Tonic triad__

d) Explain the sign at the letter **C**. __accent - stressed note__

e) Add the correct measure number inside the box at the letter **D**.

f) Name the interval at the letter **E**. __Perfect 4__

g) Identify the type/quality of the triad at the letter **F** as Major or minor. __Major__

h) Name the lowest note in this piece. __D__

i) How many triplets are in this piece? __6__

j) Explain the meaning of **Moderato**. __at a moderate tempo__

Lesson 11   Analysis - Musical Compositions

Analyze the following piece of music by answering the questions below.

- ♪ **Note:** When naming the **KEY**, look at the Key Signature. Check for the raised 7th note of the relative minor key to determine if it is Major or minor. Check the last note of the piece; it will often end on the Tonic.

1. Name the Key. __g minor__

- ♪ **Note:** When identifying the **TIME SIGNATURE**, look for the easiest measure. Confirm by checking another measure. Watch for an anacrusis (incomplete) first measure. The Time Signature is written in BOTH the Treble Clef and Bass Clef.

2. Add the correct Time Signature directly on the music.

- ♪ **Note:** **MEASURE NUMBERS** can be indicated by writing the number inside a small box above the top left of the measure. Repeat signs are NOT counted as new measures.

3. Write the measure number inside the box at the top left of the first line and at the top left of the second line.

4. When observing the repeat sign, how many measures of music are played? __6__

♪ **Note:** The **TEMPO** is on the top left above the Time Signature and indicates the speed at which the piece is performed. The **TITLE** is at the top center of the piece. The **COMPOSER'S** name is on the top right of the piece. The dates underneath the composer's name are the year of his/her birth and death. If there is only one date, it is the year of birth and the composer is still living.

5. a) Name and explain the tempo of this piece. _Andante - moderately slow, walking pace_
   b) Name the title of the piece. _The Crazy Caterpillar_
   c) Name the composer of the piece. _S. McKibbon_
   d) What year was the composer born? _1962_ Is the composer still alive? _yes_

♪ **Note:** In root position **TRIADS** (all lines or all spaces), the bottom note names the Root.
   To identify the TYPE of the triad: **Major** triad = Maj 3 + Per 5, **minor** triad = min 3 + Per 5.
   Solid (blocked) triad: 3 notes played together. **Broken** triad: 3 notes played separately.

6. Identify the Type/Quality of the triad as Major or minor. Identify the triad as Solid or Broken.
   a) The triad at **A**: Type/Quality: _minor_   Solid or Broken: _solid_
   b) The triad at **B**: Type/Quality: _Major_   Solid or Broken: _broken_

♪ **Note:** Identify the **INTERVAL** number by counting all the lines and all the spaces.
   Name the TYPE of interval: Major, minor or Perfect. (Use the Major key of the bottom note.)
   Check for any changes in clefs, or accidentals in the measure that would affect the note.
   Harmonic interval: one note ABOVE the other. **Melodic** interval: one note BESIDE the other.

7. Name the interval. Identify the interval as Harmonic or Melodic.
   a) The interval at **C** is a _Maj 2_. Harmonic or Melodic: _melodic_
   b) The interval at **D** is a _Maj 3_. Harmonic or Melodic: _harmonic_

♪ **Note:** Identifying (**d.s.**) diatonic semitones (half steps), (**e.e.**) enharmonic equivalents or
   (**w.t.**) whole tones (whole step or tone): look for intervals of a second.
   Identifying (**c.s.**) chromatic semitones: look for intervals of a first.
   Check the clef, Key Signature and any accidentals that may affect the notes.

8. Circle and label one **d.s.**, one **e.e.**, one **w.t.** and one **c.s.** found in "The Crazy Caterpillar".

♪ **Note:** When adding **RESTS**, check the Time Signature to complete the measure.

9. Add a rest under the bracket at the letter **E**. What kind of rest was used? _Eighth rest_

♪ **Note:** **TECHNICAL DEGREE NAMES**: Tonic, Subdominant and Dominant.
   Check the Key Signature to determine the key when identifying degrees.
   Tonic note is the Key note.

10. Name the notes at the following letters. Give the technical degree name for each.
    a) The note at **F** is: _D_. Technical degree name: _Dominant_
    b) The note at **G** is: _G_. Technical degree name: _Tonic_

Lesson 11 — Review Test

Total Score: ___ / 100

1. a) Write the following notes **ABOVE** the Treble Clef. Use ledger lines. Use dotted half notes.

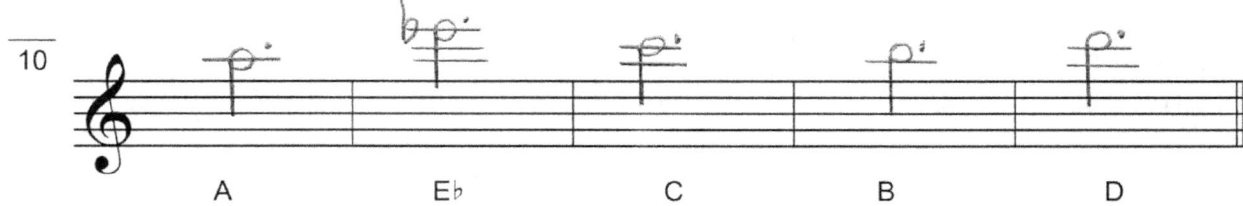

A   Eb   C   B   D

  b) Write the **ENHARMONIC EQUIVALENT** for each of the following notes. Use whole notes. Name both notes.

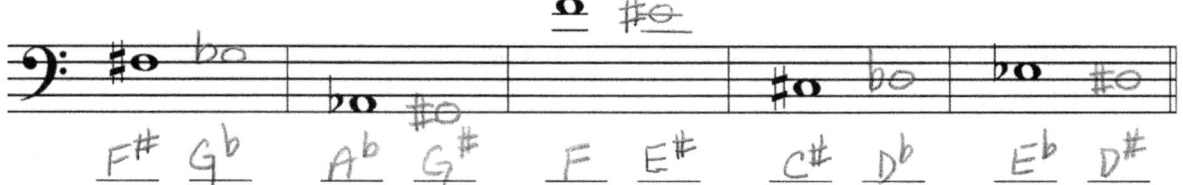

F# Gb   Ab G#   F E#   C# Db   Eb D#

2. a) Write the following **HARMONIC** intervals **ABOVE** the given notes.

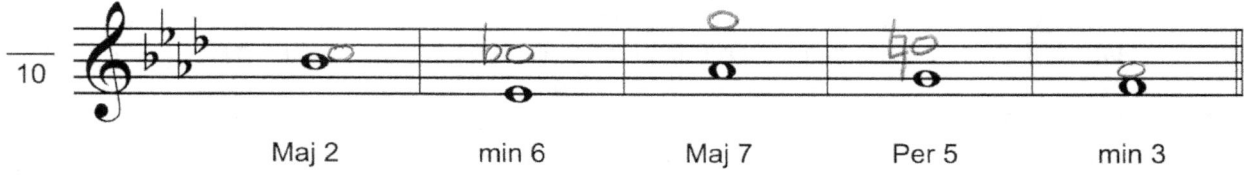

Maj 2   min 6   Maj 7   Per 5   min 3

  b) Name the following **MELODIC** intervals.

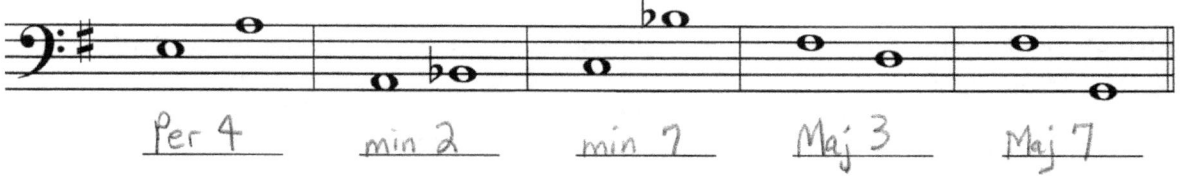

Per 4   min 2   min 7   Maj 3   Maj 7

3. Write the following **SOLID** triads in **ROOT** position in the Bass Clef using **ACCIDENTALS** instead of a Key Signature. Use whole notes.

   a) the SUBDOMINANT (iv) triad of e minor harmonic
   b) the DOMINANT (V) triad of c minor harmonic
   c) the SUBDOMINANT (IV) triad of E flat Major
   d) the DOMINANT (V) triad of d minor harmonic
   e) the TONIC (I) triad of D Major

4. Complete the **CIRCLE OF FIFTHS**:
   a) Write the order of flats and sharps.
   b) Write the Major keys on the OUTSIDE of the circle.
   c) Write the relative minor keys on the INSIDE of the circle.

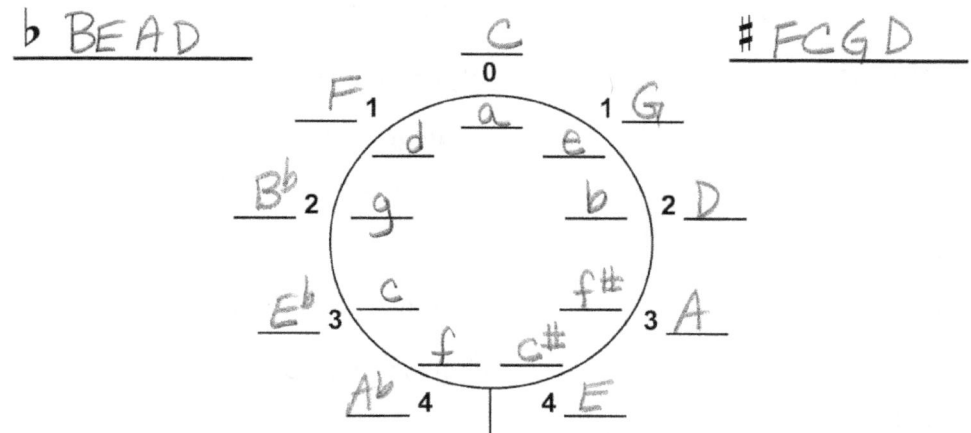

Complete the following scales by adding the correct clef, Key Signature and any necessary accidentals.

   a) g minor harmonic
   b) E flat Major
   c) d minor natural
   d) a minor melodic
   e) e minor harmonic

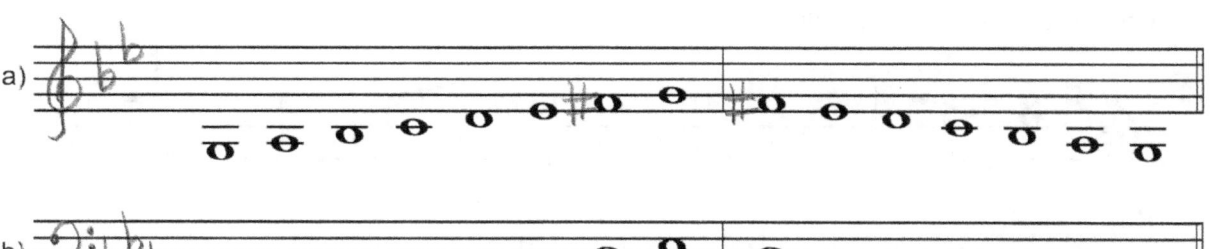

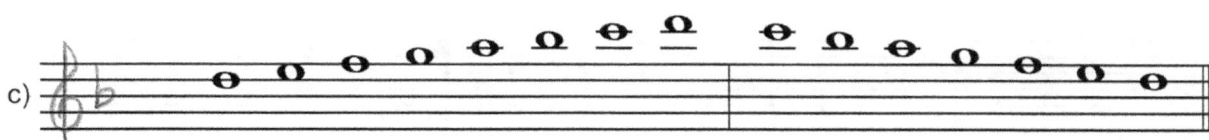

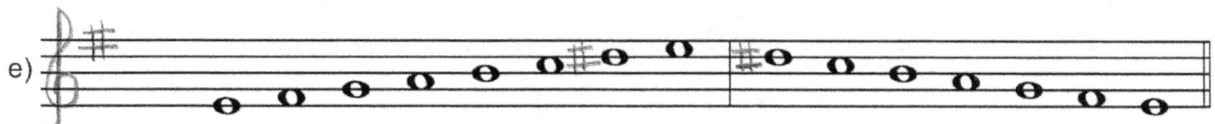

5. Match each musical term or sign with the English definition. (Not all definitions will be used.)

Term		Definition
pianissimo, *pp*	i	a) moderately slow; at a walking pace
larghetto	f	b) pedal marking
andante	a	c) moderately loud
D.C. al Fine	k	d) held, sustained
tenuto	d	e) majestic
piano, *p*	j	f) not as slow as *largo*; fairly slow and broad
Ped., ⌐⌐	b	g) becoming louder
decrescendo, decresc.	h	h) becoming softer
mezzo forte, *mf*	c	i) very soft
<	g	j) soft
		k) repeat from the beginning and end at *Fine*

6. Name the key of the following melody. Transpose it **DOWN** one octave into the **Bass Clef**, using the correct Key Signature.

Key: G Major

7. Name each of the following as: **d.s.** (diatonic semitone), **c.s.** (chromatic semitone), **w.t.** (whole tone) or **e.e.** (enharmonic equivalent).

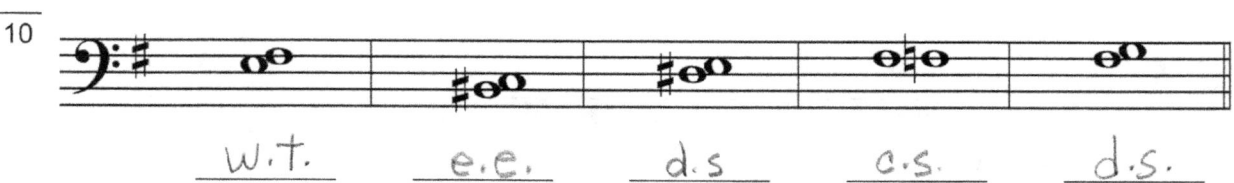

w.t.   e.e.   d.s   c.s.   d.s.

8. Name the **MINOR** key for each of the following Key Signatures. Write the SOLID **Dominant triad** in root position for each. Use whole notes.

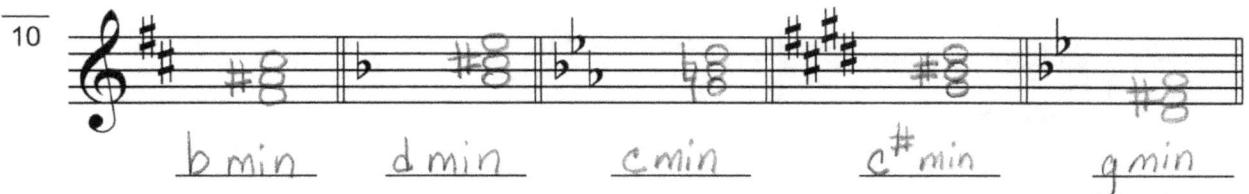

9. Write the **BASIC BEAT** and the **PULSE** below each measure. Add rests below each bracket to complete the measure. Cross off the Basic Beat as each beat is completed.

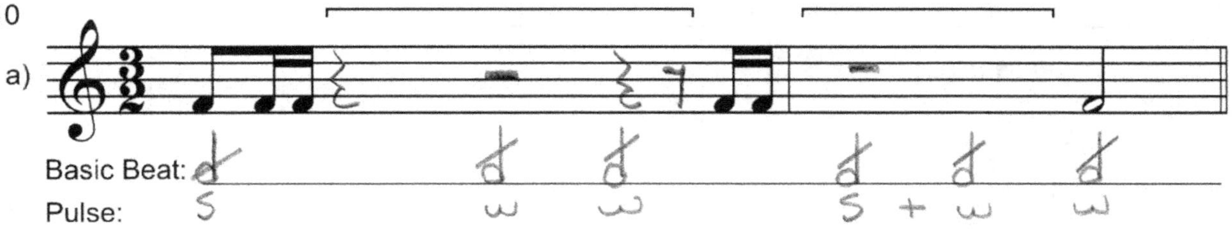

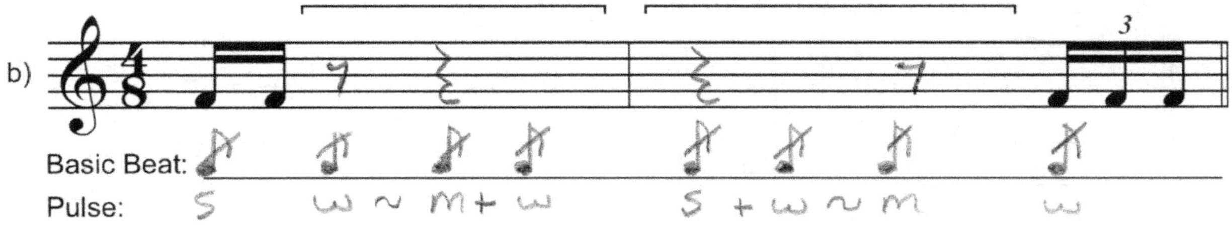

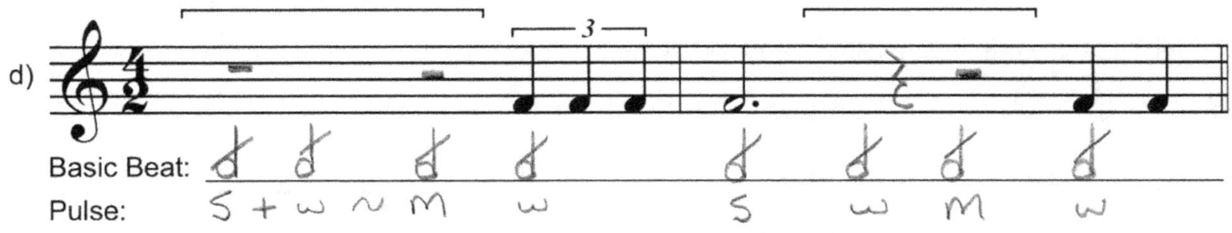

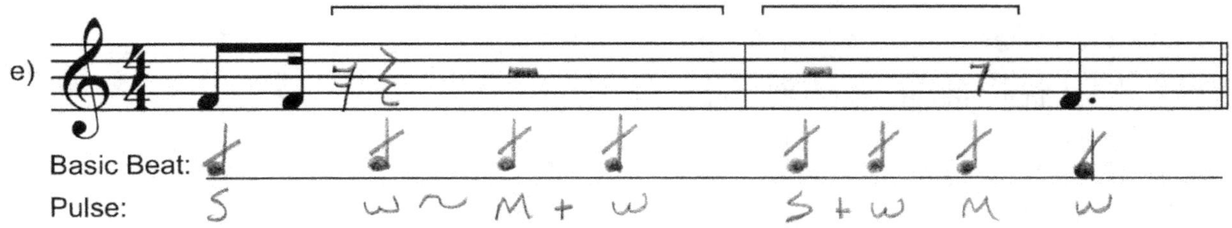

10. Analyze the following piece of music by answering the questions below.

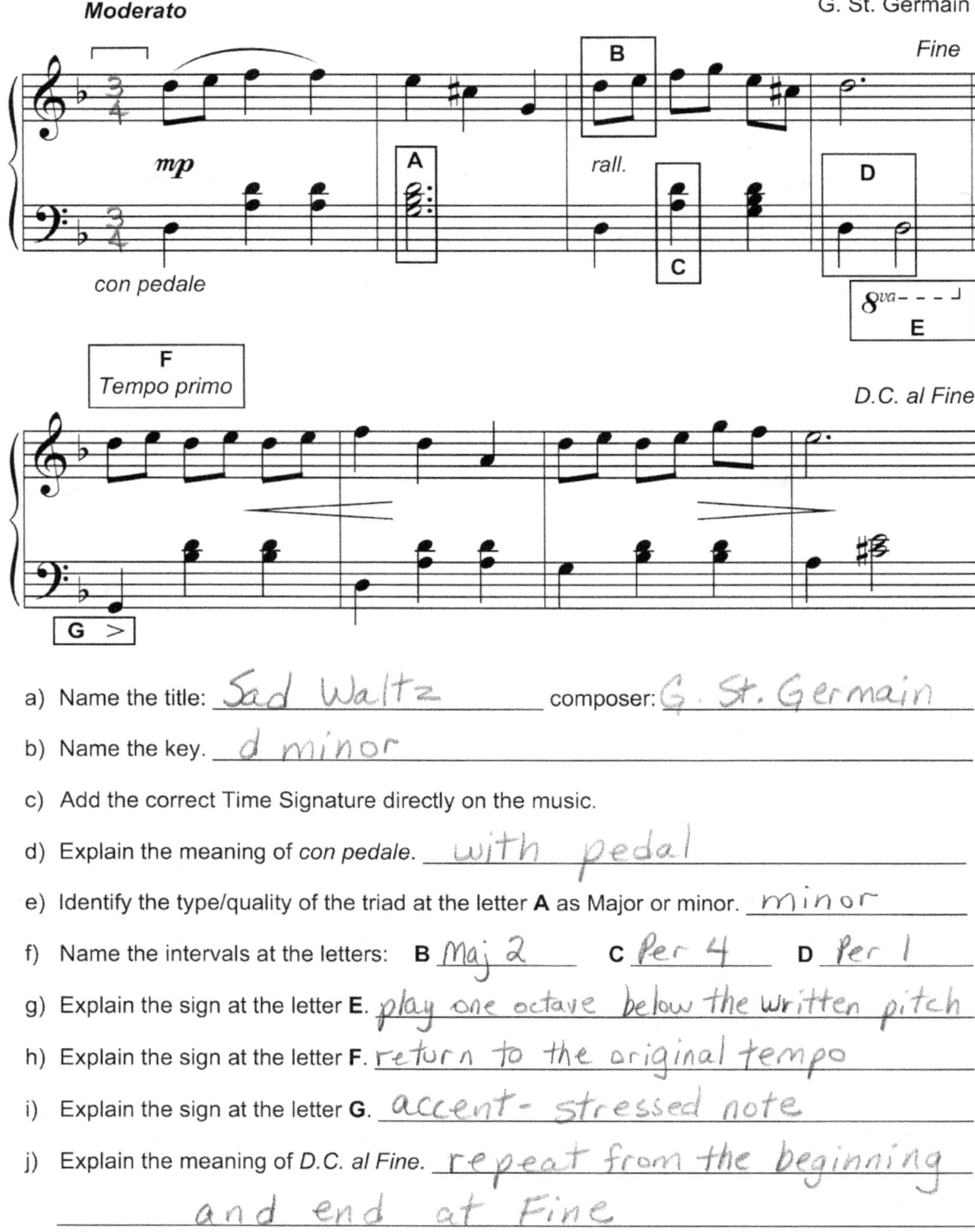

a) Name the title: **Sad Waltz** composer: **G. St. Germain**

b) Name the key. **d minor**

c) Add the correct Time Signature directly on the music.

d) Explain the meaning of *con pedale*. **with pedal**

e) Identify the type/quality of the triad at the letter **A** as Major or minor. **minor**

f) Name the intervals at the letters: **B** **Maj 2**   **C** **Per 4**   **D** **Per 1**

g) Explain the sign at the letter **E**. **play one octave below the written pitch**

h) Explain the sign at the letter **F**. **return to the original tempo**

i) Explain the sign at the letter **G**. **accent - stressed note**

j) Explain the meaning of *D.C. al Fine*. **repeat from the beginning and end at Fine**

136

Lesson 12   Musical Terms, Definitions and Signs

Articulation Terms	Definition	Sign
marcato, marc.	marked or stressed	
accent	a stressed note	
legato	smooth	
slur	play notes *legato*	
staccato	sharply detached	
tenuto	held, sustained	

1. Articulation indicates the type of touch. Write the articulation term for each definition below.

   a) play notes *legato* b) held, sustained c) sharply detached d) a stressed note

   slur   _tenuto_   _staccato_   _accent_

Signs

D.C. al *Fine*	repeat from the beginning and end at *Fine*	
D.C.	*da capo*, from the beginning	
𝄋	*dal segno*, D.S., from the sign	
M.D.	*mano destra*, right hand	
M.S.	*mano sinistra*, left hand	
8va------	*ottava*, 8va — play one octave above the written pitch	
8va------	*ottava*, 8va — play one octave below the written pitch	
Ped.	pedal marking	
L_____J	pedal marking	
‖: :‖	repeat signs: repeat the music within the double bars	
♩‿♩	tie: hold for the combined value of the tied notes	
│	bar line: a vertical line separating measures	
	measure / bar: a unit of musical time	
‖	double bar line (2 thin lines): indicates the end of a section	
‖	double bar line (final - 1 thin and 1 thick line): indicates the end of a piece	

Terms

con pedale, con ped.	with pedal	L_____J
pedale, ped.	pedal	Ped.
ottava, 8va	the interval of an octave	
tempo	speed at which music is performed	
fine	the end	

TEMPO (in order from slowest to fastest) and DYNAMICS

largo	very slow and broad; a slow and solemn tempo
larghetto	not as slow as *largo*; fairly slow and broad
adagio	slow; slower than *andante* but not as slow as *largo*
lento	slow
andante	moderately slow; at a walking pace
andantino	a little faster than *andante*
moderato	at a moderate tempo
allegretto	not as fast as *allegro*; fairly fast
allegro	fast
presto	very fast
prestissimo	as fast as possible

1. Arrange the following tempo marks in order from slowest to fastest.

    andantino   allegretto   presto   lento   larghetto

    <u>larghetto</u>   <u>lento</u>   <u>andantino</u>   <u>allegretto</u>   <u>presto</u>

Changes in Tempo

accelerando, accel.	becoming quicker
a tempo	return to the original tempo
fermata, 𝄐	a pause - hold the note or rest longer than its written value
rallentando, rall.	slowing down
ritardando, rit.	slowing down gradually
Tempo primo, Tempo I	return to the original tempo

2. Write the term or sign for each of the following definitions.

    <u>ritardando, rit.</u>   <u>fermata 𝄐</u>   <u>Tempo primo, Tempo I</u>   <u>accelerando, accel.</u>
    slowing down gradually   a pause   return to the original tempo   becoming quicker

Dynamics

crescendo, cresc.	becoming louder	<
decrescendo, decresc.	becoming softer	>
diminuendo, dim.	becoming softer	

mezzo forte, **mf**	moderately loud	*mezzo piano,* **mp**	moderately soft
forte, **f**	loud	*piano,* **p**	soft
fortissimo, **ff**	very loud	*pianissimo,* **pp**	very soft

3. Write the opposite dynamic sign for each of the following.

    a) **f** - <u>p</u>   b) **pp** - <u>ff</u>   c) **mf** - <u>mp</u>   d) *dim.* - <u>cresc.</u>   e) < - <u>></u>

STYLE in PERFORMANCE and ANALYSIS

cantabile	in a singing style
dolce	sweet, gentle
grazioso	graceful
maestoso	majestic

1. Write the definition for each of the following terms:

   a) grazioso: _graceful_

   b) cantabile: _in a singing style_

   c) maestoso: _majestic_

   d) dolce: _sweet, gentle_

2. Analyze the following piece of music by answering the questions below.

Cup of Tea — S. McKibbon

   a) Give the term for the sign at the letter **A**. _Key Signature (D Major)_

   b) Give the term for the sign at the letter **B**. _Time Signature ($\frac{4}{2}$)_

   c) Explain the term at the letter **C**. _in a singing style_

   d) Explain the term at the letter **D**. _sweet, gentle_

   e) Explain the sign at the letter **E**. _play with the left hand_

   f) Explain the sign at the letter **F**. _accent - stressed note_

   g) Explain the sign at the letter **G**. _tenuto - held, sustained_

   h) Explain the sign at the letter **H**. _play with the right hand_

   i) Identify the type of note at the letter **I**. _breve note (4 beats)_

   j) Identify the type of rest at the letter **J**. _breve rest (4 beats)_

Lesson 12 — Final Basic Exam

Total Score: ____ / 100

1. a) Write the following notes in the **Treble Clef**. Use ledger lines. Use whole notes.

   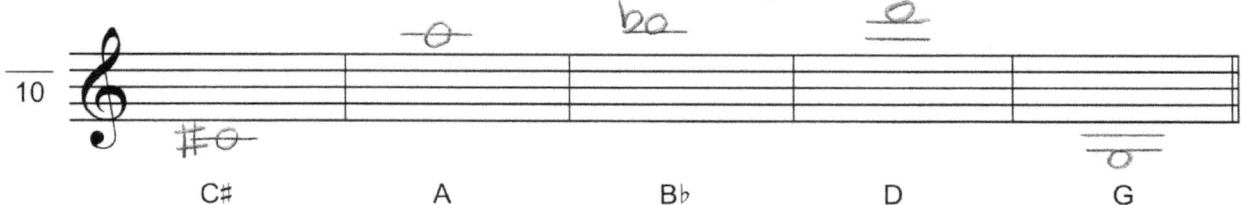

   C#   A   B♭   D   G

   b) Write the **ENHARMONIC EQUIVALENT** for each of the following notes. Use whole notes. Name both notes.

   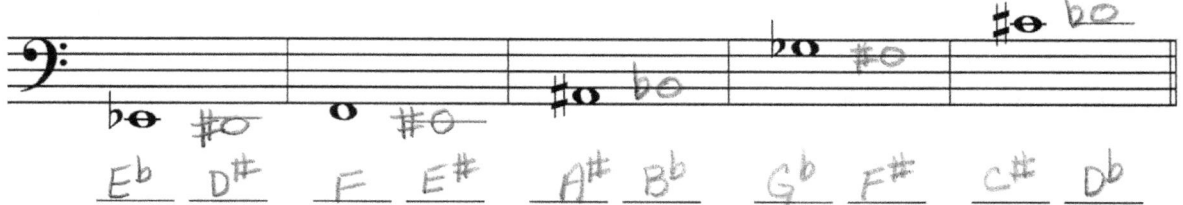

   E♭ D#   F E#   A# B♭   G♭ F#   C# D♭

2. a) Write the following **HARMONIC** intervals **ABOVE** the given notes.

   min 3   Maj 7   min 2   Per 4   Maj 6

   b) Name the following **MELODIC** intervals.

   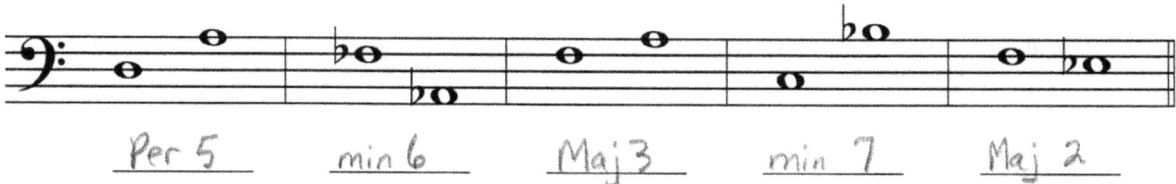

   Per 5   min 6   Maj 3   min 7   Maj 2

3. Write the following **SOLID** triads in **ROOT** position in the Treble Clef using **ACCIDENTALS** instead of a Key Signature. Use whole notes.

   a) the DOMINANT (V) triad of c sharp minor harmonic
   b) the TONIC (I) triad of A flat Major
   c) the SUBDOMINANT (iv) triad of b minor harmonic
   d) the DOMINANT (V) triad of f minor harmonic
   e) the SUBDOMINANT (IV) triad of F Major

   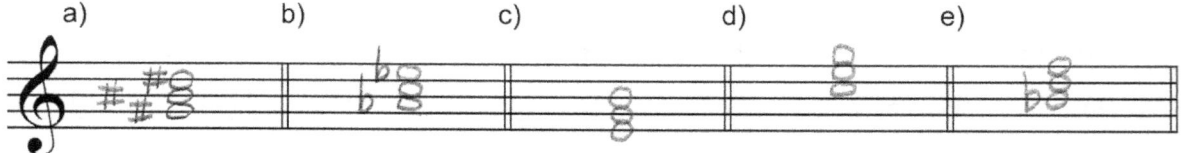

4. Complete the **CIRCLE OF FIFTHS**:
   a) Write the order of flats and sharps.
   b) Write the Major keys on the OUTSIDE of the circle.
   c) Write the relative minor keys on the INSIDE of the circle.

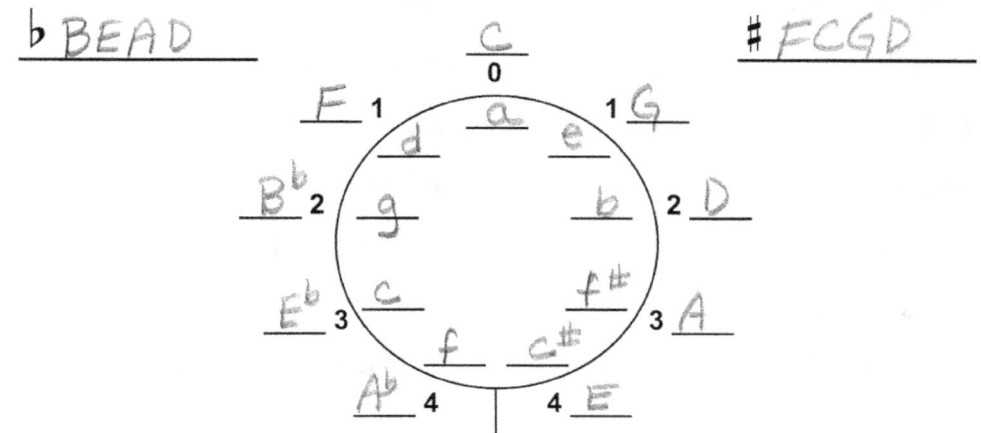

Write the following scales, ascending and descending, using the correct **KEY SIGNATURE** and any necessary accidentals for each. Use whole notes.

   a) c minor harmonic in the Treble Clef
   b) f sharp minor melodic in the Bass Clef
   c) B flat Major in the Treble Clef
   d) a minor harmonic in the Bass Clef
   e) c sharp minor natural in the Treble Clef

5. Match each musical term or sign with the English definition. (Not all definitions will be used.)

   Term   **Definition**

   crescendo, cresc.   _e_   a) slowing down
   allegretto   _i_   b) sharply detached
   a tempo   _g_   c) smooth
   rallentando, rall.   _a_   d) becoming softer
   fine   _k_   e) becoming louder
   forte, *f*   _j_   f) slow
   diminuendo, dim.   _d_   g) return to the original tempo
   legato   _c_   h) soft
   lento   _f_   i) not as fast as *allegro*; fairly fast
   piano, *p*   _h_   j) loud
                               k) the end

6. Name the key of the following melody. Transpose it **UP** one octave into the **Treble Clef**, using the correct Key Signature.

Key: _G Major_

7. Name each of the following as: **d.s.** (diatonic semitone), **c.s.** (chromatic semitone), **w.t.** (whole tone) or **e.e.** (enharmonic equivalent).

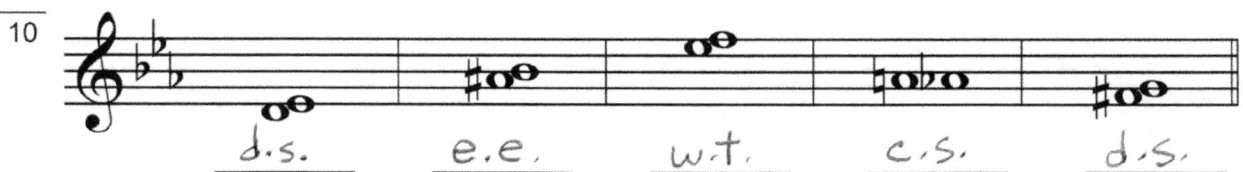

d.s.   e.e.   w.t.   c.s.   d.s.

8. a) Name the **MINOR** key for each of the following Key Signatures.
   b) Identify the technical degree name of the given note as:
      T (TONIC),   **SD** (SUBDOMINANT)   or   **D** (DOMINANT)

9. Write the **BASIC BEAT** and the **PULSE** below each measure. Add rests below each bracket to complete the measure. Cross off the Basic Beat as each beat is completed.

10. Analyze the following piece of music by answering the questions below.

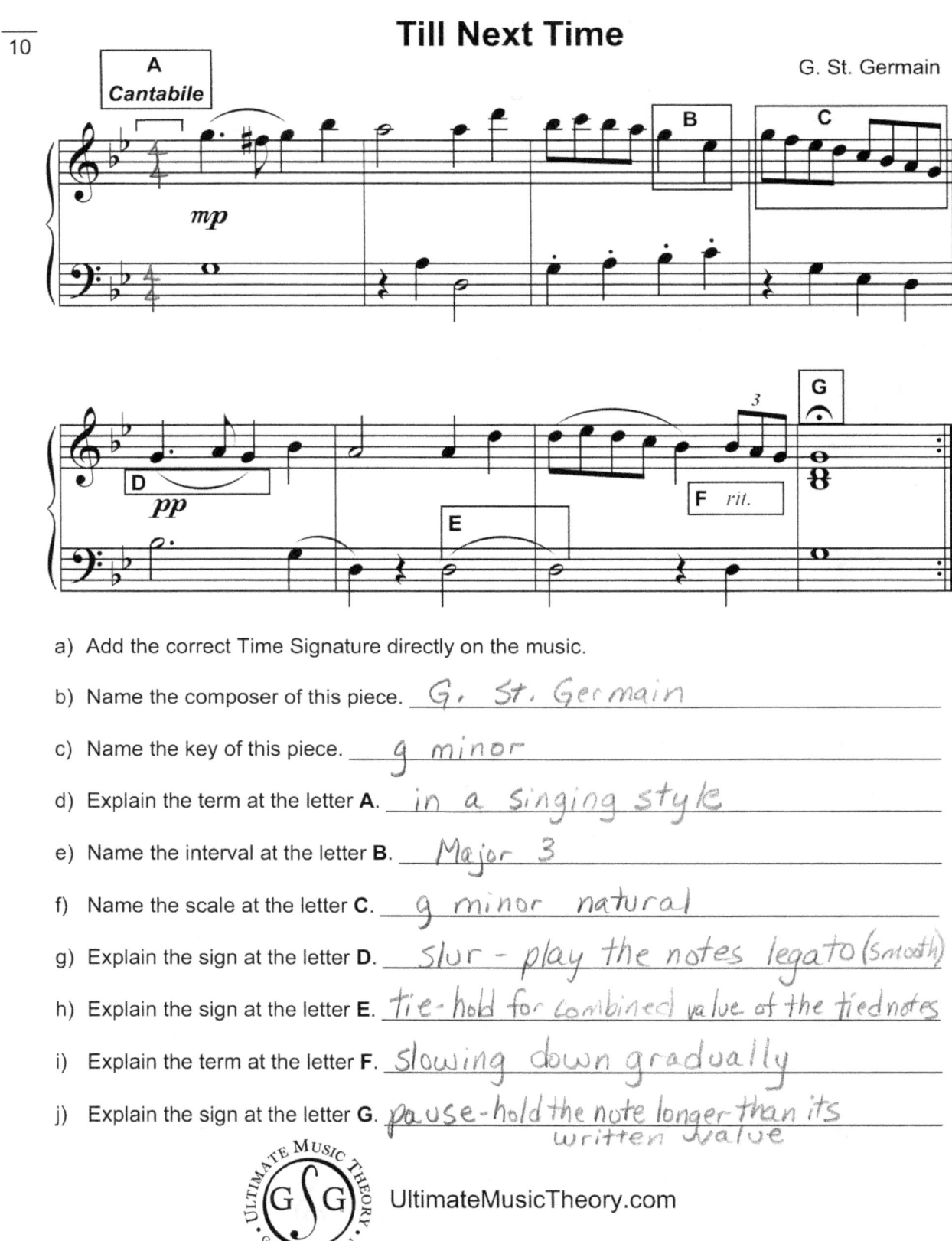

a) Add the correct Time Signature directly on the music.

b) Name the composer of this piece. __G. St. Germain__

c) Name the key of this piece. __g minor__

d) Explain the term at the letter **A**. __in a singing style__

e) Name the interval at the letter **B**. __Major 3__

f) Name the scale at the letter **C**. __g minor natural__

g) Explain the sign at the letter **D**. __slur - play the notes legato (smooth)__

h) Explain the sign at the letter **E**. __tie - hold for combined value of the tied notes__

i) Explain the term at the letter **F**. __slowing down gradually__

j) Explain the sign at the letter **G**. __pause - hold the note longer than its written value__

Ultimate Music Theory Certificate

_____

has successfully completed all the requirements of the

Basic Rudiments

_____   _____
Music Teacher   *Date*

Enriching Lives Through Music Education

ULTIMATE MUSIC THEORY GUIDE - BASIC

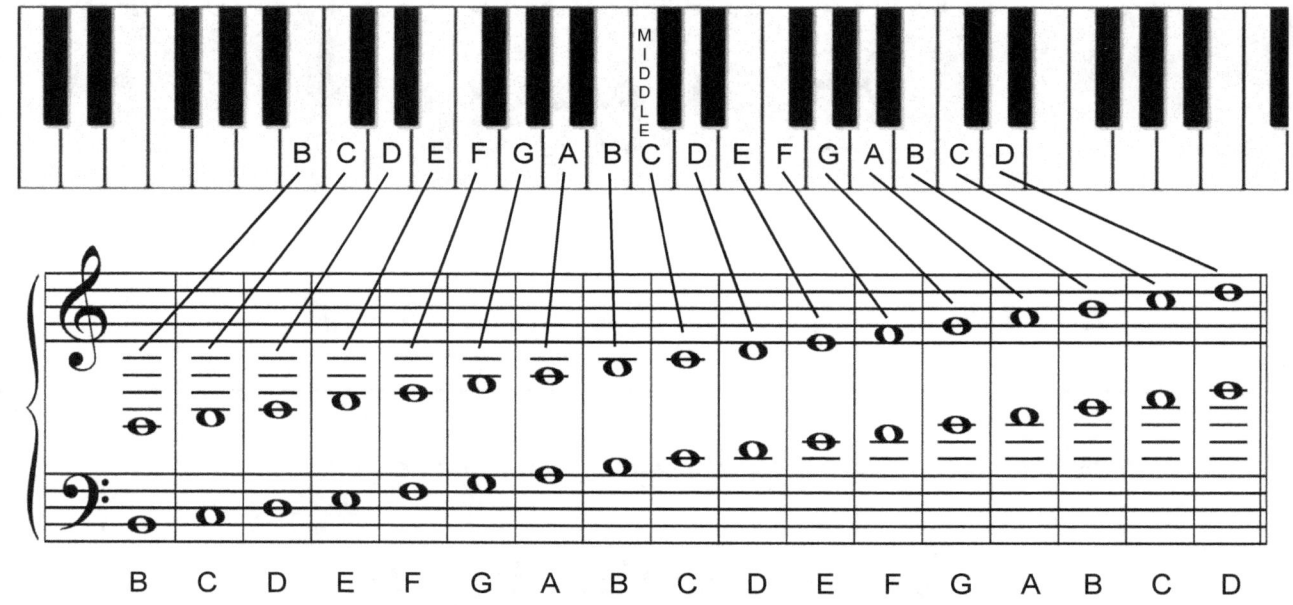

INTERVALS: An **INTERVAL** is the distance in pitch between TWO notes.

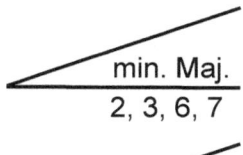

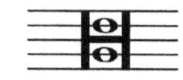

HARMONIC Interval - **H** is for Harmony
(one note ABOVE the other - together)

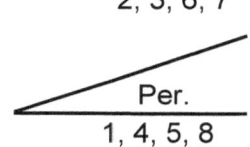

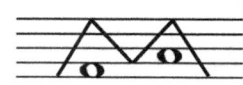

MELODIC Interval - **M** is for Melody
(one note BESIDE the other - separate)

A **Chromatic** semitone (half step) uses the SAME letter name. Example: C to C♯

A **Diatonic** semitone (half step) uses a DIFFERENT letter name. Example: C to D♭

An **Enharmonic Equivalent** is the SAME PITCH with a DIFFERENT letter name.
Example: C♯ and D♭

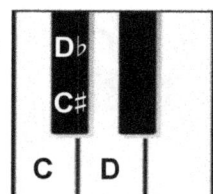

A **Whole tone** (whole step, tone) is equal to two semitones. Example: C to D

TRIADS: Broken   Solid

♪ **Note:** The **Dominant (V) Triad** is ALWAYS Major.

UltimateMusicTheory.com

ULTIMATE MUSIC THEORY CHART - BASIC
Circle of Fifths

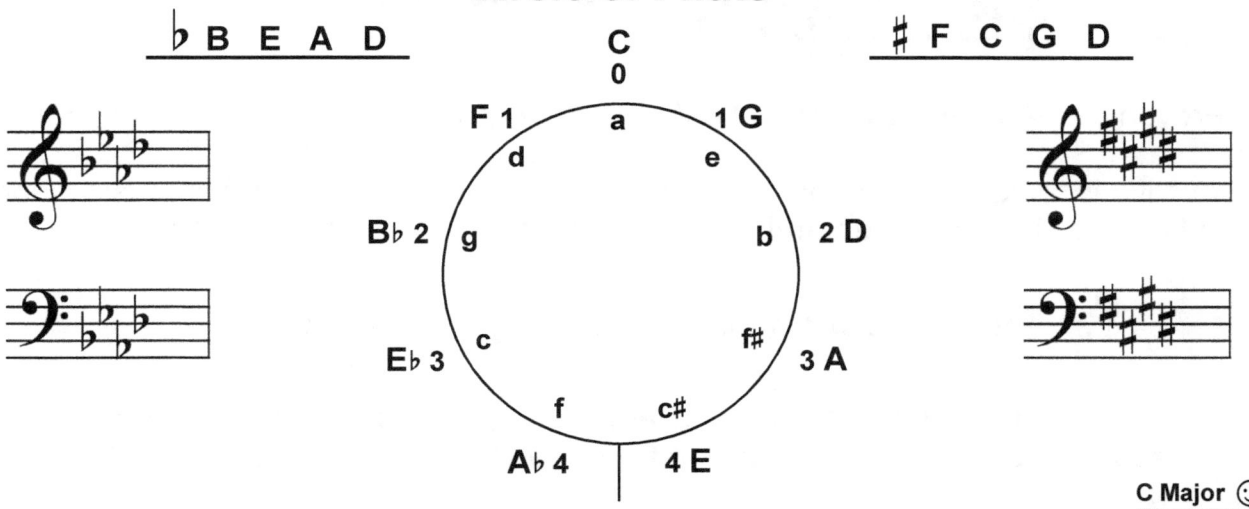

A **Major key** and its **relative minor key** have the SAME Key Signature. The distance between a Major and its relative minor key is three semitones and three letter names (a minor 3rd).

 **Natural** minor scale - Nothing added.

Harmonic minor scale - Raise the 7th note ascending and descending. (Find the 7 in the H)

Melodic minor scale - Raise the 6th and 7th notes ascending and lower the 6th and 7th notes descending. (Find the 6 and 7 in the M)

TIME SIGNATURE:

Top Number: **Pulse**

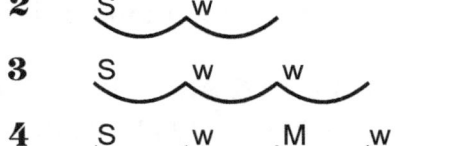

Bottom Number: **Basic Beat**

2   𝅗𝅥 = one count
4   ♩ = one count
8   ♪ = one count

¢ is a symbol for $\frac{2}{2}$ time, also called **Cut Time**

C is a symbol for $\frac{4}{4}$ time, also called **Common Time**

Breve	Whole	Half	Quarter	Eighth	Sixteenth
note/rest	note/rest	note/rest	note/rest	note/rest	note/rest

UltimateMusicTheory.com

Ultimate Music Theory Ltd. © COPYRIGHT 2021 Gloryland Publishing. All Rights Reserved.

Workbooks, Exams, Answers, Online Courses, App & More!

A Proven Step-by-Step System to Learn Theory Faster - from Beginner to Advanced.

Innovative techniques designed to develop a complete understanding of music theory, to enhance sight reading, ear training, creativity, composition and musical expression.

All UMT Series have matching Answer Books!

The UMT Rudiments Series - Beginner A, Beginner B, Beginner C, Prep 1, Prep 2, Basic, Intermediate, Advanced & Complete (All-In-One)

- ♪ 12 Lessons, Review Tests, and a Final Exam to develop confidence
- ♪ Music Theory Guide & Chart for fast and easy reference of theory concepts
- ♪ 80 Flashcards for fun drills to dramatically increase retention & comprehension

Rudiments Exam Series - Preparatory, Basic, Intermediate & Advanced

- ♪ 8 Exams plus UMT Tips on How to Score 100% on Theory Exams

Each Rudiments Workbook correlates to a Supplemental Workbook.

The UMT Supplemental Series - Prep Level, Level 1, Level 2, Level 3, Level 4, Level 5, Level 6, Level 7, Level 8 & Complete (All-In-One) Level

- ♪ Form & Analysis and Music History - Composers, Eras & Musical Styles
- ♪ Melody Writing using ICE - Imagine, Compose & Explore
- ♪ 12 Lessons, Review Tests, Final Exam and 80 Flashcards for quick study

Supplemental Exam Series - Level 5, Level 6, Level 7 & Level 8

- ♪ 8 Exams to successfully prepare for nationally recognized Theory Exams

UMT Online Courses, Music Theory App & More

- ♪ UMT Certification Course, Teachers Membership & Elite Educator Program
- ♪ Ultimate Music Theory App correlates to the Rudiments Workbooks
- ♪ Free Resources - Teachers Guide, Music Theory Blogs, videos & downloads

Go To: UltimateMusicTheory.com

Flashcards are two-sided: Question is on one side, and the Answer in square box is on the flip side.

---

slowing down gradually	becoming louder
maestoso	**pianissimo** *pp*

play one octave above the written pitch play one octave below the written pitch	becoming softer
dolce	**fortissimo** *ff*

very fast	tie: hold for the combined value of the tied notes
adagio	**mezzo piano** *mp*

hold the note or rest longer than its written value	in a singing style
allegretto	**mezzo forte** *mf*

return to the original tempo	pedal marking with pedal
allegro	**grazioso**

Ultimate Music Theory Ltd. © COPYRIGHT 2021 Gloryland Publishing. All Rights Reserved.

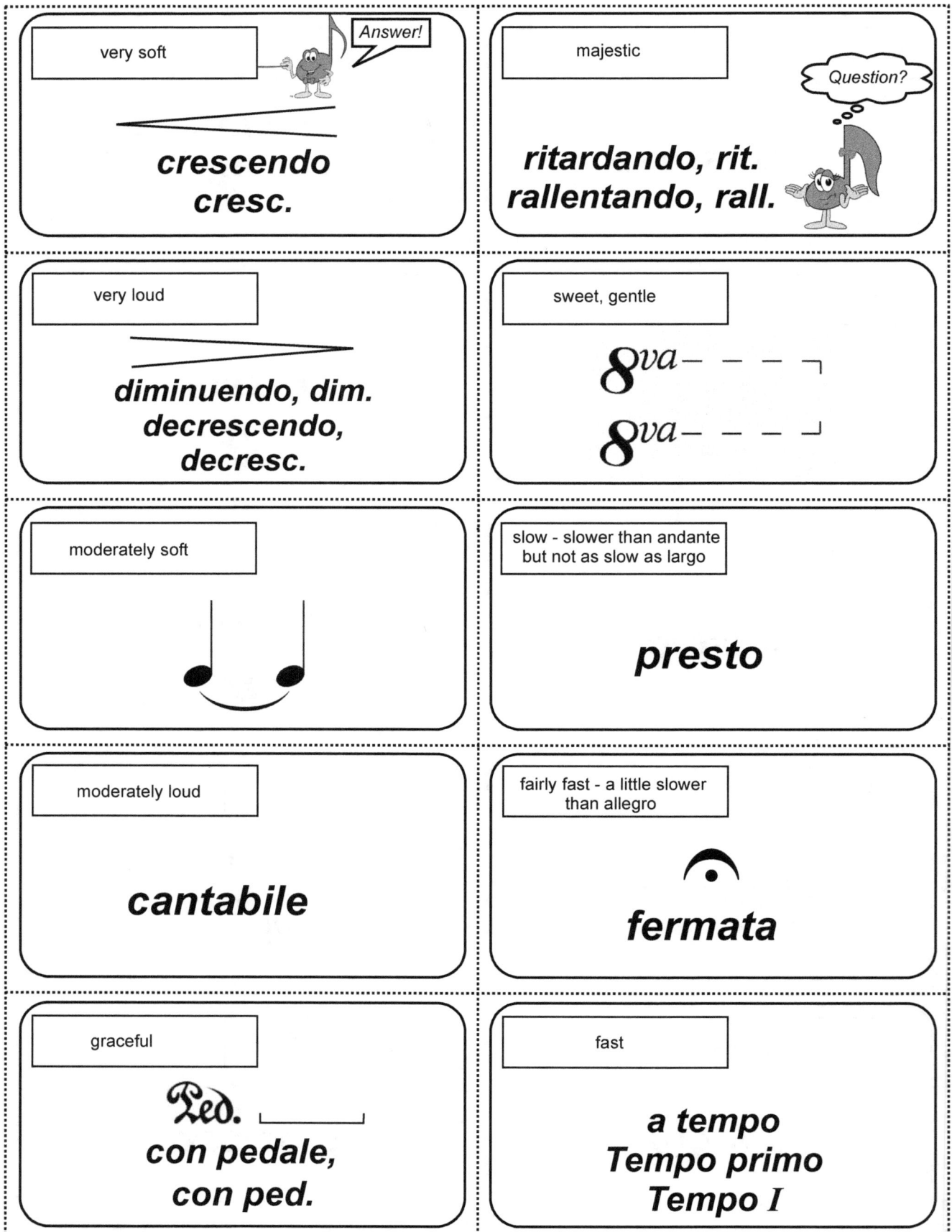

from the beginning **tempo**	a little faster than andante **largo**
held, sustained **M.S.** **mano sinistra**	a stressed note **lento**
repeat the music within the double bar lines **M.D.** **mano destra**	play the notes legato - smooth **andante**
smooth 𝄋 **dal segno, D.S.**	not as slow as largo **prestissimo**
marked or stressed **D.C. al Fine**	detached **moderato**

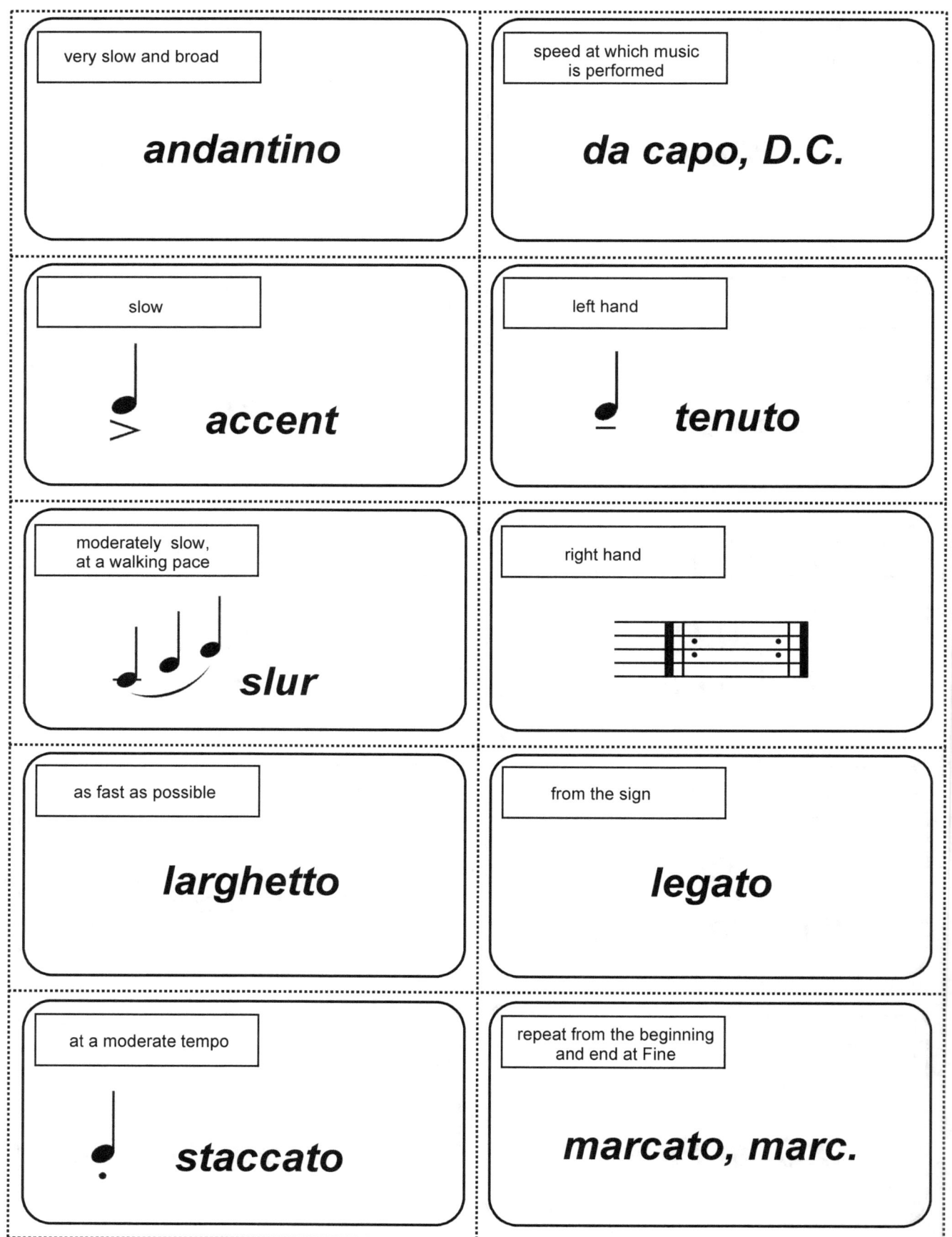

Go to: **UltimateMusicTheory.com** Read Blogs & Theory Articles, Teaching Tips, Interviews & More.

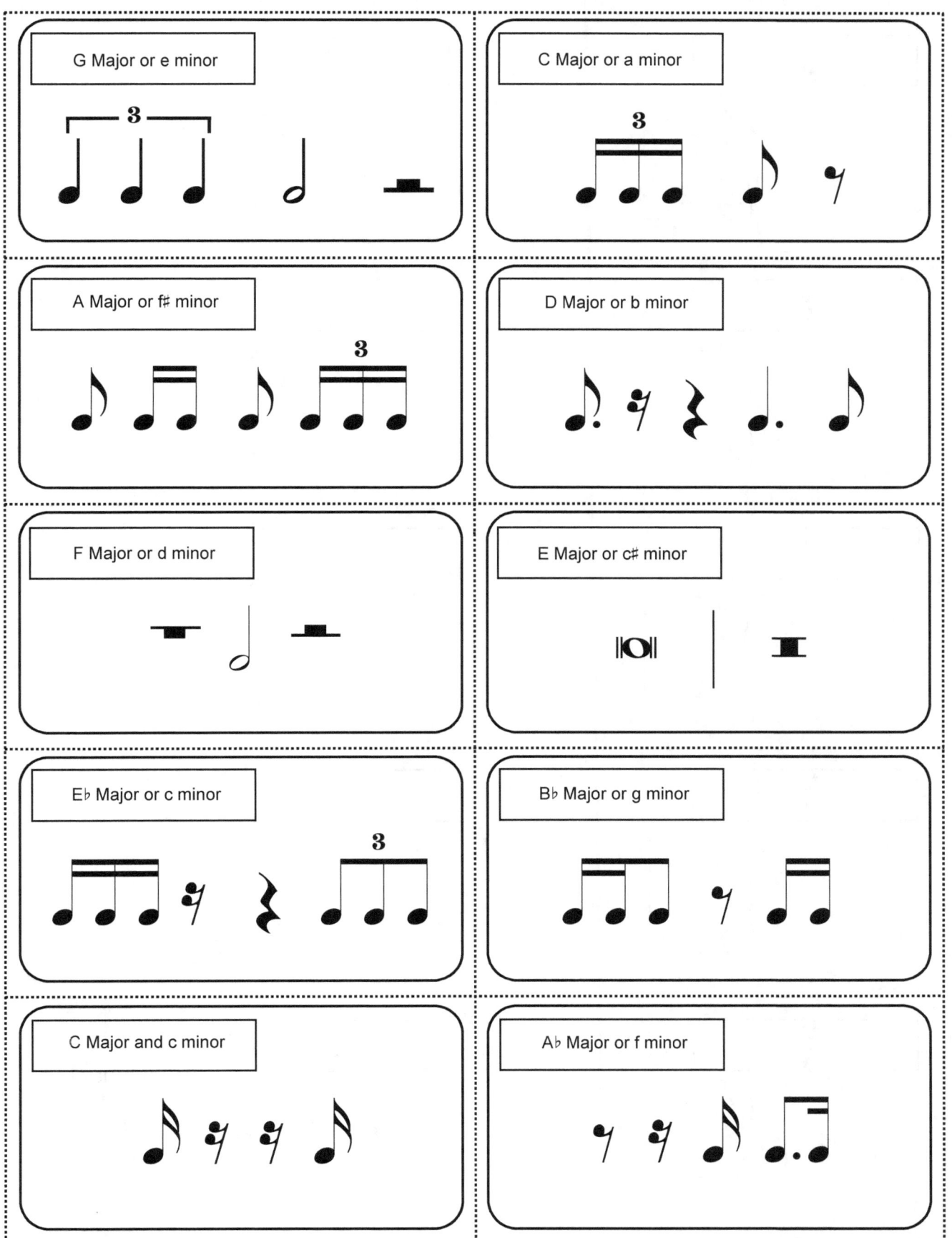

UltimateMusicTheory Ltd. © COPYRIGHT 2021 Gloryland Publishing. All Rights Reserved. 153

Go to: **UltimateMusicTheory.com** Free Resources for Worksheets, Circle of Fifths & Staff Paper.

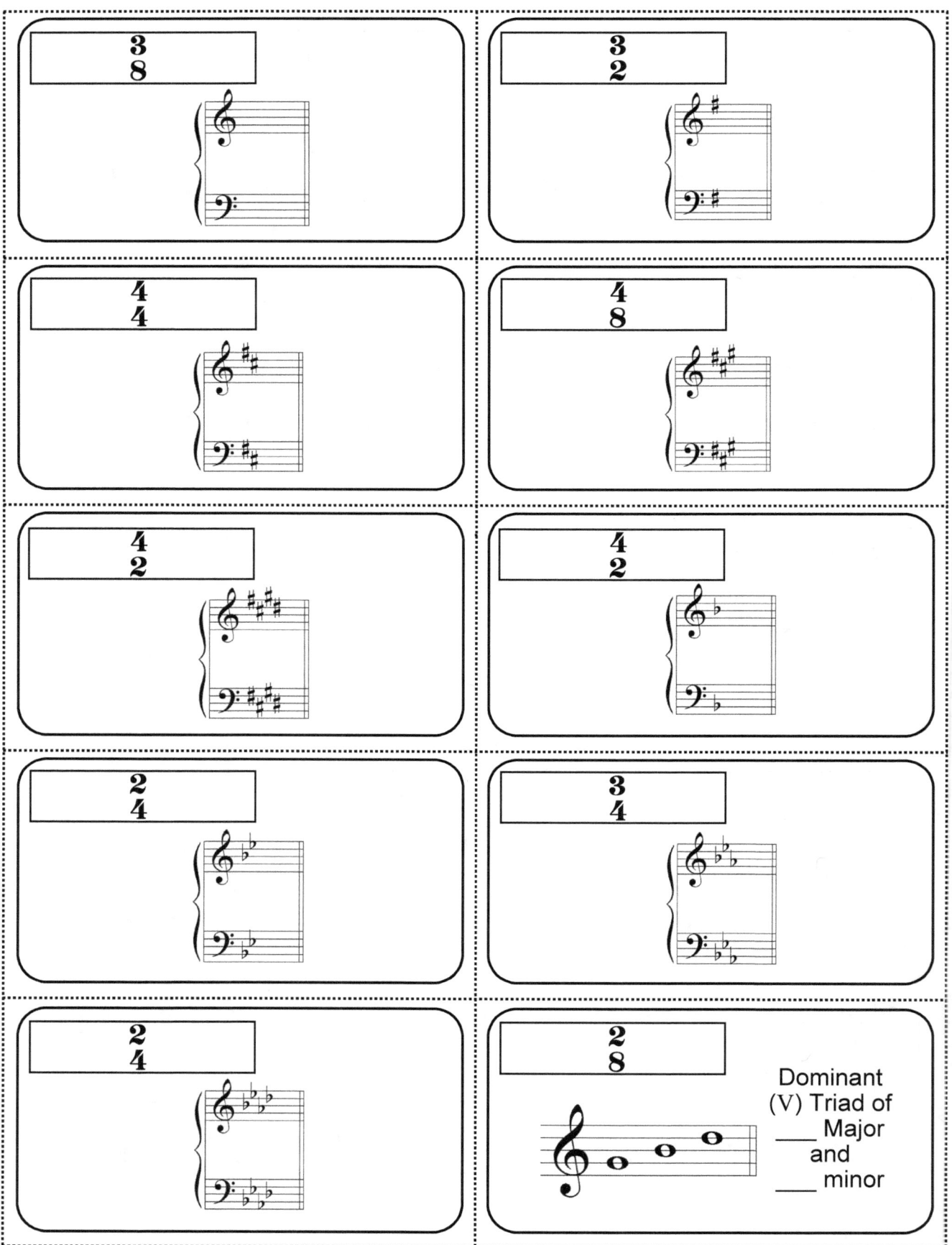

Ultimate Music Theory Ltd. © COPYRIGHT 2021 Gloryland Publishing. All Rights Reserved. 154

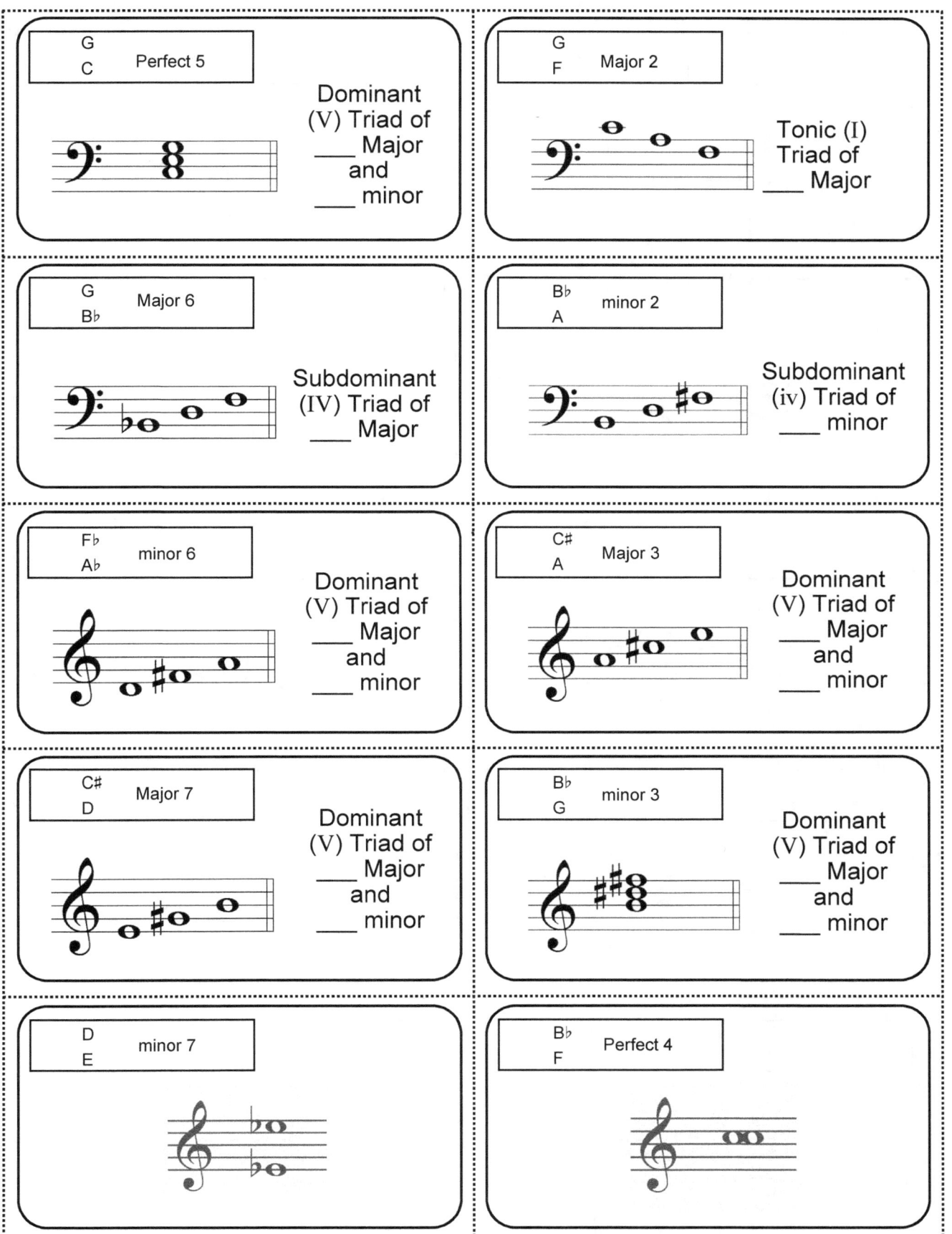

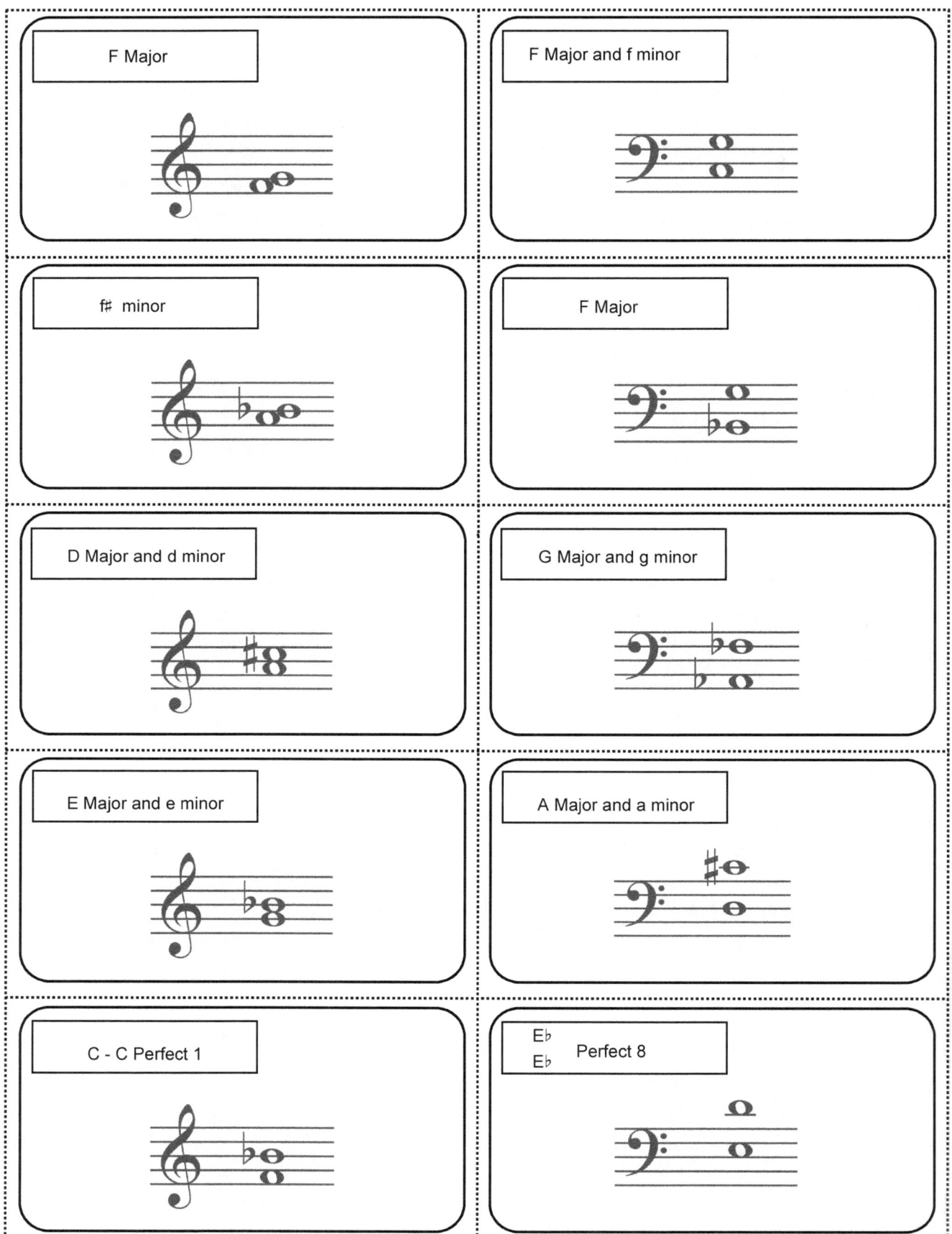

www.ingramcontent.com/pod-product-compliance
Lightning Source LLC
Chambersburg PA
CBHW060514300426

44112CB00017B/2666